ALSO BY JONATHAN SACKS

The Great Partnership

The Great Partnership

SCIENCE, RELIGION, AND THE SEARCH FOR MEANING

JONATHAN SACKS

SCHOCKEN BOOKS, NEW YORK

Library of Congress Cataloging-in-Publication Data

Sacks, Jonathan, [date]
The great partnership : Science, religion, and the search for meaning / Jonathan Sacks.
p. cm.
Includes bibliographical references.
ISBN 978-0-8052-4301-7
1. Religion and science. I. Title.
BL240.3.S23 2012   201'.65—dc23   2012006601

www.schocken.com

Jacket image (hands) illustrated by Steven Stines

Jacket design by Brian Barth

Printed in the United States of America

First American Edition

2 4 6 8 9 7 5 3 1

To my brother Brian
with love

Contents

Acknowledgements

I've been thinking about this book for over forty years, and it's impossible to thank all those who have helped me on my way. But as I make clear in the book, I owe a great debt to my philosophy teachers at Cambridge and Oxford, especially James Altham, Roger Scruton, Jonathan Glover, the late Sir Bernard Williams and Philippa Foot; to those who inspired me to become a rabbi, the late Lubavitcher Rebbe, Rabbi Menachem Mendel Schneersohn and Rabbi Joseph Dov Soloveitchik; and most of all to my teacher and mentor for twelve years, Rabbi Nachum Rabinovitch, a man to whom I owe more than I can say, not only for his insistence on fastidious scholarship, but also for his intellectual clarity and moral courage. I consider myself blessed to have been his student.

I tried out the central thesis of the book some years ago in a Credo column in *The Times*. The then Bishop of Durham, Tom Wright, himself a distinguished author, expressed an interest which encouraged me to stay with the idea. When, in 2009, Iain McGilchrist published his magisterial *The Master and His Emissary: The Divided Brain and the Making of the Western World*, I knew I was on the right lines. I benefited enormously from a conversation I had with him.

Stuart Roden persuaded me that this was a book worth writing. As always I was encouraged by the lay leaders with whom I have had the privilege to work, especially Dr Simon Hochhauser, Peter Sheldon, Professor Leslie Wagner and Sir Ian Gainsford. I could not have asked for better friends. Thanks too to my office team, especially Joanna Benarroch.

Two sad events occurred while I was writing it. My mother died, as did Marc Weinberg, son of the former director of my office, Syma Weinberg. I hope in some way what I have written is a tribute to their memory.

My thanks to my literary agent Louise Greenberg for her endless patience and tireless efforts; to my editor Altie Karper and her wonderful team at Schocken; to my publisher Ian Metcalfe and the team at Hodder, who have shown faith in their author bordering on the miraculous; and to Dayan Ivan Binstock and David Frei of the London Beth Din who read the manuscript and made many important suggestions. The errors that remain are my own: 'But who can discern their own errors? Acquit me of hidden faults' (Psalm 19:22). Finally, as always, my greatest thanks go to my wife Elaine, whose kindness makes gentle the life of this world, and whose faith in people has been my inspiration.

Jonathan Sacks
February 2011 / Adar Rishon 5771

The Great Partnership

Introduction

If the new atheists are right, you would have to be sad, mad or bad to believe in God and practise a religious faith. We know that is not so. Religion has inspired individuals to moral greatness, consecrated their love and helped them to build communities where individuals are cherished and great works of loving kindness are performed. The Bible first taught the sanctity of life, the dignity of the individual, the imperative of peace and the moral limits of power.

To believe in God, faith and the importance of religious practice does not involve an abdication of the intellect, a silencing of critical faculties, or believing in six impossible things before breakfast. It does not involve reading Genesis 1 literally. It does not involve rejecting the findings of science. I come from a religious tradition where we make a blessing over great scientists regardless of their views on religion.

So what is going on?

Debates about religion and science have been happening periodically since the seventeenth century and they usually testify to some major crisis in society. In the seventeenth century it was the wars of religion that had devastated Europe. In the nineteenth century it was the industrial revolution, urbanisation and the impact of the new science, especially Darwin. In the 1960s, with the 'death of God' debate, it was the delayed impact of two world wars and a move to the liberalisation of morals.

When we come to a major crossroads in history it is only natural to ask who shall guide us as to which path to choose. Science speaks with expertise about the future, religion with the authority of the past. Science invokes the power of reason, religion the higher power of revelation. The debate is usually inconclusive and both sides live to fight another day.

The current debate, though, has been waged with more than usual anger and vituperation, and the terms of the conflict have changed. In the past the danger – and it was a real danger – was a godless society. That led to four terrifying experiments in history, the French Revolution, Nazi Germany, the Soviet Union and Communist China. Today the danger is of a radical religiosity combined with an apocalyptic political agenda, able through terror and asymmetric warfare to destabilise whole nations and regions. I fear that as much as I fear secular totalitarianisms. All religious moderates of all faiths would agree. This is one fight believers and non-believers should be fighting together.

Instead the new atheism has launched an unusually aggressive assault on religion, which is not good for religion, for science, for intellectual integrity or for the future of the West. When a society loses its religion it tends not to last very long thereafter. It discovers that having severed the ropes that moor its morality to something transcendent, all it has left is relativism, and relativism is incapable of defending anything, including itself. When a society loses its soul, it is about to lose its future.

So let us move on.

I want, in this book, to argue that we need both religion and science; that they are compatible and more than compatible. They are the two essential perspectives that allow us to see the universe in its three-dimensional depth. The creative tension between the two is what keeps us sane, grounded in physical reality without losing our spiritual sensibility. It keeps us human and humane.

The story I am about to tell is about the human mind and its ability to do two quite different things. One is the ability to break things down into their constituent parts and see how they mesh and interact. The other is the ability to join things together so that they tell a story, and to join people together so that they form relationships. The best example of the first is science, of the second, religion.

Science takes things apart to see how they work. Religion puts things together to see what they mean. Without going into neuroscientific detail, the first is a predominantly left-brain activity, the second is associated with the right hemisphere.

Both are necessary, but they are very different. The left brain is good at sorting and analysing things. The right brain is good at forming relationships with people. Whole civilisations made mistakes because they could not keep these two apart and applied to one the logic of the other.

When you treat things as if they were people, the result is myth: light is from the sun god, rain from the sky god, natural disasters from the clash of deities, and so on. Science was born when people stopped telling stories about nature and instead observed it; when, in short, they relinquished myth.

When you treat people as if they were things, the result is dehumanisation: people categorised by colour, class or creed and treated differently as a result. The religion of Abraham was born when people stopped seeing people as objects and began to see each individual as unique, sacrosanct, the image of God.

One of the most difficult tasks of any civilisation – of any individual life, for that matter – is to keep the two separate, but integrated and in balance. That is harder than it sounds. There have been ages – the sixteenth and seventeenth centuries especially – when religion tried to dominate science. The trial of Galileo is the most famous instance, but there were others. And there have been ages when science tried to dominate religion, like now. The new atheists are the most famous examples, but there are many others, people who think we can learn everything we need to know about meaning and relationships by brain scans, biochemistry, neuroscience and evolutionary psychology, because science is all we know or need to know.

Both are wrong in equal measure. Things are things and people are people. Realising the difference is sometimes harder than we think.

In the first part of the book I give an analysis I have not seen elsewhere about why it is that people have thought religion and science are incompatible. I argue that this has to do with a curious historical detail about the way religion entered the West. It did so in the form of Pauline Christianity, a religion that was a hybrid or synthesis of two radically different cultures, ancient Greece and ancient Israel.

The curious detail is that all the early Christian texts were written in Greek, whereas the religion of Christianity came from ancient Israel and its key concepts could not be translated into Greek. The result was a prolonged confusion, which still exists today, between the God of Aristotle and the God of Abraham. I explain in chapter 3 why this made and makes a difference, leading to endless confusion about what religion and faith actually are. In chapter 4 I tell the story of my own personal journey of faith.

In the second part of the book I explain why religion matters and what we stand to lose if we lose it. The reason I do so is that, I suspect, more than people have lost faith in God, they simply do not see why it is important. What difference does it make any more? My argument is that it makes an immense difference, though not in ways that are obvious at first sight. The civilisation of the West is built on highly specific religious foundations, and if we lose them we will lose much that makes life gracious, free and humane.

We will, I believe, be unable to sustain the concept of human dignity. We will lose a certain kind of politics, the politics of the common good. We will find ourselves unable to hold on to a shared morality – and morality must be shared if it is to do what it has always done and bind us together into communities of shared principle and value. Marriage, deconsecrated, will crumble and children will suffer. And we will find it impossible to confer meaning on human life as a whole. The best we will be able to do is see our lives as a personal project, a private oasis in a desert of meaninglessness.

In a world in which God is believed to exist, the primary fact is relationship. There is God, there is me, and there is the relationship between us, for God is closer to me than I am to myself. In a world without God, the primary reality is 'I', the atomic self. There are other people, but they are not as real to me as I am to myself. Hence all the insoluble problems that philosophers have wrestled with unsuccessfully for two and a half thousand years. How do I know other minds exist? Why should I be moral? Why should I be concerned about the welfare of others to whom I am not related? Why should I limit the exercise of my freedom so that others can enjoy theirs? Without God, there is a danger that we will stay trapped within the prison of the self.

As a result, neo-Darwinian biologists and evolutionary psychologists have focused on the self, the 'I'. 'I' is what passes my genes on to the next generation. 'I' is what engages in reciprocal altruism, the seemingly selfless behaviour that actually serves self-centred ends. The market is about the choosing 'I'. The liberal democratic state is about the voting 'I'. The economy is about the consuming 'I'. But 'I', like Adam long ago, is lonely. 'I' is bad at relationships. In a world of 'I's, marriages do not last. Communities erode. Loyalty is devalued. Trust grows thin. God is ruled out completely. In a world of clamorous egos, there is no room for God.

So the presence or absence of God makes an immense difference to our lives. We cannot lose faith without losing much else besides, but this happens slowly, and by the time we discover the cost it is usually too late to put things back again.

In the third part of the book I confront the major challenges to faith. One is Darwin and neo-Darwinian biology, which seems to show that life evolved blindly without design. I will argue that this is true only if we use an unnecessarily simplistic concept of design.

The second is the oldest and hardest of them all: the problem of unjust·suffering, 'when bad things happen to good people'. I will argue that only a religion of protest – of 'sacred discontent' – is adequate to the challenge. Atheism gives us no reason to think the world could be otherwise. Faith does, and thereby gives us the will and courage to transform the world.

The third charge made by the new atheists is, however, both true and of the utmost gravity. Religion has done harm as well as good. At various times in history people have hated in the name of the God of love, practised cruelty in the name of the God of compassion, waged war in the name of the God of peace and killed in the name of the God of life. This is a shattering fact and one about which nothing less than total honesty will do.

We need to understand why religion goes wrong. That is what I try to do in chapter 13. Sometimes it happens because monotheism lapses into dualism. Sometimes it is because religious people attempt to bring about the end of time in the midst of time. They engage in the politics of the apocalypse, which always results in tragedy, always self-inflicted and often against fellow members of the faith. Most often it happens because religion becomes what it should never become: the will to power. The religion of Abraham, which will be my subject in this book, is a protest against the will to power.

We need both religion and science. Albert Einstein said it most famously: 'Science without religion is lame; religion without science is blind.'[1] It is my argument that religion and science are to human life what the right and left hemispheres are to the brain. They perform different functions and if one is damaged, or if the connections between them are broken, the result is dysfunction. The brain is highly plastic and in some cases there can be almost miraculous recovery.[2] But no one would wish on anyone the need for such recovery.

Science is about explanation. Religion is about meaning. Science analyses, religion integrates. Science breaks things down to their component parts. Religion binds people together in relationships of trust. Science tells us what is. Religion tells us what ought to be. Science describes. Religion beckons, summons, calls. Science sees objects. Religion speaks to us as subjects. Science practises detachment. Religion is the art of attachment, self to self, soul to soul. Science sees the underlying order of the physical world. Religion hears the music beneath the noise. Science is the conquest of ignorance. Religion is the redemption of solitude.

We need scientific explanation to understand nature. We need meaning to understand human behaviour and culture. Meaning is what humans seek because they are not simply part of nature. We are self-conscious. We have imaginations that allow us to envisage worlds that have never been, and to begin to create them. Like all else that lives, we have desires. Unlike anything else that lives, we can pass judgement on those desires and decide not to pursue them. We are free.

All of this, science finds hard to explain. It can track mental activity from the outside. It can tell us which bits of the brain are activated when we do this or that. What it cannot do is track it on the inside. For that we use empathy. Sometimes we use poetry and song, and rituals that bind us together, and stories that gather us into a set of shared meanings. All of this is part of religion, the space where self meets other and we relate as persons in a world of persons, free agents in a world of freedom. That is where we meet God, the Personhood of personhood, who stands to the natural universe as we, free agents, stand to our bodies. God is the soul of being in whose freedom we discover freedom, in whose love we discover love, and in whose forgiveness we learn to forgive.

I am a Jew, but this book is not about Judaism. It is about the monotheism that undergirds all three Abrahamic faiths: Judaism, Christianity and Islam. It usually appears wearing the clothes of one of these faiths. But I have tried to present it as it is in itself, because otherwise we will lose sight of the principle in the details of this faith or that. Jews, Christians and Muslims all believe more than what is set out here, but all three rest on the foundation of faith in a personal God who created the universe in love and who endowed each of us, regardless of class, colour, culture or creed, with the charisma and dignity of his image.

The fate of this faith has been, by any standards, remarkable. Abraham performed no miracles, commanded no armies, ruled no kingdom, gathered no mass of disciples and made no spectacular prophecies. Yet there can be no serious doubt that he is the most influential person who ever lived, counted today, as he is, as the spiritual grandfather of more than half of the six billion people on the face of the planet.

His immediate descendants, the children of Israel, known today as Jews, are a tiny people numbering less than a fifth of a per cent of the population of the world. Yet they outlived the Egyptians, Assyrians, Babylonians, Persians, Greeks and Romans, the medieval empires of Christianity and Islam, and the regimes of Nazi Germany and the Soviet Union, all of which opposed Jews, Judaism or both, and all of which seemed impregnable in their day. They disappeared. The Jewish people live.

It is no less remarkable that the small, persecuted sect known as the Christians, who also saw themselves as children of Abraham, would one day become the largest movement of any kind in the history of the world, still growing today two centuries after almost every self-respecting European intellectual predicted their faith's imminent demise.

As for Islam, it spread faster and wider than any religious movement in the lifetime of its founder, and endowed the world with imperishable masterpieces of philosophy and poetry, architecture and art, as well as a faith seemingly immune to secularisation or decay.

All other civilisations rise and fall. The faith of Abraham survives.

If neo-Darwinism is true and reproductive success a measure of inclusive fitness, then every neo-Darwinian should abandon atheism immediately and become a religious believer, because no genes have spread more widely than those of Abraham, and no memes more extensively than that of monotheism. But then, as Emerson said, consistency is the hobgoblin of small minds.

What made Abrahamic monotheism unique is that it endowed life with meaning. That is a point rarely and barely understood, but it is the quintessential argument of this book. We make a great mistake if we think of monotheism as a linear development from polytheism, as if people first worshipped many gods, then reduced them to one. Monotheism is something else entirely. *The meaning of a system lies outside the system. Therefore the meaning of the universe lies outside the universe.* Monotheism, by discovering the transcendental God, the God who stands *outside* the universe and creates it, made it possible for the first time to believe that life has a meaning, not just a mythic or scientific explanation.

Monotheism, by giving life a meaning, redeemed it from tragedy. The Greeks understood tragedy better than any other civilisation before or since. Ancient Israel, though it suffered much, had no sense of tragedy. It did not even have a word for it. Monotheism is the principled defeat of tragedy in the name of hope. A world without religious faith is a world without sustainable grounds for hope. It may have optimism, but that is something else, and something shallower, altogether.[3]

A note about the theological position I adopt in this book: Judaism is a conversation scored for many voices. It is, in fact, a sustained 'argument for the sake of heaven'. There are many different Jewish views on the subjects I touch on in the pages that follow. My own views have long been influenced by the Jewish philosophical tradition of the Middle Ages – such figures as Saadia Gaon, Judah Halevi and Moses Maimonides – as well as their modern successors: Rabbis Samson Raphael Hirsch, Abraham Kook and Joseph Soloveitchik. My own teacher, Rabbi Nachum Rabinovitch, and an earlier Chief Rabbi, J. H. Hertz, have also been decisive influences. Common to all of them is an openness to science, a commitment to engagement with the wider culture of the age, and a belief that faith is enhanced, not compromised, by a willingness honestly to confront the intellectual challenges of the age. For those interested in Jewish teachings on some of the issues touched on in this book, I have added an appendix of Judaic sources on science, creation, evolution and the age of the universe.

A note about style: often in this book I will be drawing sharp contrasts, between science and religion, left- and right-brain activity, ancient Greece and ancient Israel, hope cultures and tragic cultures and so on. These are a philosopher's stock-in-trade. It is a way of clarifying alternatives by emphasising extreme opposites, 'ideal types'. We all know reality is never that simple. To give one example I will not be using, anthropologists distinguish between *shame cultures* and *guilt cultures*. Now, doubtless we have sometimes felt guilt and sometimes shame. They are different, but there is no reason why they cannot coexist. But the distinction remains helpful. There really is a difference between the two types of society and how they think about wrongdoing.

So it is, for example, with tragedy and hope. Most of us recognise tragedy, and most of us have experienced hope. But a culture that sees the universe as blind and indifferent to humanity generates a literature of tragedy, and a culture that believes in a God of love, forgiveness and redemption produces a literature of hope. There was no Sophocles in ancient Israel. There was no Isaiah in ancient Greece.

Throughout the book, it may sometimes sound as if I am setting up an either/or contrast. In actuality I embrace *both* sides of the dichotomies I mention: science *and* religion, philosophy *and* prophecy, Athens *and* Jerusalem, left brain *and* right brain. This too is part of Abrahamic spirituality. People have often noticed, yet it remains a very odd fact indeed, that there is not one account of creation at the beginning of Genesis, but two, side by side, one from the point of view of the cosmos, the other from a human perspective. Literary critics, tone deaf to the music of the Bible, explain this as the joining of two separate documents. They fail to understand that the Bible does not operate on the principles of Aristotelian logic with its either/or, true-or-false dichotomies. It sees the capacity to grasp multiple perspectives as essential to understanding the human condition. So always, in the chapters that follow, read not either/or but both/and.

* * *

The final chapter of the book sets out my personal credo, my answer to the question, 'Why believe?' It was prompted by the advertisement, paid for by the British Humanist Association, that for a while in 2009 decorated the sides of London buses: 'There's probably no God. Now stop worrying and enjoy your life.' I hope the British Humanists will not take it amiss if I confess that this is not the most profound utterance yet devised by the wit of man. It reminds me of the remark I once heard from an Oxford don about one of his colleagues: 'On the surface, he's profound, but *deep down*, he's superficial.' Of course you cannot prove the existence of God. This entire book is an attempt to show why the attempt to do so is misconceived, the result of an accident in the cultural history of the West. But to take probability as a guide to truth, and 'stop worrying' as a route to happiness, is to dumb down beyond the point of acceptability two of the most serious questions ever framed by reflective minds. So, if you want to know why it makes sense to believe in God, turn to chapter 14.

Atheism deserves better than the new atheists, whose methodology consists in criticising religion without understanding it, quoting texts without contexts, taking exceptions as the rule, confusing folk belief with reflective theology, abusing, mocking, ridiculing, caricaturing and demonising religious faith and holding it responsible for the great crimes against humanity. Religion has done harm; I acknowledge that candidly in chapter 13. But the cure of bad religion is good religion, not no religion, just as the cure of bad science is good science, not the abandonment of science.

The new atheists do no one a service by their intellectual inability to understand why it should be that some people lift their eyes beyond the visible horizon or strive to articulate an inexpressible sense of wonder; why some search for meaning despite the eternal silences of infinite space and the apparently random injustices of history; why some stake their lives on the belief that the ultimate reality at the heart of the universe is not blind to our existence, deaf to our prayers and indifferent to our fate; why some find trust and security and strength in the sensed, invisible presence of a vast and indefinable love. A great Jewish mystic, the Baal Shem Tov, compared such atheists to a deaf man who for the first time comes on a violinist playing in the town square while the townspeople, moved by the lilt and rhythm of his playing, dance in joy. Unable to hear the music, he concludes that they are all mad.

Perhaps I am critical of the new atheists because I had the privilege of knowing and learning from deeper minds than these, and I end this introduction with two personal stories to show that there can be another way.

I had no initial intention of becoming a rabbi, or indeed of pursuing religious studies at all (I explain what changed my mind in chapter 4). I went to university to study philosophy. My doctoral supervisor, the late Sir Bernard Williams, described by *The Times* in his obituary as 'the most brilliant and most important British moral philosopher of his time', was also a convinced atheist. But he never once ridiculed my faith; he was respectful of it. All he asked was that I be coherent and lucid.

He stated his own credo at the end of one of his finest works, *Shame and Necessity*:

> We know that the world was not made for us, or we for the world, that our history tells no purposive story, and that there is no position outside the world or outside history from which we might hope to authenticate our activities.[4]

Williams was a Nietzschean who believed that not only was there no religious truth, there was no metaphysical truth either. I shared his admiration for Nietzsche, though I drew the opposite conclusion – not that Nietzsche was right, but that he, more deeply than anyone else, framed the alternative: either faith or the will to power that leads ultimately to nihilism. Williams's was a bleak view of the human condition but a wholly tenable one. His own view of the meaning of a life he expressed at the end of that work in the form of one of Pindar's Odes:

> Take to heart what may be learned from Oedipus:
> If someone with a sharp axe
> Hacks off the boughs of a great oak tree,
> And spoils its handsome shape;
> Although its fruit has failed, yet it can give an account of itself
> If it comes later to a winter fire,
> Or if it rests on the pillars of some palace
> And does a sad task among foreign walls,
> When there is nothing left in the place it came from.[5]

I understood that vision, yet in the end I could not share his belief that it is somehow more honest to despair than to trust, to see existence as an accident rather than as invested with a meaning we strive to discover. Sir Bernard loved ancient Greece; I loved biblical Israel. Greece gave the world tragedy; Israel taught it hope. A people, a person, who has faith is one who, even in the darkest night of the soul, can never ultimately lose hope.

The only time he ever challenged me about my faith was when he asked, 'Don't you believe there is *an obligation to live within one's time*?' It was a fascinating question, typical of his profundity. My honest answer was, 'No.' I agreed with T. S. Eliot, that living solely within one's time is a form of provincialism.[6] We must live, not *in* the past but *with* it and its wisdom. I think that in later years Williams came to the same conclusion, because in *Shame and Necessity* he wrote that 'in important ways, we are, in our ethical situation, more like human beings in antiquity than any Western people have been in the meantime'.[7] He too eventually turned for guidance to the past. Despite our differences I learned much from him, including the meaning of faith itself. I explain this in chapter 4.

The other great sceptic to whom I became close, towards the end of his life, was Sir Isaiah Berlin. I have told the story before, but it is worth repeating, that when we first met he said, 'Chief Rabbi, whatever you do, don't talk to me about religion. When it comes to God, I'm *tone deaf*!' He added, 'What I don't understand about you is how, after studying philosophy at Cambridge and Oxford, you can still believe!'

'If it helps,' I replied, 'think of me as a *lapsed heretic*.'

'Quite understand, dear boy, quite understand.'

In November 1997, I phoned his home. I had recently published a book on political philosophy which gave a somewhat different account of the nature of a free society than he had done in his own writings. I wanted to know his opinion. He had asked me to send him the book, which I did, but I heard no more, which is why I was phoning him. His wife, Lady Aline, answered the phone and with surprise said, 'Chief Rabbi – Isaiah has just been talking about you.'

'In what context?' I asked.

'He's just asked you to officiate at his funeral.'

I urged her not to let him think such dark thoughts, but clearly he knew. A few days later he died, and I officiated at the funeral.

His biographer Michael Ignatieff once asked me why Isaiah wanted a religious funeral, given that he was a secular Jew. I replied that he may not have been a believing Jew but he was a loyal Jew. In fact, I said, the Hebrew word *emunah*, usually translated as 'faith', probably means 'loyalty'. I later came across a very significant remark of Isaiah's that has a bearing on some of today's atheists:

> I am not religious, but I place a high value on the religious experience of believers . . . I think that those who do not understand what it is to be religious, do not understand what human beings live by. That is why dry atheists seem to me blind and deaf to some forms of profound human experience, perhaps the inner life: It is like being aesthetically blind.[8]

Since then I have continued to have cherished friendships and public conversations with notable sceptics like the novelists Amos

Oz and Howard Jacobson, the philosopher Alain de Botton, and the Harvard neuroscientist Steven Pinker (my conversation with Pinker figures in the recent novel by his wife Rebecca Goldstein, entitled *36 Arguments for the Existence of God*, subtitled *A Work of Fiction*).

The possibility of genuine dialogue between believers and sceptics shows why the anger and vituperation of the new atheists really does not help. It does not even help the cause of atheism. People who are confident in their beliefs feel no need to pillory or caricature their opponents. We need a genuine, open, serious, respectful conversation between scientists and religious believers if we are to integrate their different but conjointly necessary perspectives. We need it the way an individual needs to integrate the two hemispheres of the brain. That is a major theme of the book.

When he last visited us, I asked Steven Pinker whether an atheist could use a prayer book. 'Of course,' he said, so I gave him a copy of one I had just newly translated. I did not pursue the subject further but I guess, if I had asked, that he would have told me the story of Niels Bohr, the Nobel Prize–winning physicist and inventor of complementarity theory.

A fellow scientist visited Bohr at his home and saw to his amazement that Bohr had fixed a horseshoe over the door for luck. 'Surely, Niels, you don't believe in that?'

'Of course not,' Bohr replied. 'But you see – the thing is that *it works whether you believe in it or not.*'

Religion is not a horseshoe, and it is not about luck, but one thing many Jews know – and I think Isaiah Berlin was one of them – is that it works whether you believe in it or not. Love, trust, family, community, giving as integral to living, study as a sacred task, argument as a sacred duty, forgiveness, atonement, gratitude, prayer: these things work whether you believe in them or not. The Jewish way is first to live God, then to ask questions about him.

Faith begins with the search for meaning, because it is the discovery of meaning that creates human freedom and dignity. Finding God's freedom, we discover our own.

PART ONE

God and the Search for Meaning

I

The Meaning-Seeking Animal

To know an answer to the question, 'What is the meaning of human life?' *means* to be religious.

Albert Einstein[1]

The idea of life having a purpose stands and falls with the religious system.

Sigmund Freud[2]

To believe in God means to understand the question about the meaning of life.

To believe in God means to see that the facts of the world are not the end of the matter.

To believe in God means to see that life has a meaning.

Ludwig Wittgenstein[3]

When we have found all the mysteries and lost all the meaning, we will be alone, on an empty shore.

Tom Stoppard[4]

Two Stories

The first: In the beginning, some 13.7 billion years ago, there was an unimaginably vast explosion of energy, out of which the universe emerged for no reason whatsoever. In the course of time stars coalesced, then planets, then, 4.54 billion years ago, one particular planet capable of supporting life. Seven hundred million years later, inanimate matter became animate. Cells began to reproduce. Life forms began to appear, first simple, then of ever-increasing complexity. Some of these survived; others disappeared. Eventually a life form came into being capable of complex patterns of speech, among them the future tense and the ability to ask questions. For the first time something in the universe became capable of knowing that the universe existed, that it might not have done, and of asking, 'Why is it here? Why are we here?'

The formation of the universe involved massive improbabilities. Had a single one of the mathematical constants that determined the shape of the universe been slightly different – even by the order of one in a million – there would have been no stars, no planets, no life. Had the evolution of life been slightly different, had the dinosaurs not become extinct, for example, there would have been no Homo sapiens, no self-conscious being and no civilisation. But all of this was accidental, blind, mere chance. It happened. No one intended it to happen. There was no one to intend it to happen, and there is no meaning to the fact that it happened. The universe was. One day it will cease to be. To the question, 'Why are we here?' the answer is silence.

We, members of the species Homo sapiens, are wrong to believe that our questions and answers, hopes and dreams, have any significance whatsoever. They are fictions dressed up to look like facts. We have no souls. Even our selves are fictions. All we have are sensations, and even these are mere by-products of evolution. Thought, imagination, philosophy, art: these are dramas in the theatre of the mind designed to divert and distract us while truth lies elsewhere. For thoughts are no more than electrical impulses in the brain, and the brain is merely a complicated piece of meat, an organism. The human person is a self-created fiction. The human body is a collection of cells designed by genes, themselves incapable of thought, whose only purpose is blindly to replicate themselves over time.

Humans might write novels, compose symphonies, help those in need, and pray, but all this is a delicately woven tapestry of illusions. People might imagine themselves as if on a stage under the watchful eye of infinity, but there is no one watching. There is no one to watch. There is no self-conscious life anywhere else, either within the universe or beyond. There is nothing beyond sheer random happenstance. Humans are no more significant, and less successful at adapting to their environment, than the ants. They came, they will go, and it will be as if they had never been. Why are we here? We just are.

The second: The universe was called into being by One outside the universe, fascinated by being, and with that desire-to-bring-things-into-being that we call love. He brought many universes into being. Some exploded into being, then collapsed. Others continued to grow so fast that nothing coalesced into stable concentrations of matter. One, however, so closely fitted the parameters that stars and planets did form. The One waited to see what would happen next. Eventually life formed and evolved, until one creature emerged capable of communication.

The One sent messages to this creature. At first no one noticed. Thousands of years passed during which the creatures invented tools, hunted, developed agriculture, and eventually built cities and constructed cultures. They told all sorts of stories to explain why they were there, fanciful stories to be sure, for this was the childhood of civilisation. But eventually one man, Abraham, a shepherd far away from the noise of the city, listened to the silence for long enough, intently enough, to discern a message, *the* message. The one heard the One.

It was enough to send him on a journey. Where, why, to do what – of these things he had no more than a dim intuition. But he sensed that he had stumbled on something of immense significance, and he handed on the memory to his children with the instruction that they should hand it on to theirs. Eventually his descendants grew to become a nation, not numerous, not powerful; indeed they had become slaves. This time another individual, Moses, a complex figure who had spent his life among strangers as an Egyptian prince and then as a shepherd among the Midianites, heard the voice again. What it told him changed his life. Through an immense historic drama of liberation and revelation it transformed Abraham's children, by then known as the Israelites, into a covenanted nation under the sovereignty of God. Eventually it changed the world.

It said that every human being had within him or her a trace of the One who created the universe. Like the One, human beings could speak, think and communicate. They could imagine a world not present to the senses, entertain different scenarios for the future and choose between them. They could change their environment because they could change themselves. They could show that history is not destined to be an endless replay of the victory of the strong over the weak. They could construct a society built on respect for human dignity, equality and freedom, and though they failed time and again, the prophets who came after Moses never gave up the vision or the hope. Somehow they sensed that something of larger consequence was at stake.

And so the journey continued, haltingly, never without relapses and sometimes with terrible failures. The people Moses led, known to themselves as the Israelites, to others as the Hebrews, and to history as the Jews, never lost faith with that original vision even when they lost everything else: their land, their sovereignty and their freedom.

Other people in the course of time were impressed by their message and adapted and adopted it in somewhat different forms, becoming new religions in their own right. One became known as Christianity, the other Islam. Eventually it became the faith of more than half of the six billion people on the face of the planet. It did not fully transform humanity. We remain fallible people, all too often falling short of what we are called on to become. Yet those who followed Abraham's call gave rise to moments of graciousness that lifted our small and insignificant species to great heights of moral, spiritual and aesthetic beauty.

Thus the One came to be known by the many, obscurely to be sure, in visions and voices that strained against the limits of language, for the words we have to describe things within the universe are by definition inadequate to describe what lies beyond it. The closest the voice ever came to identifying itself was in the cryptic, enigmatic words *Ehyeh asher ehyeh*, 'I will be what I will be'. But in striving to listen to the more-than-human, human beings learned what it is to be human, for in discovering God, singular and alone, they eventually learned to respect the dignity and sanctity of the human person, singular and alone. We may be dust of the Earth, the debris of exploded stars, a concatenation of blindly self-replicating genes, but within us is the breath of God.

Two rival views, each coherent and consistent, each simplified to be sure, but marking out the great choice, the two framing visions of the human situation. One asserts that life is meaningless. The other claims that life is meaningful. The facts are the same on both scenarios. So is the science that explains the facts. But the world is experienced differently by those who tell the first narrative and those who tell the second.

We can imagine them arguing. The first says to the second, 'What hubris to imagine that there is a Being for whom we matter.'

The second says to the first, 'What hubris to think that what we can see and prove is all there is.'

The first says to the second, 'What abasement to believe that there is someone else who tells us what to do.'

The second says to the first, 'What abasement to believe that, given the tragic, destructive history of humankind, we know best what is best for the world.'

The first says to the second, 'Do you not recall the words of Xenophanes, that we make God in our own image? "Man made his gods, and furnished them with his own body, voice and garments." If a horse could worship, he would make his god a horse. If an ox had a god, it would be an ox.'

'You forget,' says the second, 'that Xenophanes used this argument to refute polytheism and argue for monotheism. Xenophanes was not an atheist but a believer.'

The argument is interminable, but though it is usually portrayed as an argument between religion and science, that is not what it is.

The science is the same in both stories. The difference lies in how far we are willing to push the question, 'Why?' The first story says there is no why. The second says there is. If the universe exists, and there was a time when it did not exist, then someone or something brought it into being, someone whose existence is neither part of nor dependent on the universe.

If so, why? The most economical hypothesis is that it did so because it willed so. But why would a being independent of the universe wish to bring a universe into being? There is only one compelling answer: out of the selfless desire to make space for otherness that, for want of a better word, we call love.

Such a Being would create precisely the kind of universe we inhabit, one that gave rise to stars, planets, life in endlessly proliferating diversity, and eventually the one life form capable of hearing and responding to the call of Being itself. The existence of the universe from the perspective of God, and the existence of God from the perspective of human beings, is the redemption of solitude. We exist because we are not alone. Religion is the cosmic drama of relationship.

The second story stands to the first as poetry to prose, music to speech, worship and wonder to analysis and experimentation. It has nothing to do with science, the observation and explanation of physical phenomena, and everything to do with human self-consciousness, freedom, imagination, choice, and existential loneliness, the I that seeks a Thou, the self in search of an Other. It is about the question that remains when all the science is done. When we know all that can be known about what happened and how, we may still disagree on the *meaning* of what happened.

There will be those who say, beyond the facts and the explanation of the facts, there *is* no meaning. There will be others who say there is. The universe does not come emblazoned with its purpose. To fathom it has taken much wisdom and humility and the experience of humankind over many centuries. To express it may take music and art, ritual and celebration. But to say, 'What is, is, for no other reason than it is,' is to halt prematurely the human tendency to ask and never rest satisfied with the answer, 'It just is.'[5] Curiosity leads to science, but it also leads to questions unanswerable by science.

The search for God is the search for meaning. The discovery of God is the discovery of meaning. And that is no small thing, for we are meaning-seeking animals. It is what makes us unique. To be human is to ask the question, 'Why?'

Scientists of a certain type seem to take perverse pleasure in declaring that life is in fact meaningless. Here, for example, is Jacques Monod:

> Man must at last wake out of his millenary dream and discover his total solitude, his fundamental isolation. He must realise that, like a gypsy, he lives on the boundary of an alien world, a world that is deaf to his music, and as indifferent to his hopes as it is to his sufferings or his crimes.[6]

And, more bluntly, Steven Weinberg:

> It is almost irresistible for humans to believe that we have some special relation to the universe, that human life is not just a more or less farcical outcome of a chain of accidents reaching back to the first three minutes, but that we were somehow built in from the beginning . . . It is very hard to realise that this is all just a tiny part of an overwhelmingly hostile universe . . . It is even harder to realise that this present universe has evolved from an unspeakably unfamiliar early condition, and faces a future extinction of endless cold or intolerable heat. The more the universe seems comprehensible, the more it seems pointless.[7]

Such sentiments are not new. You can find them in the Hebrew Bible, especially in the book of Ecclesiastes:

'Meaningless! Meaningless!'
says the Teacher.
'Utterly meaningless!
Everything is meaningless . . .
Man's fate is like that of the animals; the same fate awaits them both: As one dies, so dies the other. All have the same breath; man has no advantage over the animal. Everything is meaningless.' (Eccl. 1:2; 3:19)

As a mood, most of us have experienced times when that is how the world seems. In the midst of crisis or bereavement, the fabric of meaning is torn apart and we feel strangers in an alien world. Yet a mood is not a truth; a feeling is not a fact. As a general statement of the condition of the universe, there is nothing whatsoever to justify Monod's or Weinberg's conclusions. To grasp this, listen to perhaps the most eloquent account of atheism ever given, by Bertrand Russell in 'A Free Man's Worship':

> That man is the product of causes which had no prevision of the end they were achieving; that his origin, his growth, his hopes and fears, his loves and his beliefs, are but the outcome of accidental collocations of atoms; that no fire, no heroism, no intensity of thought and feeling, can preserve an individual life beyond the grave; that all the labors of the ages, all the devotion, all the inspiration, all the noonday brightness of human genius, are destined to extinction in the vast death of the solar system, and that the whole temple of man's achievement must inevitably be buried beneath the debris of a universe in ruins – all these things, if not quite beyond dispute, are yet so nearly certain that no philosophy which rejects them can hope to stand. Only within the scaffolding of these truths, only on the firm foundation of unyielding despair, can the soul's salvation henceforth be safely built.[8]

C'est magnifique. One can scarce forbear to cheer. But one can produce almost exactly the same peroration in praise of faith:

That man, despite being the product of seemingly blind causes, is not blind; that being in the image of God he is more than an accidental collocation of atoms; that being free, he can rise above his fears, and, with the help of God, create oases of justice and compassion in the wilderness of space and time; that though his life is short he can achieve immortality by his fire and heroism, his intensity of thought and feeling; that humanity too, though it may one day cease to be, can create before night falls a noonday brightness of the human spirit, trusting that, though none of our kind will be here to remember, yet in the mind of God, none of our achievements is forgotten – all these things, if not beyond dispute, have proven themselves time and again in history. We are made great by our faith, small by our lack of it. Only within the scaffolding of these truths, only on the firm foundation of unyielding hope, can the soul's salvation be safely built.

I never understood why it should be considered more courageous to despair than to hope. Freud said that religious faith was the comforting illusion that there is a father figure. A religious believer might say that atheism is the comforting illusion that there is no father figure, so that we can do what we like and can get away with: an adolescent's dream. Why should one be considered escapist and not the other? Why should God's call to responsibility be considered an easy option? Why should the belief, held by some on the basis of scientific determinism, that we have no free will and therefore no moral responsibility, not be considered the greatest escapism of them all?

There is absolutely nothing in science – not in cosmology or evolutionary biology or neuroscience – to suggest that the universe is bereft of meaning, nor could there be, since the search for meaning has nothing to do with science and everything to do with religion. We now need to see why.

The Meaning of a System

Ludwig Wittgenstein wrote:

> The sense of the world must lie outside the world. In the world everything is as it is and happens as it does happen. In it there is no value – and if there were, it would be of no value. If there is a value which is of value, it must lie outside all happening and being-so. For all happening and being-so is accidental. What makes it non-accidental cannot lie in the world, for otherwise this would again be accidental. It must lie outside the world.[9]

There is a marvellous scene in Peter Shaffer's play *Royal Hunt of the Sun* in which Pizarro, the Spanish explorer, hands Atahualpa, the Inca god-king, a Bible. Gingerly Atahualpa stares at it, smells it, feels it, licks it, puts his ear to it and eventually tosses it away. He thinks of it as a fetish, perhaps with magical properties. He has no conception of a book. Imagine what it would take to explain what a book is. The explanation would have little to do with its physical properties and everything to do with the history of writing, the development of the alphabet, and so on. Meaning, when it comes to artefacts or institutions, has little to do with the physical properties of things and everything to do with the way they symbolise and ritualise aspects of the human condition. Meaning is a phenomenon not of nature but of culture.

Imagine what it would take to explain to someone who had no conception of money, what is involved in withdrawing cash from a dispensing machine. He might watch the process a thousand times, understand precisely the physical properties of the credit card and the dispensing machine, but still have no idea of what had taken place. Explaining the transaction might include a history of the division of labour, exchange, barter, the origins of precious metals as currency, the shift from real to nominal value represented by a banknote, what a bank is, what deposits, withdrawals and credit are, and so forth.

Take a game like football. Some hypothetical visitor from a land to which football has not yet penetrated wants to understand this strange ritual which excites so much passion. You explain the rules of the game, what counts as a foul, what constitutes a goal, and so on. 'Fine,' says the visitor, 'I now understand the game. What I don't understand is why you get so excited about it.' Here you might have to launch into some larger reflection about games as ritualised conflict, and the role of play in rehearsing skills needed in actual conflict. You might even suggest that ritualised conflict reduces the need for actual conflict: the football pitch as a substitute for the battlefield.

There is an *internal logic* of the system – the laws of banking, the rules of football – but the *meaning* of the system lies elsewhere, and it can only be understood through some sense of the wider human context in which it is set. To do this you have to step outside the system and see why it was brought into being. There is no way of understanding the meaning of football by merely knowing its rules. They tell you how to play the game, but not why people do so and why they invest in it the passions they do. The internal workings of a system do not explain the place the system holds in human lives.

The meaning of the system lies outside the system. Therefore, the meaning of the universe lies outside the universe. That was the revolution of Abrahamic monotheism.

Monotheism was not a mere mathematical reduction of many gods to one God. That might have economised on temple building, but it would not have transformed the human condition. What did transform it was *the discovery of a God beyond the universe*. This idea, and this alone, has the power to redeem life from tragedy and meaninglessness.

People err in thinking that polytheism and monotheism are two species within the genus religion, variants of the same thing. That is not so at all. The gods of polytheism, in all their buzzing, boisterous confusion, were within the universe. They were subject to nature. They did not create it. They may have been stronger than human beings. They were certainly longer lived; they were immortal. But they were within the universe, and therefore in principle they could not give meaning to the universe.

The same is true for science, whose subject is the interrelationship of things within the natural world. There is a great deal of difference between giving a climatological explanation of rain, and explaining that rain is the work of the Aztec god Tleloc, the Persian god Tishtrya, Taki-Tsu-Hiko in Japan, Imdugud in Assyria, and so on through an impressive cast list of gods and goddesses of inundation. Science is not myth, myth is not science, but they are both explanations of some phenomenon within nature in terms of other phenomena within nature. In this sense, myth is proto-science. Science displaces myth.

But *neither yields meaning*, since meaning is only provided by something or someone outside the system. So, the rain falls on the righteous and wicked alike. The innocent and the guilty starve together in times of drought, and drown together in a flood. In ancient times the gods were at best indifferent, at worst actively hostile to humanity. Scientists like Jacques Monod and Steven Weinberg say the same about nature today, and within their own terms of reference they are right. Nature is sublimely indifferent to who we are and what we deserve. There is nothing moral about it; it carries no meaning within it. Myth and science in their different ways tell us how the parts are related. They cannot tell us what the totality means.

Only something or someone outside the universe can give meaning to the universe. Only belief in a transcendental God can render human existence other than tragic. Individual lives, even within a tragically configured universe, may have meaning, but life as a whole does not. Bertrand Russell was right. Take God out of the equation, and we are left with unyielding despair. On this he was more honest than most of his successors.

*   *   *

Can we prove life has a meaning? Clearly not. Imagine two people reflecting on the course of their own lives. One looks back and sees a mere series of events, with no connecting thread. The other sees a coherent narrative. Her life has a meaning. It can be told as a story. To be sure, she knows that there were distractions, setbacks, false turns, long periods in which nothing significant happened. But looking back, she can see that she was drawn to a calling, falteringly at first but then with ever-increasing confidence. The two people inhabit the same world, but they live different kinds of lives.

Almost none of the things for which people live can be proved. Consider trust. There are people whose attitude to the world is confident, positive, hopeful. They trust others. From time to time that trust is betrayed. They learn to be more circumspect. They find that certain individuals and types are best avoided. But they see these as exceptions. They do not lose their fundamental trust in people. Equally, though, we can think of people who, perhaps never having had in childhood a loving, stable relationship, see every human interaction as a potential threat. They view others with suspicion. Their assumption is that human beings are unreliable. They let you down. It is always wrong to trust and dangerous to love. All the proofs in the world will not get them to change their mind. For them to be able to trust will require not *evidence*, but *healing* – something not unlike a religious conversion.

That is at a personal level. The same applies across a broader canvas. Take history, for example. There are those who see no meaning in history whatsoever. They see it in terms of Joseph Heller's graphic description, 'a trash bag of random coincidences torn open in a wind'.[10] But there have been others – notably Tolstoy in *War and Peace* – who believed that beneath the surface of events a larger plan was unfolding, of which the participants in history were unaware.[11] The prophets believed history was a drama about redemption. For Christians it was about salvation. For the heroes of the Enlightenment it was a narrative of progress. These are not disagreements about the facts of history. They are disagreements about the interpretation of the facts of history.

We cannot prove that life is meaningful and that God exists. But neither can we prove that love is better than hate, altruism than selfishness, forgiveness than the desire for revenge. We cannot prove that the hope is truer to experience than the tragic sense of life. Almost none of the truths by which we live are provable, and the desire to prove them is based on a monumental confusion between explanation and interpretation. Explanations can be proved, interpretations cannot. Science deals in explanation. Meaning is always a matter of interpretation. It belongs to the same territory as ethics, aesthetics and metaphysics. In none of these three disciplines can anything of consequence be proved, but that does not make them insignificant. To the contrary, they represent three of the greatest repositories of human wisdom.

Often the different stances people take towards the human condition are *incommensurable*. No proof, no evidence, no court can decide between them, because people have different views as to what counts as proof, what constitutes evidence and which is the appropriate court. It is no more possible to show that one is true, the other false, than it is possible to prove the truth of optimism against pessimism, science against art, prose against poetry, courage against a play-it-safe, minimum-risk approach to life.

But the idea that *it does not matter which we choose* could not be more wrong. A life without trust or love is, most of us would feel, an impoverished thing, missing out on a range of experiences that have been held by poets and philosophers to be supreme expressions of our humanity. Life without meaning is a fearful prospect. Albert Camus, who believed that there was no meaning and that life is absurd, argued in *The Myth of Sisyphus* that the fundamental question of philosophy is, 'Why should I not commit suicide?' It is possible to live without meaning, just as it is possible to live without music, a sense of humour, or the courage to take a risk. But it cannot seriously be argued that the loss of meaning is not a loss.

*   *   *

Beliefs that lie too deep to be proved are best understood as *framing beliefs*. Like a frame, they are not part of the picture, but they give it its shape, its outline, its orientation. Every individual, and every culture, has framing beliefs that determine their fundamental stance towards the world. Those beliefs shape the way we see things, how we talk about them and the way we respond. Usually we are not conscious of them, precisely because they are frames, not part of the picture itself.[12]

One of the most significant framing beliefs is the one assumed by science: the idea that the universe is governed by certain immutable laws. As David Hume showed in the eighteenth century, the truth of this principle can never be proved. The fact that certain phenomena have occurred a million or a billion times does not entail that they will do so next time. Bertrand Russell illustrated this by life as it seems to a turkey. Every day it is fed by its owner. Being a scientific turkey, it concludes that this is a rule of nature. The Wednesday before Thanksgiving it discovers the difference between probability and certainty.[13] This, the so-called 'problem of induction', is insoluble. Science rests on the faith that, in Einstein's words, 'God does not play dice with the universe'. It cannot be proved, but it works.

There are many other unprovable framing beliefs, and they have perplexed philosophers since humans first thought systematically about such things. Is there really a world out there, or are there only our sense impressions? Are there other minds? Do we have free will? Has the universe existed for billions of years, or did it come into existence five minutes ago, together with false memories and evidence? These are staple topics of any introductory course of philosophy. Framing beliefs – that there is an external world, and other minds, and free will – lie beyond the scope of proof. Nonetheless, they are what give meaning to the chaos of experience.

I said that it is possible to live without meaning. But it will be a strange, foreshortened, defensive kind of life. We know this because of the historical parallel. The world as conceived in the twenty-first century by the new atheists is recognisably the world of ancient Greece in the third pre-Christian century, the age of the Stoics, Sceptics, Cynics and, above all, the Epicureans. Epicurus, and his Roman disciple Lucretius, believed that the material world is the only reality, that the world is made of atoms that simply reconfigure over time, and that the gods have no interest in the affairs of humankind. The Epicureans are the ancient counterparts of the new atheists in their reductive materialism and their hostility to religion. They held that there is no soul, no life after death, no meaning to history and no transcending purpose to life. The Epicurean formula for happiness is to maximise pleasure while minimising risk.

Here, roughly, is how an Epicurean would advise us to live. Do not make emotional commitments. Seize the day and harden yourself against a darker tomorrow. Do not pledge your life in marriage or suffer the burdens of bearing children. There is only one life, so there is no point in foreclosing your options or spending your time raising the next generation, for by the time your investment bears fruit you may no longer be here to see it. Do not get involved in public life: it is stressful and creates envy. Do not spend too much time on others: they seldom repay your efforts or even thank you for them. What matters is you. The others can look after themselves and if they cannot, that is their problem, not yours. Spend your time with friends. Live simply. Get used to solitude. Know that the highest form of freedom is the consciousness of necessity, and the highest form of knowledge is to know that we know nothing. Do not ask what life is for. Live it day by day. And when it becomes burdensome, end it at a time and place of your choosing.

This is a sane response to a universe without meaning. But it is also the symptom of a civilisation in advanced decline. Individuals can live without meaning. Societies in the long run cannot.

I end this chapter with the story of a man I never met, but whose life's work inspired me. His name was Viktor Frankl. Born in

Vienna in 1905, he was deported with the rest of his family to the concentration camp at Theresienstadt in 1942, and spent the next three years in extermination camps, among them Auschwitz and Dachau. He and one of his sisters were the only members of the family to survive.

Already a distinguished neurologist, he preserved his sanity in the camps by observing his fellow prisoners, as if he and they were taking part in an experiment. He noticed the various phases they went through. The first was shock and complete disillusionment. The Nazis began by dehumanising the prisoners in every conceivable way. They took from them everything that gives people a vestige of humanity: their clothes, shoes, hair, even their names. They seized Frankl's most precious possession, a scientific manuscript containing his life's work. Frankl says that at this point, 'I struck out my whole former life.'[14]

The second stage was apathy, a complete dulling of the emotions. People became automata, hardly living, merely existing from day to day. It was then that Frankl asked the fateful question. Is there any freedom left to a person who has been robbed of everything: dignity, possessions, even the power of decision itself? The Jewish victims of earlier persecutions had been given a choice: convert or die. During the Holocaust there was no choice. *What remained once you had lost everything there was to lose?* Frankl realised that there was one freedom that can never be taken away:

> We who lived in concentration camps can remember the men who walked through the huts comforting others, giving away their last piece of bread. They may have been few in number, but they offer sufficient proof that everything can be taken from a man but one thing: the last of the human freedoms – to choose one's attitude in any given set of circumstances, to choose one's own way.[15]

The freedom that remained was *the decision how to respond.* Frankl survived by constantly observing others and helping them find a reason to continue to live. One of the most deadening conditions in the camps was what he called 'futurelessness', the total absence of hope. Frankl recalls, 'A prisoner marching in a long column to a new camp remarked that he felt as if he were walking in a funeral procession behind his own dead body.'[16]

Two of his fellow inmates were contemplating suicide. By conversing with them, he was able to get each to see that they had something still to do. One had published a series of books on geography, but the series was not yet complete. A task awaited him. The other had a daughter abroad who loved him devotedly and longed to see him. A person awaited him. In both cases, what was essential was the realisation that there was something to be done that could be done by no one else.[17] This became the core of an insight Frankl was to turn, after the war, into a new school of psychotherapy. He called it *logotherapy*, from the Greek *logos*, meaning 'word' in the broadest sense – the spiritual dimension of human life, that which endows life with a sense of purpose. He summarised his teaching in the title of his most famous book, *Man's Search for Meaning*.

Homo sapiens is the meaning-seeking animal, Frankl argued. But to preserve meaning in desperate circumstances we must be able, or be helped, to do a number of things. First is the refusal to believe that we are victims of fate. We are free. Within limits, we are the authors of our lives. Second is the knowledge that there is more than one way of interpreting what happens to us – more than one way of telling the story of our life. Third, Frankl insists that *meaning lies outside us*. It is a call from somewhere else:

In the last resort, man should not ask, 'What is the meaning of my life?' but should realise that he himself is being questioned. Life is putting its problems to him, and it is up to him to respond to these questions by being responsible; he can only answer to life by answering *for* his life. Life is a task. The religious man differs from the apparently irreligious man only by experiencing his existence not simply as a task, but as a mission. This means that he is also aware of the taskmaster, the source of his mission. For thousands of years that source has been called God.[18]

To find meaning in life is to find something we are *called on to do*, something no one else can do. Discovering that task is not easy. There are depressive states in which we simply cannot do it on our own ('A prisoner cannot release himself from prison,' says the Talmud about depression[19]). But once we have found it, our life takes on meaning and we recover the will to live.

Frankl's psychotherapy is part of a wider conception I call the ethics of responsibility.[20] The word 'responsible' is related to *response*. It is an answer to a question posed by another. Responsibility is not something that comes from within, but is always a response to something or someone outside us. In *The Responsible Self*, Richard Niebuhr writes, 'Responsibility affirms: God is acting in all actions upon you. So respond to all actions as to his action.'[21] He adds, 'We are most aware of our existence in the moment, in the now, when we are radically acted upon by something from without, when we are under the necessity of meeting a challenge with an action of our own, as is the case in every important decision.'[22] The responsible life is one that responds. In the theological sense it means that *God is the question to which our lives are an answer.*

Frankl rescued lives by helping people find a reason to live, a reason that comes from outside the self. This is, if you like, a secularised version of Abrahamic monotheism, which began with a divine call. Frankl's faith, which is mine, is that the search for meaning constitutes our humanity.

So, to summarise: Science is the search for explanation. Religion is the search for meaning. Meaning is not accidental to the human condition because we are the meaning-seeking animal. To believe on the basis of science that the universe has no meaning is to confuse two disciplines of thought: explanation and interpretation. The search for meaning, though it begins with science, must go beyond it. Science does not yield meanings, nor does it prove the absence of meanings.

The meaning of a system lies outside the system. Therefore the meaning of the universe lies outside the universe. The belief in a God who transcends the universe was the discovery of Abrahamic monotheism, which transformed the human condition, endowing it with meaning and thereby rescuing it from tragedy in the name of hope. For if God created the physical universe, then God is free, and if God made us in his image, we are free. If we are free, then history is not a matter of eternal recurrences. Because we can change ourselves, we can change the world. That is the religious basis of hope.

There are cultures that do not share these beliefs. They are, ultimately, tragic cultures, for whatever shape they give the powers they name, those powers are fundamentally indifferent to human fate. They may be natural forces. They may be human institutions: the empire, the state, the political system, or the economy. They may be human collectivities: the tribe, the nation, the race. But all end in tragedy because none attaches ultimate significance to the individual as individual. All end by sacrificing the individual, which is why, in the end, such cultures die. There is only one thing capable of defeating tragedy, which is the belief in God who in love sets his image on the human person, thus endowing each of us with non-negotiable, unconditional dignity.

2

In Two Minds

For this reason a higher culture must give to a man a double-brain, as it were two brain-ventricles, one for the perceptions of science, the other for those of non-science: lying beside one another, not confused together, separable, capable of being shut off: this is a demand of health.

Nietzsche[1]

Science investigates, religion interprets . . . Religion and science are two hemispheres of human thought.

Martin Luther King, Jr[2]

Pray God us keep
From Single vision & Newton's sleep!

William Blake[3]

To cut straight to the chase, by the end of this chapter I hope to have persuaded you of a simple but fundamental proposition: *Science takes things apart to see how they work. Religion puts things together to see what they mean.*

The difference between them is fundamental and irreducible. They represent two distinct activities of the mind. Neither is dispensable. Both, together, constitute a full expression of our humanity. They are as different and as necessary as the twin hemispheres of the brain. It is, in fact, from the hemispherical asymmetry of the brain that the entire drama of the mutual misunderstanding and conjoint creativity of religion and science derive.

I want in this chapter to trace a set of intellectual journeys that will take us through a series of mental landscapes: different cognitive styles between East and West, gender differences in the way people think about moral dilemmas, a pioneering study of autism, and why people do not just construct arguments, they also tell stories. What makes these studies fascinating is that though they have different starting points, they all arrive at the same conclusion about the human mind, helping us understand why religion and science are so different. Taken together with the next chapter, they amount to a radical explanation of why that relationship has become so frayed, even adversarial, in modern times.

However, I begin with what, for me, was the 'eureka' moment. It was a discovery of seemingly surpassing triviality, but it lit up a network of neural connections, some of which I describe in this chapter. It was the clue that decoded all else. This was the discovery: alphabets without vowels, like Hebrew and Arabic, are written from right to left; alphabets with vowels, like English, are written from left to right.[4] Hardly, on the face of it, a discovery to change the world, but let's suspend judgement and explain why.

In languages where there are letters for vowels, words can be recognised and understood serially, one by one. There is limited ambiguity. But in languages like Hebrew where there are no letters for vowels, it is hard to tell, by looking at the letters on their own, what the word is and what it means. Take the English letters 'h' and 't', for example. Those sounds could combine to make hat, hot, hit, hut, heat and hate. You can only tell which by context. So reading a text in Hebrew involves a fair degree of mental activity. What has come before? What might we expect the sentence to say? What makes sense in terms of the passage as a whole? Simply knowing how to read a word involves a considered judgement based on text and context as a whole.

These different mental operations – serial processing and holistic understanding – use different parts of the brain. Specifically over the past hundred and fifty years, since Pierre Paul Broca discovered the location of language-processing skills in the left side of the brain, neuroscientists have come to understand the marked difference between the brain's two hemispheres and how they process information. The left hemisphere tends to be linear, analytical, atomistic and mechanical. It breaks things down into their component parts and deals with them in a linear, sequential way. The right brain tends to be integrative and holistic. As in E. M. Forster's phrase, it sees things steadily and sees them whole.[5] It gives an overview of a situation while the left hemisphere focuses its attention on specific details.

The right hemisphere is strong on empathy and emotion. It reads situations, atmosphere and moods. It is the locus of our social intelligence. It understands subtlety, nuance, ambiguity, irony and metaphor. It lives with the complexities the left brain tries to resolve by breaking them down into their component parts. The two hemispheres each control the opposite side of the body, so that someone who suffers a stroke in the left brain will find the right side of his body affected. Failure in the right brain will incapacitate the left.

So a language with vowels, where the words can be understood one by one, can be processed by the left brain. We read these languages from left to right, moving our head to the right, thus engaging the left brain. Languages without vowels make demands on the context-understanding, integrative functions of the right brain, so we read them from right to left, moving our head leftwards and engaging the right brain.

The Birth of the Alphabet

There is a story behind the story: about the birth of the alphabet itself. Two inventions transformed the ancient world. The first was the invention of writing, in Mesopotamia more than five thousand years ago. The birth of writing *was* the birth of civilisation, because it enabled the growth of knowledge to become cumulative. Writing enables more information to be handed on from one generation to the next than can be encompassed in a single memory. Writing seems to have been invented independently seven times: in Mesopotamian cuneiform, Egyptian hieroglyphics, the

Indus Valley script, the Minoan script known as Linear B, Chinese ideograms, and among the Mayans and the Aztecs.

Writing evolved from pictograms, simple drawings of what the symbols represent: an ox's head, a donkey, an ear of barley. They became ideograms, more abstract symbols, then syllables, when people realised that words were not just names for things but also sounds. But even at that stage there were too many symbols to learn – some 900 in cuneiform, 700 in hieroglyphics – for literacy to be widespread. It remained the closely guarded skill of a literate elite. What broke open the doors of knowledge was the invention of the alphabet, the reduction of the symbol set to a small enough number to be learned in principle by anyone. The invention of the alphabet was the birth of the possibility of universal literacy and the beginning of the end of hierarchical societies.

The first alphabet, known as proto-Sinaitic, and dated to around 1800 BCE, was discovered by the British archaeologist Flinders Petrie in 1905. He found a series of markings carved into sandstone at Serabit el-Khadem in the Sinai desert, the site of what had been turquoise mines during the age of the pharaohs. Flinders Petrie surmised that the writing may have been the work of the Hebrew slaves who worked the mines, or even that they may have made the inscriptions on their way to the Promised Land. He himself, however, was unable to decipher them and failed to recognise that they were in fact alphabetic: that symbols no longer represented objects or syllables but the *initial sound* of the syllable, so that, for example, the symbol for 'box' meant simply the sound 'b'. Not until 1916 did British Egyptologist Alan Gardiner make that discovery. There was another major find in the 1990s, at Wadi el-Hol, thirty miles north-west of Luxor, by American archaeologist John Darnell. Here too there were inscriptions carved into rock, similar to, though not identical with, those at Serabit, and of roughly the same date or slightly older.

The alphabet has the distinction of being invented only once. All others are direct or indirect descendants of that first system, used by the people of what today is the land of Israel: the Hebrews and perhaps other migrant workers, the Canaanites, Phoenicians and so on. The word 'alphabet' itself signals this: it derives from the first two letters of the Hebrew script, *aleph* and *bet*. The early alphabets, like Hebrew still today, had no letters for vowels. They came to be written from right to left.[6]

The Semitic script was brought by the Phoenicians to the Greeks at some time around the tenth century BCE. The first four letters of the Greek alphabet, *alpha, beta, gamma, delta*, precisely mirror the Hebrew *aleph, bet, gimmel, dalet*. But in the move to Greece the alphabet acquired letters to signal vowel sounds as well as consonants. Something fascinating then happened to the way Greek was written. Originally, exactly like the Canaanite-Semitic script, it was written right to left. Then, between the eighth and sixth centuries BCE, it evolved into a strange form of continuous writing, beginning from right to left, then, on reaching the end of the line, turning round and coming back, left to right, and so on. The Greeks called this *boustrophedon*, 'as an ox ploughs'. Eventually, in the fifth century, it settled into the new mode, left to right, where it has stayed ever since.

Something else of vast consequence was happening while this was taking place: the emergence of the first philosophers and scientists, the first people to think systematically about nature, matter, substance, the 'element and principle of things', and the relationship between what changes and what stays the same. Science began with Thales in the sixth century BCE, who saw water as the fundamental element. Then came Anaximander, Thales' pupil, who argued that all things derive from and ultimately return to 'the boundless'; Heraclitus, who saw nature as constant flux; Pythagoras, the mystic, who saw the universe in terms of mathematical harmony and the music of the spheres; Parmenides, who believed that reality was eternal and unchanging, so that the ever-changing world of the senses is unreal; and Democritus, who believed that the universe was composed of elementary particles he called atoms.

The same period saw the birth of philosophy – the search for the true, the good and the beautiful – which saw its supreme flowering, in the fifth and fourth centuries BCE, in the great triumvirate of Socrates, Plato and Aristotle. With Plato in particular a development took place that would shape the direction of Western thought from that day to this: a preference for the universal over the particular, the timeless over the time-bound, the abstract over the concrete particular, and the impersonal as opposed to the personal. In Plato, even love ceases to be personal. The beloved is only the starting point from which the lover passes on to contemplation of eternal beauty.

It is impossible to overstate the significance of all this for the development of Western civilisation. We owe virtually all our abstract concepts to the Greeks. The Hebrew Bible knows nothing of such ideas. There is a creation narrative – in fact, more than one – but there is no theoretical discussion of what the basic elements of the universe are. There is an enthralling story about the birth of monarchy in Israel, but no discussion, such as is to be found in Plato and Aristotle, about the relative merits of monarchy as opposed to aristocracy or democracy. When the Hebrew Bible wants to explain something, it does not articulate a theory. It tells a story. The birth of monarchy, for example, comes with sharp portraits of the people involved – Samuel, Saul and David. That is where its interest lies. There is deep ambivalence throughout the Hebrew Bible about monarchy – is it commanded, permitted, or only reluctantly conceded? – but nowhere is this given systematic expression. There is a hint here, a nuance there. The entire subject is dealt with from multiple perspectives, at a level of subtlety and ambiguity closer to great literature than either philosophy or political science.

Could it be that this difference between the two cultures has something to do with the way their respective alphabets are written? Greece, at the time the alphabet was changing from right-left to left-right, became the world's first, and greatest, left-brain civilisation. It was not only a left-brain culture. There was greatness, too, in the more right-brain fields of art, architecture and drama. But the conceptualisation and abstraction, the analysis of matter into its atomic parts, the Platonic devaluation of the personal and particular: all this comes with the unmistakable signature of the left hemisphere. The fact that this was happening at the same time, in the same place, as the emergence of the world's first fully vowelled, left-right alphabet cannot be merely coincidental.

The way we record and transmit information has a huge impact on cognitive styles. As I write, books are being published on the way the Internet, Google, Facebook and Twitter are changing the ways in which we think, with such phrases as 'information overload', 'cognitive surplus', 'attention deficit' and so on.[7] When information technology changes, so does the way we think. As Walter J. Ong put it, speaking about the transition from an oral to a literate culture, 'Writing restructures consciousness.'[8]

Here is one piece of evidence. The rabbis of the first to third centuries certainly knew, at least in a rudimentary way, about Greek philosophy and science. Israel had been under Greek rule from the days of Alexander the Great to the Maccabees' revolt against Antiochus IV in the second century BCE. Its circumambient culture was Hellenistic. Yet Jews continued to write and read from right to left, and think in right-brained ways. Here, for example, is the opening of the first great text of the rabbinic age, the Mishnah, a code of Jewish law. Its subject is prayer, and it opens with these words:

From what time does one recite the *Shema* [a central Jewish prayer] in the evening? From the time when the priests go in to eat of their heave-offering until the end of the first watch – so says Rabbi Eliezer. The Sages say: Until midnight. Rabban Gamliel says: Until the column of dawn rises. It once happened that [Rabban Gamliel's] sons came from a house of feasting. They said to [their father]: 'We have not recited the Shema.' He said to them: 'If the column of dawn has not yet risen, then you are obligated to recite it.'[9]

Note what is missing. There is no discussion of what prayer is, or why we pray. There are no general principles of any kind. Instead the Mishnah begins in the middle, with one particular prayer, the night-time *Shema*. Nor, despite the fact that this is a law code, are we given a law. Instead we find three different views as to what the law is, with no statement as to which of the three is correct or normative. This is then followed by an anecdote, which places the third opinion in the context of an actual event in the life of the person who advocated it. Decoding this Mishnah is like reading a word in an alphabet without vowels. You need to have considerable background and contextual knowledge before you can even begin to understand what is being said.

Setting aside all the qualifications and nuances, Greece and Israel in antiquity offer us the sharpest possible contrast between a strongly left-brain and a strongly right-brain culture. They were both widely literate societies, with a high regard for study and discipleship. They both valued the academy and the sage. In many respects they had the same set of priorities, with education and the pursuit of wisdom at the top. But their cognitive styles were different, just as their alphabets were written in opposite directions. They valued different things. The Greeks worshipped human reason, the Jews, divine revelation. The Greeks gave the West its philosophy and science. The Jews, obliquely, gave it its prophets and religious faith.

But I now want to survey some quite different landscapes to illustrate the difference between left- and right-brain thinking. Note that no value judgement is implied. To ask which is the more important, the right or left hemisphere, is like asking which is the more important, the right or left ventricle of the heart. We need them both. The fact that left/right brain asymmetry is a feature of human biology, as it is of some other animal species, suggests that it confers a vital adaptive advantage. Nor is the dichotomy meant to be taken literally. We know, from the earliest experiments using PET scans in the 1980s, that even a simple activity of the brain, like associating the word 'chair' with 'sit', involves both left and right brain. We have also come to understand the astonishing plasticity of the brain.[10] Children who have lost an entire hemisphere are often able to lead a fully normal life, with only minor impairments affecting peripheral vision and fine motor skills.[11]

So think of 'right' and 'left' not as precise neuroscientific descriptions, but merely as metaphors for different modes of engagement with the world.

East and West

One of the more unexpected pleasures of my undergraduate years was the presence in our college of a large number of Chinese scholars, at a time when links between China and the West were tenuous and few. The reason they were there was that the Master, Dr Joseph Needham, a brilliant biochemist, had become the world's leading authority on Chinese science and civilisation. Needham was struck by the extraordinary technical achievements of the Chinese – they had developed ink, paper, printing, porcelain manufacture, the compass, gunpowder and many other technologies long before the West, yet they had failed to develop a scientific revolution along Western lines. Needham's view was that it had something to do with the differences between thought patterns in China (Taoism, Confucianism) and the West. Europe lived with the heritage of Democritus and his successors who believed the physical universe was made up of atoms, and who thought in terms of analysis of substances into their smallest component parts. For the Chinese, by contrast, 'Their universe was a continuous medium or matrix within which interactions of things took place, not by the clash of atoms, but by radiating influences.'[12]

Many years later, University of Michigan psychologist Richard E. Nisbett was struck by a similar realisation as the result of a conversation with one of his students from China. 'The difference between you and me', said the student, 'is that I think the world is a circle, and you think it's a line.' The Chinese, he continued, 'believe in constant change, but with things always moving back to some prior state. They pay attention to a wide range of events; they search for relationships between things; and they think you can't understand the part without understanding the whole. Westerners live in a simpler, more deterministic world; they focus on salient objects or people instead of the larger picture; and they think they can control events because they know the rules that govern the behaviour of objects.'[13]

This stark contrast led Nisbett to a series of studies on the differences between Western and Eastern patterns of cognition, described in his book *The Geography of Thought*. The differences are many and striking. Shown a picture of fish in a tank, complete with plants, rocks and bubbles, American and Japanese students all mentioned seeing the fish, but the Japanese made 60 per cent more references to the background objects. Shown three objects, a chicken, a cow and a clump of grass, and asked 'Which two go together?' American children chose the chicken and the cow – both members of the same class, animal. Chinese children chose the cow and the grass – where there are cows there is grass. Researchers found that American children learn nouns faster than verbs, but that South Asian children learn verbs faster than nouns. Nouns are about classification. Verbs are about relationships.

So it goes on through a whole range of differences. Given the choice between a job offering scope for personal initiative and one with strong teamsmanship, most Americans will opt for the former, Japanese for the latter. Ask Americans, 'Tell me about yourself,' and they will tell you about themselves. Chinese, Japanese or Koreans are more likely to talk about themselves in the context of relationships, family and friends. Americans think in terms of individual rights. Chinese find the concept hard to understand: they see the self as part of a larger whole. Americans think of resolving conflict by universal principles of justice. The Chinese prefer mediation by a middleman whose goal is not fairness but animosity reduction. A famous American reading primer begins, 'See Dick run. See Dick play. See Dick run and play.' The corresponding Chinese primer reads, 'Big brother takes care of little brother. Big brother loves little brother. Little brother loves big brother.' Westerners tend to think in terms of either/or, Chinese in terms of both/and: yin and yang, feminine and masculine, passive and active, interpenetrating forces that complete one another.

As with Athens and Jerusalem, so with the West and East: there is more than one cognitive style, more than one way of seeing the world through the prism of the mind.

A Different Voice

There is also more than one way of thinking about morality. In the 1970s, at the time of 'second wave feminism', Carol Gilligan of Harvard produced a famous study, *In a Different Voice*, arguing that men and women used distinctive styles of moral reasoning. Men, she said, found their identity by separation, women by attachment. Men were more likely to feel threatened by intimacy, women by isolation. Men played competitive games in groups, regulated by rules. Women were less rule-oriented, formed smaller and closer groups, and had fewer resources for conflict resolution.[14]

When it came to thinking about moral dilemmas, she found men more likely to analyse situations in terms of rights, women in terms of responsibilities. Men's moral thinking tended to be formal and abstract, women's contextual and based on telling stories. Men spoke about justice, women about relationships. Men valued detachment and achievement, women valued attachment and care. For men morality was primarily about the public world of social power, for women it was more about the private world of interpersonal connection. Men saw morality as a set of rules for the avoidance of violence. Women were more likely to think of it as a style of relationship based on empathy and compassion. For too long, Gilligan argued, the woman's voice had been inaudible.

The male stereotype had been taken as normative. We now had to listen to another, alternative voice:

> The concept of identity expands to include the experience of interconnection. The moral domain is similarly enlarged by the inclusion of responsibility and care in relationships. And the underlying epistemology shifts from the Greek ideal of knowledge as a correspondence between mind and form to the Biblical conception of knowing as a process of human relationship.[15]

Again the contrast between ancient Greece and Israel. Gilligan's thesis proved controversial.[16] So has almost any study suggesting that gender differences are rooted in biology rather than culture. Despite this, Steven Pinker in *The Blank Slate* insists that there are such differences, and they are universal across cultures. In every society, men are more likely to compete violently, women to have more intimate social relationships. Women are 'more sensitive to sounds and smells, have better depth perception, match shapes faster, and are much better at reading facial perceptions and body language' than men. Men are more willing than women to take physical risks for the sake of status and attention. And so on.[17]

One continuing controversy turns on the gender differences in relation to the sciences and the humanities. In the United States, despite the fact that half the students on science courses are women, they make up less than 20 per cent of the workforce in science and technology and only 9 per cent in engineering. Pinker cites a study that followed a group of mathematically precocious seventh graders. The boys and girls had the same exceptional mathematical abilities, but the girls told researchers that they were more interested in people, social values and humanitarian aims. The boys declared more interest in things, theoretical values and abstract intellectual inquiry. At college the girls tended to study humanities and the arts. The boys opted for maths and science. Despite a huge effort to attract more women into the sciences and engineering, vocationalist Linda Gottfredson concluded, 'On average, women are more interested in dealing with people and men with things.'

My interest here is not with gender differences, but with cognitive styles. Just as between East and West, so between women and men, there are substantive differences in thought styles and academic specialisation between those happier taking things apart, analysing them into their components and constructing theoretical systems, and those who think in terms of human relationships, attachments, empathy and emotional literacy.

Simon Baron-Cohen on Autism

It was just this difference that led Cambridge psychologist Simon Baron-Cohen (cousin of comedian Sasha) to formulate a new theory of autism.[18] Three out of four autistic children are boys. Among those with high-functioning autism – those with normal or high IQ – or the related condition of Asperger's syndrome, the ratio of males to females is higher still: more than ten to one. Autism is marked by features suggesting diminished right-hemisphere abilities. Autistic children lack the ability to empathise. They are low on social skills. They find it difficult to make eye contact, or they stare too long. They are often good at mechanical tasks, at mathematics or memorising lists or learning foreign words. They can be obsessional. But they do not read moods or understand irony or humour or ambiguity. They tend to treat people as objects and have difficulty in developing a first-person perspective and a self-image.

Baron-Cohen's theory is that autism is a condition of hyper-maleness. His thesis is that 'The female brain is predominantly hardwired for empathy. The male brain is predominantly hard-wired for understanding and building systems.' This theory was first advanced by Hans Asperger in 1944, but his work was not translated into English until 1991. Asperger's and Baron-Cohen's theory is that empathisers and systematisers have sharply different skills. Empathisers relate to people, systematisers to things.

Empathisers have emotional intelligence; they read people's feelings. Systematisers have a more detached, scientific intelligence; they are fascinated by how things work. Almost all of us have both skills. On average women score higher than men on empathy, men higher than women on systematising, but there are many exceptions. Baron-Cohen's point is that autism is an extreme case of a high-systematising, low-empathising mind.

It is striking how closely this theory fits Carol Gilligan's on moral reasoning, and Pinker's on vocational preferences. Again my interest here is not with gender, but with the further evidence autism provides of the sharp difference between a people-centred and a systems-centred intelligence.

Jerome Bruner on Narrative

Jerome Bruner is an American cognitive psychologist and education theorist who in the late 1950s was part of a movement to bring the human, inward, reflective dimension back into psychology. At that time, in an effort to establish its credentials as a science, psychologists had tended to bypass the inner workings of the mind, focusing instead on observable behaviour, stimulus-response patterns, or even, under the impact of the development of computing, on 'information processing'. All these things, though, miss out on the central feature of the mind, the way it strives to make sense of the world. The key acts of the mind – believing, desiring, intending, choosing – have to do with the way the individual seeks to interact with the world. A focus on outward behaviour misses out on the intentionality, the what-you-are-aiming-at, of action. The task Bruner and his colleagues set was 'to establish meaning as the central concept of psychology', and to understand human beings as 'meaning-making' animals.[19]

Central to Bruner's theory, set out in his book *Actual Minds, Possible Worlds*, is the difference between two types of mental construction: *argument* and *narrative*. You can put forward a case, or you can tell a story. They are different in their methods, their inner logic and their aim. Argument appeals to verifiable truth, story appeals to verisimilitude, lifelikeness. Argument comes together with theory, analysis, logical coherence and empirical testing. Narrative speaks to the imagination and the emotions. It lends drama to believable human situations. It celebrates what James Joyce called epiphanies of the ordinary. Argument is about the universals of logic and science. Narrative is about the particularities of human experience. You can test an argument. You cannot test a story, but it can still convey powerful and revelatory truths.[20]

Bruner's point is that narrative is central to the construction of meaning, and meaning is what makes the human condition human. No computer needs to be persuaded of its purpose in life before it does what it is supposed to do. Genes do not need training in selfishness. No virus needs a coach. We do not have to enter their mindset to understand what they do and how they do it, because they do not have a mindset to enter. But humans do. We act in the present because of things we did or that happened to us in the past, and in order to realise a sought-for future. Even minimally to explain what we are doing is already to tell a story. Take three people eating salad in a restaurant, one because he needs to lose weight, the second because she's a principled vegetarian, the third because of religious dietary laws. These are three outwardly similar acts, but they belong to different stories and they have different meanings for the people involved.

There is a fundamental difference between behaviour and action. Behaviour is a physical movement, like raising a hand. An action is a movement with a purpose and an intention. I can raise my hand to ask a question, hail a taxi, demonstrate support or wave to a friend: same behaviour, different actions. Behaviour can be studied – is *best* studied – with scientific detachment, but action, to be understood, needs empathy, identification, a sense of how the agent sees herself and the world.

The difference between behaviour and action points to something else besides. The crucial differentiation between humans and all other animals is that we make meanings, and the name we give to collective systems of meanings is culture.[21] To understand human action, we need to be able to differentiate between nature and culture, and thus between the natural sciences and the humanities. Systems explain nature. Stories help us understand human nature.

Conclusion

What I hope these four stories do is to show us how, whether it registers in the form of cognitive differences between East and West, different reasoning styles between women and men, the nature of autism, or the difference between systems and stories, we are faced with a fundamental duality in the way we, as humans, relate to the world. This is rooted in biology, in the assymetrical functioning of the right and left cerebral hemispheres, and mediated through culture – through philosophy and the sciences on the one hand, through narrative, the arts and religion on the other.

There are truths we can express in systems, but others we can only tell through story. There is the kind of knowledge for which we need detachment, but another kind of knowledge we can only achieve through attachment – through empathy and identification with an other. There are truths that apply at all times and places, but there are others that are context-specific. There are truths we can tell in prose, but others for which only poetry is adequate. In her book *Poetic Justice*, Martha Nussbaum explains why judges should read novels. Only through the exercise of imaginative identification can judges balance the universality of law with a human understanding of this unique individual standing in the dock.[22]

One of the most powerful scientific ideas of the twentieth century was Niels Bohr's complementarity theory, designed to resolve one of the paradoxes of particle physics. Light cannot be both a wave and a particle, yet it behaves like both, now one, now the other. Bohr explains that the idea came to him when his son had been found guilty of a petty theft. He tried to see his son, first from the perspective of a judge, then from that of a father. He could do both, but not both at the same time. The point has been illustrated many times since, in such simple examples as the figure that, seen one way, looks like a duck and, seen another way, looks like a rabbit. We seem to be able to switch from one form of pattern recognition to another, one frame to another. It is just that we cannot see both ways simultaneously.

Complementarity theory is as true of the human mind as it is of subatomic particles. We are creative, but we are also creations. We are subjects and objects. We act and are acted on. We seek independence but also interdependence. We can switch from first- to third-person perspectives, from the observing 'I' to the observed 'Me'. We are capable of seeing a garden from the perspective of an estate agent, a horticulturalist and an impressionist painter. There is more than one way of looking at our place in the universe.

There are, of course, people incapable of complementarity: the boss who behaves at home the way he does at the office, the zealot who can only exist at the level of indignation, the academic who has no small talk, the driven success-seeker who can never relax, the petty dictator who feels the need to dominate every encounter, the religious fundamentalist who has no time for science, and the secular fundamentalist who can see nothing positive in religion.

What I have tried to show in this chapter is the profound difference between two modes of thinking, of which science and religion are the supreme exemplars. *Science takes things apart to see how they work. Religion puts things together to see what they mean.* This fundamental difference, between atomisation and integration, explanation and interpretation, between separation and detachment on the one hand, connection and attachment on the other, goes deep into who we are and how we think. Ultimately it is the difference between impersonal and personal knowledge, between understanding things and understanding people.[23]

A civilisation that had space for science but not religion might achieve technological prowess. But it would not respect people in their specificity and particularity. It would quickly become inhuman and inhumane. Think of the French Revolution, Stalinist Russia and Communist China, and you need no further proof. The world of science is an arena of causes and effects. The world of people in their glory and frailty is a domain of hopes, fears, dreams, anxieties, intentions and aspirations, all of them set within frameworks of meaning through which we discover, if we are fortunate, our purpose in life, that which we are called on – by God, by nature, by the still small voice – to do.

I began this chapter with a sharp contrast between the Greece of the philosophers and the Judaism of the Bible and the post-biblical sages. I suggested, speculatively, that it might be related to the difference between the Greek and Hebrew languages in their written forms. Could it be that a simple contrast between left-to-right and right-to-left might account for the vast difference between these two cultures? It would be strange to find that so much turned on so slight a detail.

Yet the story I am about to tell in the next chapter is stranger still by far, because it tells of how a right-brain spirituality was introduced to the West in a left-brain language, leading to a unique synthesis between the worlds of Athens and Jerusalem that survived for seventeen centuries, and then began to crumble. It sheds new light on the relationship between religion and science, showing us that there is more than one way it can be construed. But it begins with the too-little-reflected-on story of how the West received its religion in translation.

3

Diverging Paths

Be indulgent in cases where, despite our diligent labour in translating, we may seem to have rendered some phrases imperfectly. For what was originally expressed in Hebrew does not have exactly the same sense when translated into another language. Not only this book, but even the Law itself, the Prophecies, and the rest of the books differ not a little when read in the original.

Prologue to Ecclesiasticus

Translating from one language to another . . . is like looking at Flemish tapestries from the wrong side.

Cervantes[1]

In entering the Greek world, Plato's turf, the early Christians mixed biblical ideas into a Greek framework that often distorted their original meaning.

Harvey Cox[2]

I want in this chapter to tell three stories, one about the birth of Christianity, a second about a curious incident in the history of Judaism, a third about the wrestling match between science and religion since the seventeenth century. The issues they touch on are vast and I can only deal with them in the broadest of brushstrokes. Almost every sentence of this chapter needs qualification and nuance. But the stories are so strange and their significance so little appreciated that they helped me, as I hope they will help you, understand how people came to think that you can prove or disprove the existence of God by a combination of science and philosophy.

The first is the strangest of them all, a fortuitous, unpredictable event that has influenced the entire trajectory of Western civilisation for close to two thousand years and has had a profound bearing on our understanding of the relationship between religion and science.

The West owes its development to two cultures, ancient Greece and ancient Israel, Hellenism and Hebraism, the heritages respectively of Athens and Jerusalem. The difference between them was one of the great tropes of nineteenth-century cultural analysis. Herder and Heine wrote about it in Germany, Renan in France and Matthew Arnold, in *Culture and Anarchy*, in England.[3] They were the first two cultures to make the break with myth, but they did so in different ways, the Greeks by philosophy and reason, the Jews by monotheism and revelation.

There were times when the relationship between them was warm. The Jews respected Greek science. In return, Aristotle's disciple Theophrastus spoke of the Jews as a nation of philosophers. But there were also tensions, especially when Israel came under Seleucid rule in the second century BCE. One Seleucid ruler, Antiochus IV, attempted to Hellenise the Jews, banning the public practice of Judaism and erecting a statue of Zeus in the precincts of the Temple in Jerusalem. The Jews successfully fought a war of freedom that we still recall on the festival of Hanukkah. A century later, however, Pompey invaded Israel, conquered Jerusalem, and the land came under Roman rule.[4]

By then and throughout the remaining Second Temple period the Jewish people was hopelessly factionalised. Some favoured accommodation with Rome, others active rebellion. Some believed in politics as usual, others were convinced that an apocalypse was in the making that would lead to the messianic age and 'the kingdom of heaven', when idolatry would cease, and Israel would recover its sovereignty and be free to pursue its vocation as a holy nation.

There was also a major cultural struggle. Many Jews in Israel and the Diaspora had become deeply Hellenised. Meanwhile, as we know from Philo, Josephus and other contemporary observers, many Gentiles in the Hellenistic world had adopted at least some Jewish practices and become half-converts, 'God-fearers', Jewish sympathisers if not full Jews. In the opposite direction there were Jews – the rabbis – who believed the faith would only survive by turning inwards and strengthening the key institutions of the Jewish home, the synagogue and the House of Study. It was against this complex and fraught backdrop that Christianity was born.

Jesus was a Jew. He lived in the land of Israel, mainly in the Galilee area, in and among Jews. He spoke to them as a Jew. He read the Bible and almost certainly prayed in Hebrew. Most of his words, phrases, concepts and ideas are familiar to anyone acquainted with the rabbinic Judaism of the time.

Jesus spoke Aramaic, the language of Jews living in Israel at the time. This was the language of the school and the marketplace, into which the Bible was orally translated, line by line, when read in the synagogue, for the benefit of those who did not understand the original. Later it would become the language of the Talmud.

Whenever we hear the direct, untranslated speech of Jesus in the Gospels, he is speaking Aramaic. When he brings back a dead girl to life, he says *Talita kum*, the Aramaic for 'Little girl, get up.' When he prays to God in Mark 14:36, he uses the word *Abba*, Aramaic for 'Father'. During the Sermon on the Mount he criticises those who call other people *Raca*, an Aramaic insult meaning 'empty one'. Most famously, at the crucifixion he cries out, in its standard Aramaic translation, the line from Psalm 22, 'My God, my God, why have you forsaken me?' The Aramaic, *Eli, Eli lama sabachtani*, is very close to the Hebrew, *Eli, Eli lama azavtani*.

Jesus spoke Aramaic and Hebrew. *But every book of the New Testament was written in Greek*. That is the extraordinary fact. Even the Hebrew Bible was known to Christians for centuries in Greek only, in the form of the Septuagint, the translation into koine Greek made in Ptolemaic Egypt in the third century BCE.

The New Testament is, through and through, a Greek document, not a Hebrew or Aramaic one. The testimony of perhaps the greatest Christian biblical scholar of our time, James Barr, is particularly striking. Arguing that the New Testament 'is much more Greek in its terms, its conceptuality, and its thinking than main trends of modern biblical theology have tended to allow', he continues:

> My own experience makes this to me undeniable. If one has spent most of one's life, as I have, working on Hebrew and other Semitic-language texts, and then returns after some absence to a closer study of the New Testament, the impression of the essentially Greek character of the latter is overwhelming . . . The attempt, at one time popular and influential, to argue that, though the words might be Greek, the thought processes were fundamentally Hebraic, was a conspicuous failure.[5]

Barr's statement, made in the course of his 1991 Gifford Lectures, is all the more striking since it was he who, thirty years earlier, in his influential *The Semantics of Biblical Language*, argued against contrasting Greek and Hebrew modes of thought in terms of the structure of their respective languages.

The reasons for this strange turn of events are well known. In the first decades after Jesus' death the Church might have gone in either of two directions. It might have become a Jewish sect, the Jerusalem church, under Jesus' brother James. In the event, however, it was Paul who found a ready audience among the Hellenistic Gentiles of the Mediterranean, especially those who had already shown an interest in elements of Jewish practice and faith. It was the Greek- not the Hebrew-and-Aramaic–speaking population that proved to be the fertile soil in which Christianity took root and grew.

We do not know whether Jesus spoke or understood Greek. It is likely that he knew a few words, the kind you might use in the market or the street, but there is no evidence that he thought, taught or prayed in Greek, and the balance of probability is over-whelmingly against it. It is an open question whether he would have understood the New Testament. We have here, in other words, a unique phenomenon in the history of religion: *a religion whose sacred texts are written in what to its founder would have been a foreign and largely unintelligible language.*

Had the languages in question been closely related, part of the same linguistic family, this might have been of little conse-quence. But first-century Greek and Hebrew were not just differ-ent languages. They represented antithetical civilisations, unlike in their most basic understanding of reality. In terms of the last chapter, Greek philosophy and science – the Greece of Thales and Democritus, Plato and Aristotle – was a predominantly left-brain culture, the Israel of the prophets a right-brain one. At precisely the time Greek came to be written left-to-right and Athens became a literate rather than an oral culture, it became the birthplace of science and philosophy, the two supremely left-brain, conceptual, analytical ways of thinking.

Western civilisation was born in the synthesis between Athens and Jerusalem brought about by Pauline Christianity and the conversion of Emperor Constantine in 312, turning a small and often persecuted sect into the official religion of the Roman Empire. It was an astonishing, improbable event and it eventually transformed the world. Christendom drew its philosophy, science and art from Greece, its religion from Israel. But from the outset it contained a hairline fracture that would not become a struc-tural weakness until the seventeenth century. It consisted in this, that though Christians encountered philosophy, science and art in the original Greek, they experienced the religion of their founder in translation.

Greek is a language into which the personal religious back-ground of Jesus does not go. It was the natural language of thought of Paul, the writers of the Gospels, the authors of the other books of the New Testament, the early Church Fathers and the first Christian theologians. It was their genius that shaped a new religious movement that was to prove the most successful in the entire history of the spiritual quest of humankind. But it contained one assumption that would eventually be challenged from the seventeenth century until today, namely that science and philosophy on the one hand, and religion on the other, belong to the same universe of discourse.

They may. But they may not. It could be that Greek science and philosophy and the Judaic experience of God are two different languages that – like the left- and right-brain modes of thinking we encountered in the last chapter – only imperfectly translate into one another. Recognising this now might leave science freer to be science, and religion to be religion, without either challenging the integrity of the other.[6]

The Christianity that eventually emerged from the tradition of Paul, Augustine, Anselm and Aquinas had strong Judaic elements. It spoke of faith, hope, charity, righteousness, love, forgiveness, the dignity of the human person and the sanctity of life. It valued humility and compassion. It spoke of a God who loves his creatures. But it also contained strands that were undeniably Greek and in striking contrast with the way Jews read the Hebrew Bible. The following are some of them.

The first and most obvious is *universality*. Judaism is a principled and unusual combination of universality and particularity: the universality of God, and the particularity of the ways in which we relate to God. The God of Israel is the God of all humanity, but the religion of Israel is not, and is not intended to be, the religion of all humanity. You do not have to be part of the Sinai covenant, or even the covenant of Abraham, to reach heaven and achieve salvation.

Pauline Christianity rejected this. The upside of this is its inclusivity, expressed most famously in Paul's striking statement, 'There is neither Jew nor Gentile, neither slave nor free, nor is there male and female' (Galatians 3:28). The downside is its denial of any other route to salvation. *Extra ecclesiam non est salus*: 'Outside the Church there is no salvation.' Universality is supremely characteristic of Greek thought in the classic age between the sixth and third pre-Christian centuries (though of course it was not applied in their religious understanding). Above all it is the legacy of Plato, who utterly devalued particulars in favour of the universal form of things. For Plato truth is universal and eternal or it is not truth at all. In that sense, Paul and Plato are soulmates.

The second is *dualism*. To a far greater extent than Judaism, Christianity after Paul develops a series of dualisms, between body and soul, the physical and the spiritual, Earth and heaven, this life and the next, with the emphasis on the second of each pair. The body, says Paul in Romans, is recalcitrant. 'What I want to do I do not do, but what I hate I do' (Romans 7:15). There is nothing like this in Jewish literature. To be sure there is the 'evil inclination', but no suggestion that because of our embodied condition we are slaves to sin. The entire set of contrasts – soul as against body, the afterlife as against this life – is massively Greek with much debt to Plato and traces of Gnosticism. Paul's occasionally ambivalent remarks about sexuality and marriage also have no counterpart in mainstream Judaism.

Third is the Pauline reinterpretation, one of the most radical in the history of religion, of the story of Adam and Eve and 'the Fall', and the consequent *tragic view of the human condition*. There is no such interpretation of the passage in the Hebrew Bible. According to Judaism we are not destined to sin. In the very next chapter, before Cain murders his brother Abel, God reminds him of his essential freedom: 'Sin is crouching at your door; it desires to have you, but you can dominate it' (Genesis 4:7). The collective forgiveness of humankind occurs, in the Hebrew Bible, after the Flood. 'Never again,' says God, 'will I curse the ground because of humans, even though every inclination of the human heart is evil from childhood' (Genesis 8:21).

The human tragedy as described by Paul is more Greek than Jewish, and as for the idea of inherited sin, it is already negated in the sixth pre-Christian century by both Jeremiah and Ezekiel.[7]

Of course, in Christianity, tragedy is avoided by salvation; but salvation in this sense, the existential deliverance of the human person from the grip of sin, does not exist in Judaism. We choose. Sometimes we choose wrongly. We atone (in biblical times through the Temple service, post-biblically by repentance) and God forgives.

Fourth is the potential for the separation, unknown in Judaism, between 'faith' and 'works'. In Judaism the two go hand in hand. Faithfulness is a matter of how you behave, not what you believe. Believing and doing are part of a single continuum, and both are a measure of a living relationship characterised by loyalty. In general one of the great differences between classical Greek and Hebraic thought is the immense emphasis in the latter on the *will*. We are, in a Jewish view, what we choose to be, and it is in the realm of choice, decision and action that the religious drama takes place. The Greek view emphasises far more the role of fate and the futility of fighting against it. Under its influence Christianity became more a religion of acceptance than protest – the characteristic stance of the Hebrew prophets.

The fifth and most profound difference lies in the way the two traditions understood the key phrase in which God identifies himself to Moses at the burning bush. 'Who are you?' asks Moses. God replies, cryptically, *Ehyeh asher ehyeh*. This was translated into Greek as *ego eimi ho on*, and into Latin as *ego sum qui sum*, meaning 'I am who I am', or 'I am he who is'. The early and medieval Christian theologians all understood the phrase to be speaking about ontology, the metaphysical nature of God's existence. It meant that he was 'Being-itself, timeless, immutable, incorporeal, understood as the subsisting act of all existing'. Augustine defines God as that which does not change and cannot change. Aquinas, continuing the same tradition, reads the Exodus formula as saying that God is 'true being, that is being that is eternal, immutable, simple, self-sufficient, and the cause and principal of every creature'.[8]

But this is the God of Aristotle and the philosophers, not the God of Abraham and the prophets. *Ehyeh asher ehyeh* means none of these things. It means 'I will be what, where, or how I will be'. The essential element of the phrase is the dimension omitted by all the early Christian translations, namely the future tense. God is defining himself as the Lord of history who is about to intervene in an unprecedented way to liberate a group of slaves from the mightiest empire of the ancient world and lead them on a journey towards liberty. Already in the eleventh century, reacting against the neo-Aristotelianism that he saw creeping into Judaism, Judah Halevi made the point that God introduces himself at the beginning of the Ten Commandments not as God who created heaven and Earth, but by saying, 'I am the Lord your God, who brought you out of Egypt, out of the land of slavery.'⁹

Far from being timeless and immutable, God in the Hebrew Bible is active, engaged, in constant dialogue with his people, calling, urging, warning, challenging and forgiving. When Malachi says in the name of God, 'I the Lord do not change' (Malachi 3:6), he is not speaking about his essence as pure being, the unmoved mover, but about his moral commitments. God keeps his promises even when his children break theirs. What does not change about God are the covenants he makes with Noah, Abraham and the Israelites at Sinai.

So remote is the God of pure being – the legacy of Plato and Aristotle – that the distance is bridged in Christianity by a figure that has no counterpart in Judaism, the Son of God, a person who is both human and divine. In Judaism we are *all* both human and divine, dust of the Earth yet breathing God's breath and bearing God's image. These are profoundly different theologies.

The unique synthesis of Athens and Jerusalem that became Christianity led to the discipline of theology and thus to the intellectual edifice of Western civilisation between the fourth and seventeenth centuries. It was a wondrous achievement, a cathedral of the mind. It brought together the Judaic love of God and the Hellenistic love of nature and human reason. It led to philosophical proofs of the existence of God. There was the cosmological argument: the universe must have a cause that is not itself caused. Or the contingency of being must be rooted in necessary being. Or the moving stars must have an unmoved mover. There was the ontological argument: the most perfect being must necessarily exist since otherwise it would be imperfect. There was the argument from design. As Cicero put it, 'When you see a sundial or a water-clock, you see that it tells the time by design and not by chance. How then can you imagine that the universe as a whole is devoid of purpose and intelligence, when it embraces everything, including these artifacts themselves and their artificers?'[10]

There is natural law. Contemplation of nature tells us how to behave in such a way as to align ourselves with the order of the universe. It leads us to cultivate virtue, pursue justice and have concern for the common good. And there is natural theology. God's purposes can be read in creation, for God wrote two books, one in words called the Bible, the other in works called the universe. So wrote Hugh of St Victor in the twelfth century, as did Francis Bacon in the seventeenth, ushering in the age of science.[11]

It was, to repeat, a wondrous creation – but it was as much Greek as Judaic. The philosophical proofs for the existence of God derived ultimately from Plato and Aristotle. Natural law came from the Stoics. The idea that purposes are inherent in creation – that nature is teleological – was Aristotelian. It combined left-brain rationality with right-brain spirituality in a single, glorious, overarching structure. We may never see its like again.

The second story began for me in 1993 when I was privileged to receive an honorary doctorate from Cambridge University together with, among others, James Watson, co-discoverer of DNA. It gave me the opportunity of saying the ancient blessing, coined by Judaism's sages some two thousand years ago and still to be found in all Jewish prayer books, thanking God for bestowing his wisdom on human beings. Essentially it is a blessing to be said on seeing a great scientist, although the word 'scientist' was not coined until many centuries later, and it reflects a time when religion and science were seen not as adversaries but as respected friends.

I thought hard about that blessing because it is so unexpected. The Talmud says it is to be said on seeing 'one of the sages of the nations of the world'.[12] The sages they were referring to were either Greek or Roman. Remember that the Greeks, under the Seleucid Antiochus IV, had banned the public practice of Judaism. Centuries later, the Romans had destroyed the Temple and razed Jerusalem. These were Israel's enemies, politically, militarily, above all culturally and spiritually. The Greeks were polytheists. The Romans had a disturbing tendency to turn caesars into gods. For the sages to institute a blessing – a religious act of thanksgiving – over their scholars showed a remarkable open-mindedness to wisdom whatever its source. 'Accept the truth, whoever says it,' said Maimonides.[13] There is religious dignity and integrity to science.

No less remarkable is the way in which the rabbis of that era recognised that when it came to science, their own views might simply be wrong. There is a talmudic passage – it reads somewhat quaintly nowadays – in which the rabbis are discussing the question of where the sun goes at night. First they give their own opinion, then they cite the Greek view, that of Ptolemy. They then conclude, 'And their view seems more plausible than ours.'[14] That is the way the Talmud tells the story. They are right. We are wrong. End of discussion.

Similarly, on a more religiously sensitive matter, the rabbinic literature records a conversation between Rabbi Judah the Prince, head of the Jewish community in the early third century, and Antoninus, a Roman sage, about when the soul enters a child. Rabbi Judah says, at birth. Antoninus says, at conception. The rabbi then astonishingly declares that Antoninus is right. Thereafter, when he repeats the teaching, the rabbi is careful to say, 'Antoninus taught me this.'[15] This was a religious attitude to science both open-minded and willing to learn.

Yet I remained puzzled about one of the most curious facts in the intellectual history of Judaism. The first chapter of Genesis with its momentous simplicity – 'And God said let there be . . . and there was . . . and God saw that it was good' – was described by Max Weber and more recently by Peter Berger as the origin of Western rationality.[16] Unlike all the cosmological myths of the ancient world, there is no clash of the gods and their rivals, no cosmic battles like those of Tiamat and Marduk, Seth and Osiris, Kronos and Zeus. There is no myth at all. God speaks and the universe comes into being. The universe has been stripped of its overlay of mystery and caprice. It has been, in Weber's famous word, 'disenchanted'. Genesis 1 is the beginning of the end of the mythic imagination.

It made science possible. No longer was the universe seen as unpredictable. It was the work of a single, rational creative will. Nor was it – as were the gods of myth – at best indifferent, at worst actively hostile to human beings. Genesis spoke of a God who endowed humanity with his image. Evidently he wanted humans to be, in at least some respect, god-like. Had we the evidence of Genesis 1 alone, we could have predicted that the people who lived by this book would have become a nation of scientists.

The curious incident is that they did not. The Greeks did. Jews knew that they did. As we have seen, they admired their work and even coined a blessing over its practitioners. Yet neither in the biblical nor in the early rabbinic age did Jews evince a sustained, widespread, focused interest in science. It is as if from the outset Jews knew that science – what they called 'wisdom' – was one thing, and religion another. Science was about natural law, religion about moral law. Natural laws are laws that predict and explain, moral laws are laws that command or constrain. Science was about things, religion about people and their freely chosen acts. Having established the preconditions of science, Jews evinced no further interest in it at least until the Middle Ages.

Why then is Genesis 1 there? The most obvious reason is that it is not a myth but a polemic against myth. Unlike the gods of myth, God is not part of nature. He is the author of nature which he created by a free act of will. By conferring his image on human-kind, God gives us freedom of the will. This generates the entire moral world of the Bible with its vision of the human person as a responsible, choosing moral agent. Rejecting myth, the Bible discovers freedom.

Second is the insistence on the goodness of the world. Seven times we read that 'God saw that it was good'. This too was revolutionary. Most religions, ancient and modern, have contrasted this world and the next, Earth and heaven, the world of the senses and that of eternity, this life and the afterlife. Here is chaos, there is order. Here is suffering, there is its reward. To a quite remarkable degree the Hebrew Bible is reticent about life after death and never uses it to reconcile people with their condition on Earth. The religious drama takes place here. This world, this life, is where we meet God and either do or fail to do his will. The universe is good, but humans are free to do evil. This frames the entire religious drama of humankind.

Third is the orderliness of the universe. Gone is the mythic mindset of ever-threatening chaos. The narrative is tightly structured. For three days God creates domains – light and dark, sea and sky, sea and dry land. For the next three days he populates those domains with moving things: the sun, moon and stars, fish and birds, land animals and man. The seventh day, the day of rest, is holy: an enduring symbol of the world at peace with itself and its maker. The implication is clear. God creates order; it is man who creates chaos.

Equally radical is the fact that, since God created everything, he is God of everywhere. For the first time, God and religion are de-territorialised. There is no longer a god of this place and a god of that; a god of these people as opposed to those. Abrahamic universalism is born here. This will prove crucial in the book of Exodus when God intervenes to deliver one nation out of another, what we would call today an international intervention in defence of human rights. His authority extends, as it were, not only over the Promised Land but also over Egypt. God is the God of everyone, though not necessarily in the same way. Unlike Plato, the Hebrew Bible emphasises *both* the universal *and* the particular.

It is a worldview of extraordinary simplicity and power. The buzzing confusion of the polytheistic pantheon has disappeared and the entire universe has been cleared for the drama between the lone God and lonely humanity, who have, as it were, only each other for company. Nature has been demystified and demythologised. All Earthly power has been relativised, allowing for the desacralisation of kingship and the eventual secularisation of the political domain.

So Genesis 1, a text that might have been a prelude to science, turns out not to lead in that direction at all. Its frame of reference is moral and spiritual. It is about freedom and order and goodness. It is about a God who creates and makes a being, Homo sapiens, able to create; a God who is free and bestows on his most cherished creation the gift of freedom. Virtually everything that follows in the Bible is about this personal relationship between Creator and creation, at times tender, often tense. To be sure, from time to time the Hebrew Bible expresses wonder at the divine wisdom within creation – the wisdom tracked by science – but that is not where its interest lies.

I have told this second story to show that there was an alternative to the synthesis that eventually emerged in Christianity, namely the way taken by the Judaism of the Hebrew Bible and the rabbinic sages. It saw science as an autonomous activity with its own dignity. It was the wisdom of the Greeks, not the gift of the Jews. Science reveals the wisdom of God in creation, and wisdom is itself the gift God gave humanity when he made us in his image and likeness, which Rashi, the classic Jewish commentator, reads as 'with the capacity to understand and discern'.

But there is a difference between wisdom and Torah.[17] Wisdom tells us how the world is. Torah tells us how the world ought to be. Wisdom is about nature. Torah is about will. It is about human freedom and choice and the way we are called on to behave. Wisdom is about the world God makes. Torah is about the world

God calls on *us* to make, honouring others as bearers of God's image, exercising our freedom in such a way as not to rob others of theirs.

The difference between the two is freedom. The natural universe is as it is because that is how it is. The planets are not free in their movements. Chemical elements do not choose which way to combine. Genes do not make decisions. But we are free; we do choose; we do make decisions. If the movements of the planets fail to obey Aristotle's law of circular motion, that is not because they are disobedient but because Aristotle's law is wrong. But if human beings fail to obey the laws against murder, robbery or theft, that is not because there is something wrong with the laws but because there is something wrong with us.[18] Moral laws are not scientific laws. They belong to a different world, the human world, the world of freedom, God's most fraught and fateful gift. The Hebrew Bible is entirely about this drama of human freedom. Hence the possibility of admiring science as wisdom while at the same time seeing it as a separate discipline best left to scientists.

The third story is simply told. We still do not know what it was about the seventeenth century that led to the rise of experimental science. Some claim it was religion: Protestantism in general or Calvinism in particular. Others claim it was the waning of religion. Some say it was an attempt to repair the Fall of man, who had been exiled from Eden for wrongly eating of the tree of knowledge. Some say it was the attempt to build an Earthly paradise by the use of purely secular reason.[19] Stephen Toulmin has argued, convincingly in my view, that it was the impact of the wars of religion of the sixteenth and seventeenth centuries that led figures like Descartes and Newton to seek certainty on the basis of a structure of knowledge that did not rest on dogmatic foundations.[20]

One way or another, first science, then philosophy, declared their independence from theology and the great arch stretching from Jerusalem to Athens began to crumble. First came the seventeenth-century realisation that the Earth was not the centre of the universe. Then came the development of a mechanistic science that sought explanations in terms of prior causes, not ultimate purposes.

Then came the eighteenth-century philosophical assault, by Hume and Kant, on the philosophical arguments for the existence of God. Hume pointed up the weakness of the argument from design. Kant refuted the ontological argument.

Then came the nineteenth century and Darwin. This was, on the face of it, the most crushing blow of all, because it seemed to show that the entire emergence of life was the result of a process that was blind.

We think of these as shaking the religious worldview of the Bible, but in fact they were something else entirely. For it was the Greeks who saw the Earth as the centre of the celestial spheres. It was Aristotle who saw purposes as causes. It was Cicero who formulated the argument from design. It was the Athenian philosophers who believed that there are philosophical proofs for the existence of God.

The Hebrew Bible never thought in these terms. The heavens proclaim the glory of God; they do not prove the existence of God. All that breathes praises its Creator; it does not furnish philosophical verification of a Creator. In the Bible, people talk *to* God, not *about* God. The Hebrew word *da'at*, usually translated as 'knowledge', does not mean knowledge at all in the Greek sense, as a form of cognition. It means intimacy, relationship, the touch of soul and soul. God, for the Bible, is not to be found in nature for God transcends nature, as do we whenever we exercise our freedom. In Hebrew the word for universe, *olam*, is semantically related to the word 'hidden', *ne'elam*. God is present in nature but in a hidden way.

So the shaking of the foundations that took place between the seventeenth and nineteenth centuries was, in reality, the undermining and eclipse of the Greek rationalist tradition, not of the Judaic basis of faith itself, which, while respecting and honouring science as a form of divine wisdom, never allied itself to one particular scientific tradition and specifically distanced itself from certain aspects of Greek culture.

That means that the original basis of Abrahamic monotheism remains, whatever the state of science. For religious knowledge as understood by the Hebrew Bible is not to be construed on the model of philosophy and science, both left-brain activities. God is to be found in relationship, and in the meanings we construct when, out of our experience of the presence of God in our lives, we create bonds of loyalty and mutual responsibility known as covenants. People have sought in the religious life the kind of certainty that belongs to philosophy and science. But it is not to be found. Between God and man there is moral loyalty, not scientific certainty.

Construe knowledge on the basis of science and, with the best will in the world, you will discover at best only one aspect of God, the aspect the Hebrew Bible calls *Elokim*, the impersonal God of creation as opposed to the personal God of revelation.[21] This is Spinoza's and Einstein's God, and they were indeed two profoundly religious individuals – Novalis called Spinoza a 'God-intoxicated man'. They could see God in the universe, and find awe at the universe's complexity and law-governed order. What they could not conceive was God as the consecration of the personal, the Divinity that underwrites our humanity.

Elokim, the God of creation whose signature we can read in the natural world, is common ground between the God of Aristotle and the God of Abraham. These two great conceptions came together for almost seventeen centuries in Christianity and for a short period between the eleventh and thirteenth centuries in Islam (Averroes) and Judaism (Maimonides). But since the seventeenth century science and religion have gone their separate ways and the old synthesis no longer seems to hold.

But most of the Bible is about another face of God, the one turned to us in love, known in the Bible by the four-letter name that, because of its holiness, Jews call *Hashem*, 'the name'. This aspect of God is found in relationship, in the face of the human other that carries the trace of the divine Other. We should look for the divine presence in compassion, generosity, kindness, understanding, forgiveness, the opening of soul to soul. We create space for God by feeding the hungry, healing the sick, housing the homeless and fighting for justice. God lives in the right hemisphere of the brain, in empathy and interpersonal understanding, in relationships etched with the charisma of grace, not subject and object, command and control, dominance and submission.

Faith is a relationship in which we become God's partners in the work of love. The phrase sounds absurd. How can an omniscient, omnipotent God need a partner? There is, surely, nothing he cannot do on his own. But this is a left-brain question. The right-brain answer is that there is one thing God cannot do on his own, namely have a relationship. God on his own cannot live within the free human heart. Faith is a relationship of intersubjectivity, the meeting point of our subjectivity with the subjectivity, the inwardness, of God. God is the personal reality of otherness. Religion is the redemption of solitude.

Faith is not a form of 'knowing' in the sense in which that word is used in science and philosophy. It is, in the Bible, a mode of *listening*. The supreme expression of Jewish faith, usually translated as 'Hear, O Israel, the Lord our God, the Lord is one' (Deuteronomy 6:4), really means 'Listen, O Israel'.[22] Listening is an existential act of encounter, a way of hearing the person beneath the words, the music beneath the noise. Freud, who disliked religion and abandoned his Judaism, was nonetheless Jewish enough to invent, in psychoanalysis, the 'listening cure': listening as the healing of the soul.[23]

It may be that we are already embarked on a fourth story. Again, for me it began with an episode in Cambridge. I had been taking part in a debate on religion and science. This was just before the appearance of the string of books by the new atheists, and at the time I thought the subject was so *passé* that I assumed only a handful of people would turn up. To my surprise I discovered that the organisers had taken the largest auditorium in the university, and it was filled to overflowing.

My opponent, the professor of the history of science, the late Peter Lipton, was generous and broad-minded. We found ourselves agreeing on almost everything – so much so that the chair of the proceedings, Lord Robert Winston, Britain's most famous television scientist and a deeply religious Jew, said after about half an hour, 'In that case, I'm going to disagree with both of you.' It was a good-natured and open conversation and left most of us feeling that religion and science, far from being opposed, were on the same side of the table, using their distinctive methods to help us better understand humanity, nature and our place in the scheme of things.

As we were leaving, a stranger came up to me, gentle and unassuming, and said, 'I've just written a book that I think you might find interesting. If I may, I'll send it to you.' I thanked him and some days later the book arrived. It was called *Just Six Numbers*, and with a shock of recognition I realised who the stranger was: Sir Martin, now Lord, Rees, Astronomer Royal, Master of Trinity College, Cambridge and President of the Royal Society, the world's oldest and most famous scientific association. Sir Martin was, in other words, Britain's most distinguished scientist.

The thesis of the book was that there are six mathematical constants that determine the physical shape of the universe. Had any one of them been even slightly different, the universe as we know it would not exist. Nor would life. It was my first glimpse into the new cosmology and the string of recent discoveries of how improbable our existence actually is. James Le Fanu, in his 2009 book *Why Us?*, adds to this a slew of new findings in neuroscience and genetics to suggest that we are on the brink of a paradigm shift that will overturn the scientific materialism of the past two centuries:

The new paradigm must also lead to a renewed interest in and sympathy for religion in its broadest sense, as a means of expressing wonder at the '*mysterium tremendum et fascinans*' of the natural world. It is not the least of the ironies of the New Genetics and the Decade of the Brain that they have vindicated the two main impetuses to religious belief – the non-material reality of the human soul and the beauty and diversity of the living world – while confounding the principle tenets of materialism: that Darwin's 'reason for everything' explains the natural world and our origins, and that life can be 'reduced' to the chemical genes, the mind to the physical brain.[24]

There may be, in other words, a new synthesis in the making. It will be very unlike the Greek thought-world of the medieval scholastics with its emphasis on changelessness and harmony. Instead it will speak about the emergence of order, the distribution of intelligence and information processing, the nature of self-organising complexity, the way individuals display a collective intelligence that is a property of groups, not just the individuals that comprise them, the dynamic of evolving systems and what leads some to equilibrium, others to chaos. Out of this will emerge new metaphors of nature and humanity, flourishing and completeness. Right-brain thinking may reappear, even in the world of science, after its eclipse since the seventeenth century. Right and left may be in closer alignment than they have been. I say more on the new science in chapters 11 and 14.

What I have sought to show in this chapter, however, is that there is a significant history to the Western experience of God and religion on the one hand, philosophy and science on the other. They came together in the grand, unique synthesis of Christianity from Paul, through the Church Fathers and the scholastics, to the seventeenth century. Since then they have been progressively separated, but they may be coming together again in ways we cannot foresee. There always was, though, an alternative, the road less travelled, adhered to by a tiny people, the Jews.

On this view, religion, faith and God are not among the truths discovered by science or philosophy in the Greek and Western mode. They are about meaning. Meaning is made and sustained in conversations. It lives in relationships: in marriages, families, communities and societies. It is told in narrative, invoked in prayer, enacted in ritual, encoded in sacred texts, celebrated on holy days and sung in songs of praise.

The left brain, with its linear, atomising, generalising powers, is effective in dealing with things. It is not best at dealing with people. It does not understand the inner life of people, their hopes and fears, their aspirations and anxieties. Religion consecrates our humanity. In discovering God, singular and alone, our ancestors discovered the human individual, singular and alone. For the first time in history sanctity was conferred on the human individual as such, regardless of class, caste, colour or creed, as God's image and likeness, God's beloved.

Science takes things apart to see how they work. Religion puts things together to see what they mean. They speak different languages and use different powers of the brain. We sometimes fail to see this because of the way the religion of Abraham entered the mainstream consciousness of the West, not in its own language but in the language of the culture that gave birth to science. Once we recognise their difference we can move on, no longer thinking of science and religion as friends who became enemies, but as our unique, bicameral, twin perspective on the difference between things and people, objects and subjects, enabling us to create within a world of blind forces a home for a humanity that is neither blind nor deaf to the beauty of the other as the living trace of the living God.

4

Finding God

God lives where we let Him in.

Rabbi Menahem Mendel of Kotzk

It was as though a more complex interlocutor had spoken.

Jorge Luis Borges, 'The Approach to Al-Mu'tasim'

But the Lord God called to the man, 'Where are you?'

Genesis 3:9

'Thank God for atheists!' was my first response to philosophy. I was the first member of my family to go to university, and it hit me like a cold shower. Those were the days – Oxford and Cambridge in the 1960s – when the words 'religion' and 'philosophy' went together like cricket and thunderstorms. You often found them together but the latter generally put an end to the former. Philosophers were atheists, or at least agnostics. That, then, was the default option, and at the time I did not know of any exceptions.

The first thing we did, a kind of nursery-slope exercise, was to refute all the classic proofs for the existence of God. Kant had disproved the ontological argument. Hume had shown that for any supposed miracle, the evidence that it had not happened was always greater than the evidence that it had. Darwin had shown the error in the 'argument from design'. For me, far from being a threat, this was like an immersion in a *mikveh*, a ritual bath. I felt purified.

All these arguments, by then deemed to be fallacious, were in any case wholly alien to the religion I knew and loved. They were

Greek, not Hebraic. They carried with them the scent of Athens, not Jerusalem. They were beautiful but misconceived. As Judah Halevi put it in the eleventh century, they were about the God of Aristotle, not the God of Abraham. Now, every thinking Jew – none more than Maimonides – loves Aristotle, and every feeling Jew loves Socrates, who comes across the pages of history exactly like a rabbi, always asking unsettling questions. Socrates is that most Jewish of figures, an irrepressible iconoclast. But Greece is Greece, Jerusalem is Jerusalem, and the two are not the same.

The ontological argument struck me as philosophical legerdemain of the lowest kind. It states, roughly, that if we can conceive of the greatest possible being, then it must exist, because if it did not exist, it would not be the greatest possible being. It immediately occurred to me that by the same token you could prove that the cruellest possible being exists, because if it does not exist, how cruel could it really be? At best, it qualified as a not-very-good Woody Allen–type joke. The idea that you can pass from concept to existence in that kind of way is actually a kind of magical thinking: the belief that saying, or thinking, makes it so. That is what Wittgenstein set himself against when he called philosophy 'the battle against the bewitchment of our intelligence by means of language'.[1]

As for the argument from design – the world looks as if it was designed, therefore it had a Designer – it was wobbly to begin with. Had John Stuart Mill not put the contrary case with immense passion and power?

> Nature impales men, breaks them as if on the wheel, casts them to be devoured like wild beasts, burns them to death . . . starves them with hunger, freezes them with cold, poisons them by the quick or slow venom of her exhalations, and has hundreds of other hideous deaths in reserve . . . If there are any marks at all of special design in creation, one of the things most evidently designed is that a large proportion of all animals should pass their existence in tormenting and devouring other animals . . . [I]f

Nature and Man are both the works of a Being of perfect goodness, that Being intended Nature as a scheme to be amended, not
imitated, by man.[2]

But is that not precisely what the rabbis meant when they said
that Abraham encountered God in the vision of 'a palace in
flames', meaning, yes, there was order, but there was also disorder, violence, chaos, injustice?[3] God told Abraham to leave home
and travel 'to the land I will show you', but no sooner had he
arrived than there was a famine in the land and he had to leave.
Design there may be, but it is not obvious, not on the surface,
certainly not self-evident.

As for Mill's conclusion – 'If Nature and Man are both the
works of a Being of perfect goodness, that Being intended Nature
as a scheme to be amended, not imitated, by man' – that is
precisely what the rabbis had in mind when they spoke of people
becoming 'God's partner in the work of creation'. They believed
that God left the world incomplete to be completed by humanity.
That, in Judaism, is not heresy but mainstream belief.

As for miracles, David Hume would surely have enjoyed the
approach of Moses Maimonides, who argued that miracles are
not a proof of anything, since there is always the possibility that
they have been performed by magic, optical illusion or the like.
The Israelites did not believe in Moses because of the miracles
he performed, he says in his code of Jewish law.[4] Why then did
Moses perform them? Because they answered a physical, not a
metaphysical need. Why did he divide the Red Sea? Because the
Israelites needed to get to the other side. Why did he produce
manna from heaven and water from a rock? Because the people
were hungry and thirsty. Believe in miracles, said Maimonides,
and there is a danger you will believe in false prophets.

Lest it be thought that Maimonides was a lone voice, consider
the Bible itself. Two prophets, Elijah and Elisha, both raise the
dead to life (1 Kings 17:17–24; 2 Kings 4:8–37). Yet neither the
biblical text nor later Jewish tradition made any great fuss over

this. The real miracle in both cases – as it is in the stories of the patriarchs and matriarchs in Genesis, and of Hannah in the book of Samuel – is that infertile women were able to have children in the first place. In that sense, modern fertility treatments, including in vitro fertilisation, are our miracles. We should not need supernatural intervention to see children as the gift of God.

The Babylonian Talmud displays a fascinating attitude towards the miraculous. It tells the story of a man whose wife died giving birth. The man was so poor he was unable to pay for a wet-nurse. A miracle happened, says the Talmud, and his own breasts sprouted milk (male lactation is, in fact, a natural though rare occurrence). What is fascinating is what the Talmud says next: 'Rav Joseph said: Come and see how great is this man that such a miracle was performed for him. Abbaye said to him: To the contrary, come and see how lowly was this man, that he needed the natural order to be changed for him.'5

Abbaye believed, with many of the sages, that we should not need miracles, nor should we rely on them. Judaism is a religion that celebrates law: the natural law that governs the physical universe, and the moral law that governs the human universe. God is found in order, not in the miraculous suspension of that order. If you read closely the book of Exodus, the book that contains the most and greatest miracles, you will see that none induced lasting faithfulness on the part of the Israelites. Within three days of the division of the Red Sea they were complaining about the water (Exodus 15:22–24). Forty-one days after the revelation at Mount Sinai, they were making a golden calf (Exodus 32). Faith is about seeing the miraculous in the everyday, not about waiting every day for the miraculous.

So my induction into godless philosophy did wonders for my faith. It cleared the garden of religion from the covering of weeds that was disfiguring the lawn and hiding the flowers. Nor did I expect otherwise. If God created the world, then his existence must be compatible with the world. If he created human intelligence, his existence must not be an insult to the intelligence. If the greatest gift he gave humanity was freedom, then religion could not establish itself by coercion. If he created law-governed order, then he could not have asked us to depend on events incompatible with that order.

Oddly enough, it was the atheist Bernard Williams, who later became my doctoral supervisor, who really clarified the issue for me. In what must have been one of his first published articles, 'Tertullian's Paradox', he delivered a devastating onslaught against irrationalism in the religious life.[6] His target was the famous statement made by Tertullian in the third century: *Certum est, quia impossibile*, 'It is certain because it is impossible.' Faith transcends understanding.

Williams rightly argued that, once you start down this road, there is no way of distinguishing between holy nonsense and unholy nonsense. If a belief cannot be stated coherently, then what is it to believe in it? Faith would then become 'whistling in the dark without even the knowledge that what one is whistling is a tune'.

Maimonides had made almost exactly the same point eight centuries earlier. In *The Guide for the Perplexed* he referred to people who objected to giving reasons for the divine commandments, on the grounds that if their logic could be understood by mere mortals, then there was no reason for believing they were divine. Maimonides dismissed such views as unworthy of consideration, because they resulted in making God lower than mere mortals. Shall we really say that human beings do things for a reason while God does not?[7]

Williams's second point, though, was deeper. Religious believers were called on to believe two things that *cannot both be true*. On the one hand God is eternal, unchangeable and beyond time. On the other, God is involved in history. Williams spoke about the central events of Christianity, but the same is true in Judaism. God speaks to Abraham, gives him a child, is with Joseph in Egypt, summons Moses at the burning bush, and rescues the Israelites from slavery. Williams, with great elegance and subtlety, in effect said: you cannot have it both ways. Either God is within history or he is beyond history, but not both.

Given that this was the only theological statement of Williams I know of, written when he was relatively young – twenty-five – it may have been that this was one of the reasons he decided to abandon his faith, though this is mere speculation on my part. To me, however, it suggested exactly the opposite, the first intimation of the argument I have set out in the previous three chapters. What Williams saw as a contradiction *within* faith, I recognised as a contradiction *between* the Jewish and Greek conceptions of God. The changeless, unmoved mover was the God of Plato and Aristotle. The God of history was the God of Abraham. They simply did not belong together. Williams the atheist helped me clarify, and thereby strengthen, my faith. He did more – but of that anon.

What led me to examine my faith in depth was not the success of philosophy in refuting proofs for the existence of God. It was its failure to say anything positive of consequence about the big questions of life: Who am I? Why am I here? To what story do I belong? How then shall I live?

I loved philosophy and still do. I read it, teach it and cherish it. At Cambridge, and later at Oxford, I was taught by people of awesome brilliance, especially by my undergraduate tutor Roger Scruton, for whom I have a deep affection and admiration. But philosophy in the late 1960s and early 1970s had reached a dead end. Under the influence of the Vienna Circle and Logical Positivism, it had given up on the big questions. Instead philosophers spent their time focusing on the meaning of words. Instead of asking what is right and wrong, it asked, 'What do we *mean* when we say this is right, that is wrong?' It seemed less like the search for wisdom than a kind of high-minded lexicography, as if the great arguments that had divided serious minds for twenty-five centuries could be resolved, or dissolved, by mere reflection on what words mean.

Besides which, it often seemed to turn out that they did not mean anything at all. 'Right' and 'wrong', it was argued, were nothing more than an expression of emotion or perhaps not even that. The combination of technical virtuosity and naiveté was sometimes staggering. G. E. Moore had argued that morality was a matter of intuition, as if it was not patently obvious that people in different cultures and ages had different moral intuitions. A. J. Ayer, in a mere twenty pages of *Language, Truth and Logic*, consigned the entire worlds of aesthetic and moral judgement, metaphysics and religion to the wastepaper basket on the grounds that they consisted of statements that could not be conclusively verified and were therefore meaningless. Either this was a joke whose point I could not see, or it was philistinism on a stunning scale.

Slowly it began to dawn on me that I would have to turn to religion, not philosophy, to find the wisdom I sought. I was beginning to see why. Philosophy aimed at universality – at propositions that were true in all places, at all times. But *meaning is expressed in particularity*. There is no universal meaning. There are universal rules. 'Treat others as you would wish to be treated' – the so-called Golden Rule – is one. 'Do not cause suffering where it can be avoided' is another. But they are too few, thin and abstract to constitute a way of life.

There was a witty philosophy professor at Columbia University, Sidney Morganbesser, who is said to have taught this point to his students by taking them to a restaurant, summoning a waiter, and ordering soup. 'And which soup would you like?' asked the waiter. 'We have chicken soup, fish soup, leek soup, lentil soup and a very fine borsht.'

'I don't want any of those,' said Morganbesser, 'I just want soup.'

Whether or not the waiter got the joke, the students eventually did. There may be a Platonic essence of soup – soup in general, the universal form of soup – but it belongs strictly to a Platonic heaven. Down here, if you want to drink soup, it has to be of a particular kind. The same, I realised, applies to meaning. Science may be universal, but meaning is not. The great error of the Enlightenment was to confuse the two.

One of the great joys of my life was to discover, some years later, that some great thinkers had reached the same conclusion: Alasdair MacIntyre in *After Virtue*, Michael Walzer in *Spheres of Justice*, Stuart Hampshire in *Morality and Conflict*, Michael Sandel in *Liberalism and the Limits of Justice*, all of them appearing in the early 1980s. Together they gave back to philosophy its history and substantive particularity.

Something else happened in 1967 that led to a real crisis of faith: not faith in God but faith in human beings. It is hard for anyone who did not live through them to describe the mood that prevailed among Jews in the tense weeks before the Six Day War. Arab armies were massing on Israel's borders. Egypt's President Gamal Abdel Nasser had closed the Straits of Tiran and was threatening to drive Israel into the sea. It seemed, not just to us but to Jews throughout the world, that there was a real danger that Israel would be totally annihilated. The little synagogue in Thompson's Lane was full day after day. Jews we had never seen there before were praying daily for Israel's safety. As it happened, Israel won a swift victory. But it was a transformative moment for my generation. We who had been born after the Holocaust had just lived through the fear of a second Holocaust, and nothing would be the same again.

At about the same time I encountered the English don George Steiner. We debated one another at the Cambridge Union. He had just published a book of essays, *Language and Silence*, and this too made a great impression on me. What he wrote about the Holocaust was about the failure, in Germany, of the humanities to humanise. 'We know now,' he wrote, 'that a man can read Goethe or Rilke in the evening, that he can play Bach and Schubert, and go to his day's work at Auschwitz in the morning.' This was new to me, and the more I have read in the intervening years, the more disturbing it becomes.[8]

The Holocaust did not take place long ago and far away. It happened in the heart of rationalist, post-Enlightenment, liberal Europe: the Europe of Kant and Hegel, Goethe and Schiller, Beethoven and Brahms. Some of the epicentres of antisemitism were places of cosmopolitan, avant-garde culture like Berlin and Vienna. The Nazis were aided by doctors, lawyers, scientists, judges and academics. More than half of the participants at the Wannsee Conference in January 1942, who planned the 'final solution to the Jewish question', the murder of all Europe's Jews, carried the title 'doctor'. They either had doctorates or were medical practitioners.[9] This was devastating to me. I have known people who lost their faith in God during the Holocaust, and others who kept it. But that anyone can have faith in humanity after Auschwitz to me defies belief.

Much has been written about the history of hate that Hitler exploited. There have been libraries of books about Christian, racial and (sadly and more recently) Islamist antisemitism. Far too little, however, has been written about a fourth kind, which played its own part in the centuries leading up to the Holocaust, namely *philosophical* antisemitism.

It can be found in virtually all of the great continental philosophers of the Enlightenment and beyond. Voltaire called the Jews 'an ignorant and barbarous people, who have long united the most sordid avarice with the most detestable superstition'. Fichte (1762–1814) wrote that the only way of making Jews civilised was to amputate their Jewish heads. Immanuel Kant spoke privately of Jews as 'the vampires of society' and argued for the 'euthanasia' of Judaism.

Hegel took Judaism as his model of a 'slave morality'. Nietzsche accused Jews of giving the world an ethic of kindness and compassion which he saw as the 'falsification' of natural morality, namely the will to power. The most virulent of the philosopher antisemites, whose work was regularly cited by the Nazis, was Schopenhauer. He spoke of Jews as 'no better than cattle' and 'scum of the Earth' and said they should be expelled from Germany. The logician Gottlob Frege wrote in 1924 (he was in his mid-seventies at the time) that it was a 'misfortune that there are so many Jews in Germany and that in future they will have full political equality with German citizens'.[10]

Martin Heidegger, the greatest German philosopher of the twentieth century, joined the Nazi Party in 1933. Shortly after joining the party he became rector of the University of Freiburg. Among his first declarations was the statement that 'The Führer alone *is* the present and future German reality and its law.' After the war Heidegger made no attempt to apologise for his involvement with the Nazis, his admiration for Hitler, or his betrayal of Jewish colleagues. Jonathan Glover summarises his response as a 'mixture of silence and grandiose evasion'.[11]

This cries out for explanation. The philosophers of the Enlightenment believed that prejudice belonged to religious sentiment and that it could be cured by an age of reason, in which, in the words of the revolutionary French National Assembly, 'All men are born, and remain, free and equal in rights.' Why did this dream fail so consistently and so profoundly?

The Enlightenment was a 'dream of reason'. Reason is universal. It applies at all places, in all times. Prejudice, so Voltaire and others argued, comes from the particular: the local, the church, the neighbourhood, the community, even the family, the things that make us different, attached to this, not that. Tolerance would therefore come only when men and women learned to worship the universal, 'humanity'.

That is a dream destined to fail *because* it is universal. Its immense power, evident in science, is that it leads us to seek universal patterns, chains of cause and effect, in the phenomena of nature from the cosmos to the genome. But the human person is not entirely a phenomenon of nature. Yes, we are bodies, the 'quintessence of dust'. But we also have minds, and whether or not the mind is coextensive with the brain, it allows human beings to do something no other life form known to us does: to become self-conscious, to feel lonely not just alone, to question, think, plan, choose, and ask 'Why?'

To think, we must use language and everything that goes with language: communities, cultures, conventions and codes, the things that make us different. *Languages and cultures are always particular.* Between Babel and the end of days, there is no universal language. To universalise, to apply modes of thought that work for science to human beings, is to dehumanise human beings. Hence philosophy in the Platonic-Cartesian-Kantian mode is no defence against genocide. Allied to hate, it makes it possible.

So my encounter with philosophy, which I still love and cherish, taught me the limits of philosophy. I needed something more. The question was, where to find it? Where do you find God?

There is a short story by the Argentinian poet Jorge Luis Borges called 'The Approach to Al-Mu'tasim'.[12] In it Borges imagines a young man who finds himself in a poor neighbourhood of Bombay. He is a fugitive – from what, we never learn. He takes refuge among 'people of the vilest class' and gradually adjusts to them 'in a kind of contest of infamy'. He hides himself in their midst and becomes like them. One day he is in the middle of a conversation when he senses in one of the people with whom he is talking a discrepant note – a tone of voice, an inflection, that does not belong:

> All at once – with the miraculous consternation of Robinson Crusoe faced with the human footprint in the sand – he perceives some mitigation in this infamy: a tenderness, an exaltation, a silence in one of the abhorrent men. 'It was as if a more complex interlocutor had joined the dialogue.'

He knows that the man with whom he is conversing is incapable of 'this momentous decorum'. He infers that he has been influenced by someone else. He is 'the reflection of a friend, or of the friend of the friend'. He senses a trace, perhaps many times removed, of a remarkable presence. 'Rethinking the problem he arrives at a mysterious conviction: some place in the world there is a man from whom this clarity emanates; some place in the world there is a man who is this clarity.' He resolves to dedicate his life to finding this man.

That is how I have sought God, not through philosophical proofs, scientific demonstrations or theological arguments; not through miracles or mysteries or inner voices or sudden epiphanies; not by ceasing to question or challenge or doubt; not by blind faith or existential leap; certainly not by an abandonment of reason and an embrace of the irrational. These things have brought many people to God. But they have also brought many people to worship things that are not God, like power, or ideology, or race. Instead I have sought God in people – people who in themselves seemed to point to something or someone beyond themselves. In 1931, in his notebook, Wittgenstein wrote the following sentence: 'Amongst Jews "genius" is found only in the holy man.'[13] In the summer of 1968 I set off in search of holy men.

I went to America. That might seem a strange choice, but I was looking for Jewish thinkers unafraid to confront the challenges of philosophy. The mid-1960s had witnessed, in both Britain and the United States, a 'death of God' controversy, in both cases started not by atheists but by theologians. An American-Jewish magazine, *Commentary*, had published a series of Jewish responses from leading rabbis,[14] and I decided to meet as many of them as I could. So I bought a Greyhound bus ticket and spent the whole of that summer travelling from city to city in Canada and the United States, meeting rabbis and asking them the big questions.

Wherever I went, two names kept coming up in conversation. One was Rabbi Joseph Soloveitchik, the leading thinker of American Orthodoxy. Heir to one of the leading dynasties of East European talmudic scholarship, he had ventured out into Western philosophy and written a doctorate on post-Kantian epistemology. Coming to the United States with the rise of Nazism, he had taught several generations of modern Orthodox rabbis. Of all contemporary Jews literate in the two worlds of Talmud and philosophy, he was the greatest.

The other was the Lubavitcher Rebbe, Rabbi Menachem Mendel Schneersohn. Already a legend, he had done what no previous Jewish leader had ever tried to do. He had sent emissaries throughout the world, seeking out lost and disaffiliated Jews and, wherever possible, bringing them back to faith. Eventually other individuals and organisations followed his lead, but he was the first, and the people I met spoke about him with awe.

Not only were these two – one in the arena of thought, the other in leadership – the greatest rabbis alive, they were also living remnants of the world Jewry had lost, the talmudic academies and Hassidic courts of Eastern Europe, more than 90 per cent of which were destroyed in the Holocaust. I was determined, whatever the practical difficulties, to meet them, and eventually I did. In both cases, it did not take long to realise that I was in the presence of greatness.

Rabbi Soloveitchik, formidably erudite in every branch of philosophy, spoke about the need to create a new kind of Jewish thought, based not on philosophical categories but on *halakhah*, Jewish law. Law was the lifeblood, the DNA, of Judaism, and it was more than mere regulation of conduct. It was a way of being in the world. Jewish philosophy in the past had based itself on its Western counterpart, and in so doing had failed to express what was unique about Judaism, its focus on the holy deed. For two hours he spoke with an intellectual passion and depth far beyond anything I had experienced in Cambridge.

My encounter with Rabbi Schneersohn was unlike any other. The first half of our conversation proceeded conventionally. I asked the questions, he gave answers. Then, unexpectedly, he reversed the roles and started asking me questions. How many Jewish students were there at Cambridge? How many were actively identified with Jewish life? What was I doing to engage them? This was something for which I was not prepared. I was on a private intellectual quest, with no larger intention. I was interested in *my* Jewish identity, not that of others.

I began my reply with a typical English evasion: 'In the situation in which I find myself . . .' The Rebbe allowed the sentence to go no further. 'You do not *find* yourself in a situation,' he said. 'You *place* yourself in a situation; and if you placed yourself in one, you can place yourself in another.' We were losing Jews, he said, and each of us had a responsibility to do something about it. Years later, I summed up that moment by saying how wrong people were to think of him as a leader with thousands of followers. A good leader, I said, creates followers. A great leader creates leaders. The Rebbe created leaders on a scale unprecedented in Jewish history.

These were life-changing encounters. Rabbi Soloveitchik had challenged me to think. Rabbi Schneersohn had challenged me to lead. In both – though neither spoke of it – I sensed the extent of what Jewish life had lost in the Holocaust. In both too I felt the scale of the challenge in the present, as Jews were losing interest in Judaism, nowhere more so than on campus in their college years. Both conveyed the gravitas and depth of the Jewish soul. There was something in them that was more than them, as if an entire tradition spoke through their lips. This was not 'charisma'. It was a kind of humility. In their presence you could feel the divine presence. At university I had found intellectual agility, subtlety, wit, the rapier thrust of trained, honed, razor-sharp minds. But these were holy people. Somehow you felt larger because of them.

I went back to Cambridge, finished my degree, began a doctorate under Bernard Williams, then went to Oxford where I studied briefly with the Catholic philosopher Philippa Foot, who did much to bring virtue ethics back into moral thought, and then, for two years, I taught philosophy. But the memory of those two meetings stayed with me, challenging me to learn more about Judaism. So in 1973 I said goodbye to everything I had dreamed of doing as an academic, and began serious Judaic study. Five years later I became a rabbi. Thirteen years after that I became Chief Rabbi. God kept calling and I kept following, hoping that at least some of the time I was going in the right direction.

I have sought God in the meanings that have inspired people to live in such a way that their lives seem to point to something larger than themselves, what Matthew Arnold called 'the power not ourselves that makes for righteousness', and what the rabbis meant when they said 'the divine presence spoke through them'. It can be a gentleness, a tenderness, a generous embrace. It can be an affirmation, someone who gives you the confidence to be yourself. It can be a forgiveness, a way of saying, yes, you know and I know that it was wrong, but that was yesterday, and you have work to do today, and perhaps tomorrow will bring the chance to heal what you harmed. It is hard to define what it is that makes you feel, as did Borges' young man, that you are seeing the trace of another, greater presence, but you do, at least if you have accustomed yourself to search for it.

People within the Abrahamic monotheisms have always known that for most of us, most of the time, God, more infinite than the universe, older and younger than time, cannot be known directly. He is known mainly through his effects, and of these the most important is his effect on human lives. That is what I sensed on meeting the Lubavitcher Rebbe and Rabbi Soloveitchik. In them it was obvious. It is why they commanded so much respect within the American Jewish community. But over the years I have learned to find it so much more widely, in communities that care, in the kindness of strangers, in people who touch our lives, perhaps only momentarily, doing the deed or saying the word that carries us to safety across the abyss of loneliness or self-doubt.

It is where I find God in Jewish history. There is a grandeur, a nobility, a heroic passion about Jews that does not seem to come naturally to this fractious, quarrelsome, stiff-necked people. We catch traces of it in a Hebrew fugitive tending his father-in-law's sheep in the desert in Midian, in a village herdsman from Tekoah, a water-drawer from Babylon, a wine-seller in eleventh-century France, in a hundred eighteenth-century villages in Russia – in short, in Moses, Amos, Hillel, Rashi, the followers of the Baal Shem Tov, and others in every generation. Time and again, often in circumstances of back-breaking poverty, the Jewish spirit has caught fire and produced words and deeds of incandescent beauty. Their kingdom bounded by a nutshell, Jews counted themselves kings of infinite space.

I find no way of accounting for this in terms of what Jews were, or where they lived, or what happened to them. Somehow they were touched by a sense of destiny, a vision of God and the world, that transfigured them – even at times against their will – into a people that defied the normal rules of the decline and fall of civilisations. Their very existence seemed to testify to something vast and unfathomable that knowingly or otherwise they carried in their midst. They became what Isaiah called 'God's witnesses'. Their history, their survival against the odds, their intellectual flights and utopian endeavours, became a signal of transcendence.

But you have to be very narrow indeed not to see beauty and wisdom in faiths other than your own. I have been inspired by seeing Sikhs offering hospitality to the poor in Amritsar, Christians building homes for the homeless throughout the world, Hindus practising *sewa*, compassion to the distressed, by the majestic wisdom of the great Chinese Confucian and Taoist traditions, and the courage of the many Muslims I know who fight the extremists in their own communities. The statement that every human being is in God's image precedes both the universal covenant with Noah in Genesis 9 and the particular covenant with Abraham in Genesis 17, to tell us that our humanity precedes our religious identity, whatever that identity may be.

Why is it that we say we see something distinctive in these lives and not, say, in a politician hoping for our vote, or a lawyer doing her job, or even a soldier risking his life for the sake of his country? Because the scientists and philosophers are to this extent right, that people generally act on the basis of rational self-interest.

Consciously or otherwise, we seek to hand on our genes to the next generation. Individually and as groups, tribes, nations and civilisations, we are engaged in a Darwinian struggle to survive. All this we know, and though the terminology may change from age to age, people have known it for a very long time indeed.

But here and there we see acts, personalities, lives, that seem to come from somewhere else, that breathe a larger air. They chime with the story we read in chapter 1, about a God who creates in love, who has faith in us, who summons us to greatness and forgives us when, as from time to time we must, we fall, the God whose creativity consists in self-effacement, in making space for the otherness that is us. This has nothing whatsoever to do with the physical laws, Darwinian or otherwise, governing biology, and everything to do with the making of meaning out of the communion of souls linked in loyalty and love. Stephen Jay Gould and Richard Lewontin see such flowerings of the spirit as 'spandrels', decorative motifs that have nothing to do with the weight-bearing architecture of life.[15] Like most people, I see them as the redemption of life from mere existence to the fellowship of the divine. As Isaiah Berlin said, there are people tone deaf to the spirit. There is no reason to expect everyone to believe in God or the soul or the music of the universe as it sings the improbability of its existence.

God is the distant voice we hear and seek to amplify in our systems of meaning, each particular to a culture, a civilisation, a faith. God is the One within the many; the unity at the core of our diversity; the call that leads us to journey beyond the self and its strivings, to enter into otherness and be enlarged by it, to seek to be a vehicle through which blessing flows outwards to the world, to give thanks for the miracle of being and the radiance that shines wherever two lives touch in affirmation, forgiveness and love.

How then are we to understand the rationality or otherwise of religious faith? Ironically, again it was Bernard Williams who led me to the answer. In one of his most famous essays, 'Moral Luck', he wrote about the painter Paul Gauguin. At the age of thirty-seven, in the midst of a successful career as a stockbroker, Gauguin left his wife and five children to work full time as a painter, first in Paris, then in Arles, and finally in Polynesia where he died.

Williams asked the question: What would have had to have been the case for Gauguin's decision to be justified? He became one of the greatest artists of his time, and that leads us to think he was right to do what he did. But he might not have become a great artist. He might simply have lacked the ability, the gift. But Gauguin could not know this in advance. None of us can. We do not know what we could become until we try to become it. It was luck that justified Gauguin's decision. So there is a place for luck in the moral life.[16]

That seems to me a faulty analysis. Whether or not Gauguin became a great artist has no bearing whatsoever on the moral question of whether he was justified in leaving his wife and family. We might well say that as an artist he was admirable, but as a human being less so. History is littered with such examples. Yeats put it best:

> The intellect of man is forced to choose
> perfection of the life, or of the work,
> And if it take the second must refuse
> A heavenly mansion, raging in the dark.[17]

So I could not see that the Gauguin case introduced luck into morality. But there was another conclusion to be drawn altogether.

The Gauguin case showed that there can be key decisions, life-changing, 'existential' as we used to call them, that cannot be rational because not all the facts on which a rational decision depends are knowable in advance. Gauguin may have suspected that he had artistic genius, but he could not know until he had taken the risk of dedicating himself totally to art. I may know who and what I am. I cannot know in advance who or what I could become. There are certain risks you have to take, such that only in retrospect can you know whether you were right to take them, and perhaps not even then. Neither Gauguin nor Van Gogh lived to see their genius recognised.

This is not a minor fact about humanity. It lies at the heart of all creative endeavour. Crick and Watson could not know in advance that they would discover DNA when they began to search for it. Columbus could not have known he would discover America before he set sail for it. As Karl Popper said in *The Poverty of Historicism*, the future cannot be predicted, because how it will happen depends on discoveries that cannot be predicted, because if they could be predicted they would already have been discovered. That is why every attempt to foretell 'the shape of things to come' is at best guesswork, and usually bad guesswork.

What Gauguin had was *faith*: faith in himself, in his art, in his vocation. Externally, his fate may seem like luck: so Williams argued. But to Gauguin himself, luck was the last thing he had in mind. Does anyone engaged in scientific research, or writing a novel, or starting a new business, or getting married, believe in luck? Hardly. If luck were what governed the universe, we would all be Stoics or Epicureans, guarding ourselves against outrageous fortune by avoiding worst-case scenarios and minimising risks. Luck is precisely the wrong concept to invoke if we seek to understand those who take great risks in a cause to which they feel themselves called.

What they have is faith: faith that effort is rewarded, that dedication is worthwhile, that there is no creativity without risk and no risk without occasional failure. Faith is not a spurious knowledge of things we might be able to demonstrate through scientific means. Nor is it belief in the irrefutable, always insulated against the possibility of being proved wrong. Faith is the human response to the phenomenon that defines the human condition: the constitutive uncertainty of our lives as we walk towards the undiscovered country called the future.

We know much, but there is one thing we can never know: what tomorrow may bring. Faith is what allows us to face the future without fear: 'Though I walk through the shadow of death I will fear no evil for you are with me.' That was the faith that moved Abraham and Sarah to leave their land, their birthplace and their father's house, to travel to an unknown destination in response to a divine call. It moved Moses to abandon life as an Egyptian prince or a Midianite shepherd, to lead his people to freedom. Faith is what moves people to great achievement that defies probability and predictability.

Faith is not certainty. It is the courage to live with uncertainty. Faith is never easy. The great heroes of the moral life, like the great artists and scientists and thinkers, like anyone who has undertaken to live a life of high ideals, know failure after failure, disappointment after disappointment. What made them great is that they refused to despair. Like Jacob wrestling with the angel, they said to fate, 'I will not let you go until you bless me' (Genesis 32:26). Judaism is built on that faith. Jews refused to let go of God, and God refused to let go of them. They wrestle still. So do all who have faith.

Science is about explanation. Religion is about meaning. To find meaning in life, as Viktor Frankl discovered in Auschwitz, is to hear a call. 'In the last resort, man should not ask, "What is the meaning of my life?" but should realise that he himself is being questioned.'[18] God is calling each of us to a task – asking each of us as he asked the first humans, 'Where are you?' – but to hear the call we have to learn to listen. We can never be sure that we heard correctly. We can never know that it really was the voice of God, which is why humility not arrogance, and risk not certainty, are the deepest marks of faith. Nor can we be sure in advance that the journey we take will lead to the destination we seek. That – the Gauguin problem – is why we need faith. I owe that discovery to my teacher, Bernard Williams, perhaps the greatest atheist of our time.

Everything I have learned about faith in a lifetime tells me that the science of creation – cosmology – wondrous though it is, takes second place to the sheer wonder that God could take this risk of creating a creature with the freedom to disobey him and wreck his world. There is no faith humans can have in God equal to the faith God must have had in humankind to place us here as guardians of the vastness and splendour of the universe. We exist because of God's faith in us. That is why I see in the faces of those I meet a trace of God's love that lifts me to try to love a little as God loves. I know of nothing with greater power to lift us beyond ourselves and to perform acts that carry within them a signal of transcendence. God lives wherever we open our eyes to his radiance, our hearts to his transforming love.

PART TWO

Why It Matters

5

What We Stand to Lose

The absence of God, when consistently upheld and thoroughly examined, spells the ruin of man in the sense that it demolishes or robs of meaning everything we have been used to think of as the essence of being human: the quest for truth, the distinction of good and evil, the claim to dignity, the claim to creating something that withstands the indifferent destructiveness of time.

Leszek Kolakowski[1]

When I was a student, a friend of mine, an Orthodox Jew who had lost his faith, decided to conduct a scientific experiment to prove, once and for all, whether God existed or not. He waited until the Sabbath, when Jews are forbidden to switch electricity on or off, and then, in his room, switched on the light. God – somewhat to his relief – did not strike him down. Nothing happened except that the light went on. He had proved to his satisfaction that God did not exist.

Now that he has returned to his faith, he has worked out that things are not quite that simple. When you stop believing in God, there is no sudden explosion of light or darkness. The world continues on its accustomed course. The sky does not fall. The sun still shines. Life goes on. But something is lost nonetheless, something important that gives life connectedness, depth and a sense of purpose; that gives you a feeling of participating in something vast and consequential.

When we lose God, what else do we lose? What do we lose collectively and individually? That is the question I pose in the chapters that follow.

The loss is not immediately obvious, but our human worth is subtly undermined. Politicians value us for how we vote, economists for how we earn, advertisers for how we buy, people in the arts and entertainment for how we spend our leisure. Outside religion there is no secure alternative base for the unconditional source of worth that in the West has come from the idea that we are each in God's image. Though many have tried to create a secular substitute, none has ultimately succeeded.[2] None has stood firm under pressure. That has been demonstrated four times in the modern world when an attempt was made to create a social order on secular lines: the French Revolution, Stalinist Russia, Nazi Germany and Communist China. When there is a bonfire of the sanctities, lives are lost.

We are unlikely to go down that road for the foreseeable future, but civilisations can end not with a bang but with a whimper. They can die so slowly that very few notice they are dying. When religious faith goes, five things happen, gradually and imperceptibly. First there is a loss of belief in human dignity and the sanctity of life. This is not immediately obvious, because the new order announces itself as an enhancement of human dignity. It values autonomy, choice and individual rights. It creates a culture of individualism. So, at first, human dignity seems to do better in a secular culture than in a religious one.

But eventually people discover that in the new social order they are more vulnerable and alone. Marriages break up. Communities grow old and weak. People lack deep, stable structures of support. They become members of the lonely crowd or the electronic herd. They float on a tide of fashion. They dress in strangely uniform ways. They think in strangely uniform ways. It takes far more courage to defy the consensus than it used to when conscience was given dignity by faith. Wherever you look, in the arts, in music, in poetry, in the way people spend their free time, life seems more superficial than it once did. It has become a play of surfaces. Ultimately, life itself becomes disposable, in the form of abortion and euthanasia. That is often the first warning signal.

The second sign is the loss of the politics of covenant, the idea that society is a place where we undertake collective responsibility for the common good. Citizenship in such a society has a moral dimension. It involves loyalty and the willingness to sacrifice for the sake of others. The politics of covenant has deep religious roots, although they are almost never visible on the surface. When those roots are lost, in its place comes the politics of contract, in which the state becomes a supplier of services in return for taxes, and political parties vie on the basis of offering either a better service or a lower cost. People become cynical about politicians and increasingly care less about politics and more about private life. Society dissolves into a series of pressure groups and no longer deeply enters our identity. Being British or French or Italian comes to seem more like *where* you are than *who* you are.

The third sign is a loss of morality. This does not mean that people become immoral. Some people do that, whether they are religious or secular; most do not, whether they are religious or secular. I do not believe that you need to be religious to be moral: I take that as a slander against humanity. What happens, though, is that words that once meant a great deal begin to lose their force – words like duty, obligation, honour, integrity, loyalty and trust. If you can do it and get rewarded for it and other people do it anyway, you will be regarded as odd if you do not on the grounds that it is dishonourable or would betray a trust or 'that's not how decent people behave'. People may respect you, but they will think you an odd survival of an earlier age.

The fourth sign is the loss of marriage. Relationships in a secular society are no longer consecrated. They become multiple forms of friendship, that can break and reconfigure without too much emotional distress. The idea of marriage as a commitment, a loyalty at the deepest level of our being, becomes ever harder to sustain. So fewer people marry, more marriages end in divorce, fewer people – men especially – have a lifelong connection with their children, and the bonds across the generations grow thin. Compare all those sonnets about love from the seventeenth to nineteenth centuries with the lyrics of a contemporary pop song about sex, and a certain difference may strike you. Those who live in the world of the latter may well find it difficult to understand what those earlier writers were talking about.

The fifth is the possibility of a meaningful life. By this I do not mean life as a personal project. That is available to us in today's secular culture. I mean life with a meaning that comes from outside us, as a call, a vocation, a mission. To be sure, you can be completely secular and still feel a sense of vocation – to teach, to heal, to fight injustice or poverty. But there is some kind of transcendence functioning here, because life as such does not call. The universe is silent. Nature is dumb. Life makes no demands of us. The concept of 'being called' is one of the last relics of religious memory within a secular culture. A totally secular order would not have space for it or find it meaningful.

As I wrote in the Introduction, I do not mean any of this in an absolute either/or sense. There are people who are completely secular and live happy and purposeful lives. More than that: they often live altruistic and heroic lives. Human goodness is widely distributed, and I have no respect for religious people who cannot see this. There are also religious people who live miserable and guilt-haunted lives. There are secular societies, many of them, in which there is far greater freedom than in religious societies. In fact, our image of a religious society in the twenty-first century is of a repressive, rights-denying, even brutal regime, and I have nothing to say in defence of such societies. They break the rule of Abrahamic faith, set out in chapter 13, that religion should never wield power. Religion, as I explain it there, is a principled opposition to the will to power. Faith is about the forms of gracious coexistence that abjure the use of power.

We need some kind of balance: a public space in which we are each accorded equal respect regardless of our beliefs or lack of them, and a variegated but vigorous civil society where we associate in families, congregations, communities, neighbourhoods and schools, often though not always held together by religious bonds, places where we feel the radiance of the divine presence blessing our life together and connecting us across time and space to our several larger, extended families of faith. These are the places where meaning is made, where we discover the sacred space where self and other meet in divine embrace.

It took the West a long time to develop this balance, but we are in danger of forgetting what happens, not immediately but in the long run, when we lose it.

Friedrich Nietzsche was the most honest atheist of modern times. He was one of the very few who truly understood how momentous an event it would be for European civilisation to lose the spiritual foundation on which it had been built since the conversion of Emperor Constantine in 312. In the famous passage in which, in *The Gay Science*, he has a madman first pronounce the words 'God is dead', he expresses real terror:

> God is dead. God remains dead. And we have killed him. How shall we comfort ourselves, the murderers of all murderers? What was holiest and mightiest of all that the world has yet owned has bled to death under our knives: who will wipe this blood off us? What water is there for us to clean ourselves? What festivals of atonement, what sacred games shall we have to invent? Is not the greatness of this deed too great for us? Must we ourselves not become gods simply to appear worthy of it?[3]

There is an unmistakable echo of Macbeth in these lines and, like Lady Macbeth, Nietzsche eventually went mad, spending the last eleven years of his life clinically insane. Nietzsche published *The Gay Science* in 1882, by which time he knew that many significant intellectuals had lost their faith: in Britain they included George Eliot and Matthew Arnold as well as the man who greatly influenced his thought, though he was reluctant to admit it – Charles Darwin.[4]

Nietzsche thought that the British completely failed to understand the gravity of what was happening. He singled out George Eliot, whom he called an 'English shallowpate', for failing to realise that if you lose Christian faith, you will inevitably lose Christian morality. 'If one breaks out of it a fundamental idea, the belief in God, one thereby breaks the whole thing to pieces: one has nothing of any consequence left in one's hands.'[5] Europe, Nietzsche believed, would have no real choice but to go back to the Greek-Dionysian ethic he espoused, namely the will to power.

Nietzsche was not a minor figure in the history of European thought. He was by far the most prophetic moralist, or anti-moralist, of modern times. My doctoral supervisor Bernard Williams admired him greatly and said he wished he could quote him every twenty minutes. No one saw more clearly the consequences of abandoning Christian ethics, and Nietzsche unhesitatingly drew the Darwinian conclusion. The strong must eliminate the weak. The Christian principle of caring for the weak was against nature and against the logic of power. The Christian idea of the universal love of humanity means, in practice, 'the preference for the suffering, underprivileged, degenerate: it has in fact lowered and weakened the strength, the responsibility, the lofty duty to sacrifice men'.[6]

There is a terrifying passage in *The Will to Power*, written in 1888:

The biblical prohibition 'thou shalt not kill' is a piece of naiveté compared with the seriousness of the prohibition of life to decadents: 'thou shalt not procreate'. – Life itself recognizes no solidarity, no 'equal rights', between the healthy and the degenerate parts of an organism: one must excise the latter – or the whole will perish. – Sympathy for decadents, equal rights for the ill-constituted – that would be the profoundest immorality, that would be antinature itself as morality![7]

Once the Christian conscience was eliminated, human beings would be forced to become brutal, ruthless, hard; impose their will on others; eliminate the handicapped and those deemed subhuman; and give full reign to the violence that Christian compassion had emasculated for so long.

Nietzsche had a premonition that some vast tragedy was going to play itself out in Germany once the full consequence of the death of Christianity had been absorbed. He wrote, 'One day my name will be associated with the memory of something tremendous – a crisis without equal on Earth, the most profound collision of conscience, a decision that was conjured up against everything that had been believed, demanded, hallowed so far. I am no man, I am dynamite.'[8]

Had he been entirely alone in this judgement, one might have said this was madness, despite the fact that it actually happened and that *the most objectionable passages in Nietzsche's writings also turned out to be the most prophetic*. But one other genius, the poet Heinrich Heine, saw the same thing in 1843, forty-five years before Nietzsche, in one of the most prescient pieces ever written:

A drama will be enacted in Germany compared to which the French Revolution will seem like a harmless idyll. Christianity restrained the martial ardor of the Germans for a time but it did not destroy it; once the restraining talisman is shattered, savagery will rise again . . . the mad fury of the berserk, of which Nordic poets sing and speak . . . The old stony gods will rise from the rubble and rub the thousand-year-old dust from their eyes. Thor with the giant hammer will come forth and smash the gothic domes.

The German thunder . . . rolls slowly at first but it will come. And when you hear it roar, as it has never roared before in the history of the world, know that the German thunder has reached its target.[9]

Although Heine's views had nothing in common with Nietzsche's, on this one point their judgement concurred. It would happen when Christian ethics lost their power, when people could no longer hear the divine 'Thou shalt not'.

To be sure, religion has done a great deal of harm. On that I am in complete agreement with the atheists. It is a point that must trouble every religious conscience, and it cannot be glossed over. But Europe has been through a nightmare in the twentieth century, a barbarism without precedent or parallel, and it happened not inadvertently, but in the very spirit of its most profound anti-religious thinker. Of course, Nietzsche was not a Nazi. He condemned antisemitism. He broke with Wagner because of the latter's antisemitism. All this is true and important. But Nietzsche, together with Schopenhauer – who really was an antisemite – provided Nazism with its intellectual foundations. That may never be forgotten as long as human beings care for the future of humanity.

We are unlikely to go down precisely that road again. There are other, less disastrous ways for civilisations to die. But die they do. Will and Ariel Durant, a husband-and-wife team of historians, spent forty years between 1935 and 1975 writing their massive and award-winning history of humankind, *The Story of Civilization*. They believed that 'a great civilization is not conquered from without until it has destroyed itself from within', and in the fifth volume they wrote the following extraordinarily germane analysis of the civilisational dynamic that has played itself repeatedly:

> [A] certain tension between religion and society marks the higher stages of every civilization. Religion begins by offering magical aid to harassed and bewildered men; it culminates by giving to a people that unity of morals and belief which seems so favorable to statesmanship and art; it ends by fighting suicidally in the lost cause of the past. For as knowledge grows or alters continually, it clashes with mythology and theology, which change with geological leisureliness. Priestly control of arts and letters is then felt as a galling shackle or hateful barrier, and intellectual history takes on the character of a 'conflict between science and religion'.

Institutions which were at first in the hands of the clergy, like law and punishment, education and morals, marriage and divorce, tend to escape from ecclesiastical control, and become secular, perhaps profane. The intellectual classes abandon the ancient theology and – after some hesitation – the moral code allied with it; literature and philosophy become anticlerical. The movement of liberation rises to an exuberant worship of reason, and falls to a paralyzing disillusionment with every dogma and every idea. Conduct, deprived of its religious supports, deteriorates into epicurean chaos; and life itself, shorn of consoling faith, becomes a burden alike to conscious poverty and to weary wealth. *In the end a society and its religion tend to fall together*, like body and soul, in a harmonious death. Meanwhile among the oppressed another myth arises, gives new form to human hope, new courage to human effort, and after centuries of chaos builds another civilization.[10]

The passage is all the more remarkable since Will Durant himself, who had at one stage contemplated entering the priesthood, lost his own religious faith.

I fear for the future of the West if it loses its faith. You cannot defend Western freedom on the basis of moral relativism, the only morality left when we lose our mooring in a sacred ontology or a divine-human covenant. No secular morality withstood Nazi Germany or Stalinist Russia. No secular morality today has the force to withstand the sustained onslaught of ruthless religious extremism. Neither market economics nor liberal democracy has the power, in and of itself, to inspire people to make sacrifices for the common good. In the multicultural nation states of contemporary Europe, it is increasingly difficult to know whether there remains a compelling sense of the common good.

The Judeo-Christian ethic is not the only way of structuring a society and ordering a life. But it is the only way that has succeeded in the long run in the West, the only way that has given rise autonomously to the scientific and industrial revolutions, parliamentary democracy and liberty of conscience, the only system that has combined strong individualism with a social conscience and a highly active civil society. We stand to lose much if that ethic is lost. We will lose our sense of human dignity, our distinctive politics of the common good, our morality of obligation and responsibility, our respect for marriage and parenthood as a covenantal bond, and our best hope for a meaningful life. Such will be my argument in the next five chapters.

6

Human Dignity

What is man that You are mindful of him, and the son of man that You visit him? Yet You have made him little lower than the angels, and have crowned him with glory and honour.

Psalm 8

This laboriously won *self-contempt* of man.

Nietzsche, On the Genealogy of Morals[1]

Man is an invention of recent date. And one perhaps nearing its end.

Michel Foucault[2]

Pico della Mirandola (1463–94) was one of the moving spirits of the Italian Renaissance. Born into an aristocratic family, he was a child prodigy, mastering Latin and Greek at an early age and winning the title of papal protonotary when he was only ten. Initially intending a career in the Church, he went to the University of Bologna to study law, but widened his interests to include philosophy, which he pursued at the universities of Ferrara and Padua.

In 1486 he completed his monumental 900 Theses, *Conclusiones philosophicae, cabalasticae et theologicae*, on the entire range of human knowledge. To accompany them he wrote his *Oration on the Dignity of Man*, widely regarded as a manifesto of the Renaissance. In it he argued that the human person was the centrepiece of creation, the one being other than God himself who had no fixed nature. Endowed with freedom, he could rise higher than the angels or fall lower than the animals. This is how he imagines God addressing the first human:

Adam, we give you no fixed place to live, no form that is pecu-
liar to you, nor any function that is yours alone ... All other
things have a limited and fixed nature prescribed and bounded
by our laws. You, with no limit or no bound, may choose for
yourself the limits and bounds of your nature. We have placed
you at the world's center so that you may survey everything
else in the world. We have made you neither of heavenly nor of
Earthly stuff, neither mortal nor immortal, so that with free
choice and dignity, you may fashion yourself into whatever form
you choose. To you is granted the power of degrading yourself
into the lower forms of life, the beasts, and to you is granted the
power, contained in your intellect and judgment, to be reborn
into the higher forms, the divine.[3]

Human dignity never received a higher expression. Pico's *Oration*
reminds us that Renaissance humanism was initially a *religious*
humanism. Its heroes, Michelangelo, Da Vinci, Brunelleschi,
Ghiberti and their contemporaries, were enthralled by the possibilities of science and technology. They explored perception and
rediscovered perspective. They studied techniques of construction and produced architectural masterpieces like Michelangelo's
design for St Peter's, Rome. Da Vinci studied human anatomy
and used it in his sketches and paintings. Fascinated by the possibilities of technology, his notebooks are full of inventions centuries ahead of their time, from submarines to flying machines.
Yet they were also often deeply religious individuals and this is
reflected in their work: in Michelangelo's Sistine Chapel ceiling,
Da Vinci's *The Last Supper* and Ghiberti's bronze doors for the
Baptistry of the cathedral in Florence. They combined a passion
for science and religion together and saw no conflict or contradiction between them.

The Italian Renaissance was in part the rediscovery by Christian
Europe of the classical tradition of ancient Greece and Rome,
but there was another element that we can sense clearly in Pico's
words. For what they express is the standard Jewish reading of

the creation of the first humans. There is no reference to original sin. The human person is in the image and likeness of God, never more so than when he uses his intelligence and understanding to fathom the universe. Our freedom and creativity are what connect us to the divine.

How did Pico arrive at this interpretation, previously excluded from Christian theology as the Pelagian heresy? Almost certainly it was the result of his encounter, in Padua, with a Jewish scholar named Rabbi Elijah del Medigo, who taught him Hebrew and Aramaic, introduced him to the Babylonian Talmud and the classic Jewish Bible commentaries and even gave him tuition in Kabbalah, Jewish mysticism.[4] Such encounters happened rarely. Christians did not seek out Jewish scholarship. Jews for their part were reticent in teaching Christians. Both men eventually suffered for their friendship. Pico was accused of heresy and del Medigo regarded with suspicion by the Italian Jewish community.

The *Oration* was a turning point in the history of the West, for it marked a break with that strand in Christian thought that owed as much to Plato as to Paul: the contrast between body and soul, flesh and spirit, the darkness of Earth and the radiance of heaven. The human person is tainted with sin. The human arena is marked by corruption. Only by divine grace can people achieve anything. We are fallen, frail, without the capacity to redeem ourselves; we are sinners all.

That is not what Pico heard in the opening chapters of Genesis, and as a result he was able to develop a religious humanism that was to have an extraordinary influence on the artists of the Renaissance. The years that followed were the most creative in the long story of the complex interweaving of Athens and Jerusalem within the European soul. The Greek passion for beauty met the biblical sense of human possibility and the encounter led in art, architecture and literature to incandescent masterpieces of the mind, imperishable fragments of infinity. Pico understood that one of the driving themes of the Hebrew Bible is that it is precisely in our freedom that the human person most resembles God.

The Fall

Five hundred years later we encounter a quite different evaluation of the nature and dignity of humankind. Published in 1997 by members of the International Academy of Humanism, its signatories included Francis Crick, co-discoverer of DNA, Richard Dawkins, the sociobiologist E. O. Wilson, Kurt Vonnegut the novelist, and the philosopher W. V. Quine. The subject at hand was the permissibility or otherwise of research into human cloning. The signatories all supported such research, and explained why:

> What moral issues would human cloning raise? Some religions teach that human beings are fundamentally different from other mammals – that humans have been imbued with immortal souls by a deity, giving them a value that cannot be compared to that of other living things. Human nature is held to be unique and sacred ... As far as the scientific enterprise can determine, Homo sapiens is a member of the animal kingdom. Human capabilities appear to differ in degree, not in kind, from those found among the higher animals. Humankind's rich repertoire of thoughts, feelings, aspirations, and hopes seems to arise from electrochemical brain processes, not from an immaterial soul that operates in ways no instrument can discover ... A view of human nature rooted in humanity's mythical past ought not to be our primary criterion for making moral decisions about cloning.[5]

We are, on this view, not distinctive at all. We are part of nature, nothing more. There is nothing corresponding to the soul, nor is there anything in the 'rich repertoire' of works of the human spirit to differentiate us in kind from other forms of life. Our hopes, dreams and ideals 'arise from electrochemical brain processes' – implying that this is all they are. Striking is the sheer loss of the sense of grandeur and possibility that drove Renaissance humanism. This loss of dignity is deeply embedded in popular science. We have become 'the naked ape', 'a gene's way of making another gene', an organism among organisms, without freedom or virtue, neither sacred nor unique. Reviewing this history of the descent of man, it is hard not to feel that we have lost more than we have gained. For what does it profit humanity if it gains the world and yet loses its soul? How did it happen?

It was a drama in several acts, extended over several centuries. First came Copernicus's discovery that the Earth was not the centre of the universe. The sun did not revolve around man's habitation; it was the Earth that circled the sun. In the fullness of time that initial paradigm shift was amplified many times over. Even the solar system is not the centre of the galaxy, and even the galaxy is only one of more than a hundred billion others. In space, the wide Earth turned out to be a speck of dust on the surface of infinity.

What applied to space applied to time also. Newton, in the seventeenth century, could still believe that the Earth was some six thousand years old, spending a fair proportion of his time trying to work out the exact date of its birth. Yet as rock strata began to be understood, and fossils were found, the birth had to be pushed back further and further, to hundreds of thousands of years, then to millions, then to 4.54 billion, in a universe 13.7 billion years old.

If so, then the opening chapters of the Bible could not be read literally. The universe was not created in six days. The entire history of humanity was an eyelid's blink in eternity, if that. The universe had managed to survive for billions of years without Homo sapiens. How then could we claim to be the ultimate purpose of creation?

Then came Spinoza, who taught us that to the extent that we are physical beings we are subject to physical laws, all of which have the character of necessity. Therefore freedom – the single greatest gift of God to humanity, separating us from the animals – is an illusion. There is, in fact, only one form of freedom: the consciousness of necessity. The philosopher grows wise by knowing that things could not have been otherwise.

Spinoza set the stage for a whole series of determinists of different kinds, each finding the course of history in some other shaping force, but all agreed that we are what we are because we could not be otherwise than we are, and that all thoughts to the contrary are mere illusion.

Marx argued that the whole of human history was shaped by economic forces, and by the desire of a dominant class to maintain hegemony. Religion, which taught otherwise, was itself the tool of the ruling classes, used by them to teach the poor to accept their fate as the will of God, and to live with suffering in this world in the hope, even promise, of reward in the world to come.

Then came Darwin, with the shocking revelation that human beings were not even *sui generis*, a class on their own. Not only were they not the image of God, they were just one branch of the primates, close cousins to the apes and chimpanzees. There might be differences of degree between humans and others, but not of kind. Other animals, said Darwin, felt feelings, used language, even had self-consciousness.

Then came Freud with the revelation of a subterranean channel of dark instinctual drives running beneath the surface of our minds. We are driven by Eros and Thanatos, the sex instinct and the death instinct. We want to murder our father and marry our mother. In fact, this was the source of religion itself. Long ago the younger males of the tribe gathered together to murder their father, the alpha male. Having done the deed, they then experienced overwhelming remorse – the return of the repressed – and that is what God and the voice of conscience are.[6] Religion, said Freud, is the obsessional neurosis of humankind.[7]

Finally – at least thus far – came the neo-Darwinians with their assault on one thing humans could still pride themselves on, their altruism, their willingness to sacrifice themselves for the sake of others. Not so, argued the sociobiologists. The human person is, after all, just a gene's way of making another gene. Whatever stories we tell ourselves, our apparently altruistic acts are only ways of ensuring our genetic survival into the next generation. We only really help kin and in precise proportion as they share our genes. 'Scratch an altruist,' said Michael Ghiselin, 'and watch a hypocrite bleed.'[8]

Nor was this all. What riveted the neo-Darwinians was the implication that evolution proceeded by mere chance, random genetic mutation, which produced the variety on which natural selection could work. Stephen J. Gould drew the conclusion that if the tape of evolution were to be replayed there would be no certainty that Homo sapiens would emerge.[9] So not only were human beings not made by an act of special divine creation, their very existence was pure accident.

So we are nothing, our planet is insignificant, our existence a mere caesura in time. Our noblest thoughts conceal base intentions. There is no freedom, just necessity. There is no truth, just hegemonic narrative. There is no moral beauty, just a sordid struggle to survive. It is all very much like Hamlet on a bad hair day: 'To me, what is this quintessence of dust?'[10]

There is something surpassingly odd about this. During the entire period that this drama of disillusionment was being enacted, human powers of understanding, explanation and control were expanding beyond all previous imaginings and at an ever faster rate. How is it that *the higher human achievements become, the lower the human self-image sinks*?

As always, the most insightful observer was Nietzsche:

Has not man's self-deprecation, his *will* to self-deprecation, been unstoppably on the increase since Copernicus? Gone, alas, is his faith in his dignity, uniqueness, irreplaceableness in the rank ordering of beings, – he has become *animal*, literally, unqualifiedly and unreservedly an animal, man who in his earlier faiths was almost God ('child of God', 'man of God') . . . since Copernicus, man seems to have been on a downward path,

– now he seems to be rolling faster and faster away from the centre – where to? into nothingness? into 'piercing sensation of his nothingness'?[11]

Nietzsche called this a 'laboriously won *self-contempt* of man', for there is nothing self-evident about it. Is it the scientific equivalent of original sin? Have scientists become a new priesthood, offering salvation from humankind's ever more drastically fallen state? Nietzsche wrote *On the Genealogy of Morality*, from which this quote was taken, in 1887. Yet scientific self-abasement – the systematic insistence that we are 'nothing but' reproductive units blindly replicating ourselves – has continued unabated ever since.

It is totally unwarranted. The fact that we occupy a small space in the universe and a small stretch of the totality of time says nothing about our significance or lack of it. Yes, we have dark drives, but we also have high ideals, and sometimes the force of the latter can lift us above the pull of the former. There is no logic that forces us to accept the 'hermeneutics of suspicion'[12] of the Marxists, Freudians and neo-Darwinians, that we do not really mean what we say, that all human communication is either deception or self-deception. In plain language, this is mere cynicism and its effect is to undermine the trust on which human relationships and institutions depend.

This is more than mere nit-picking. Marxism and Darwinism came with the highest price in human lives ever exacted by ideas. Let me be clear. There is no suggestion whatsoever that Marx and Darwin would have approved of the use others made of their ideas. They would have been horrified. But we may not forget that Marxism led to Soviet Communism and Stalinist Russia, and social Darwinism was one of the main inspirations behind Nazi Germany in general and Hitler in particular.

How many people died as a result of Marxist teachings we will never know. During the years of Stalin alone, an estimated 20 million people died in mass executions and forced movements of populations. Many died as a result of deliberately created famine, others in the course of slave labour. In the early 1930s the Central Committee of the Communist Party took the decision to shift from 'restricting the exploiting tendencies' of the *kulaks* – peasants considered 'bourgeois' – to 'liquidating them as a class', leading to a programme of mass murder on an almost unimaginable scale.

It was a regime of unmitigated brutality and ruthlessness. Stalin had many of his leading colleagues, including Trotsky, assassinated. The regime maintained a constant atmosphere of fear through the secret police, informants and show trials. Those who perpetrated these crimes knew that one day they might suffer the same fate themselves. It was the longest nightmare yet undertaken with high ideals, and it took a very long time indeed before Marxist fellow travellers in the West acknowledged that they had been worshipping what André Gide, Arthur Koestler and others eventually called 'the god that failed'.

As for Nazi Germany, we do no service to the cause of understanding either to isolate it as a unique instance of human depravity or to normalise it under Hannah Arendt's phrase 'the banality of evil'. There were many influences on Hitler and his supporters and it would be wrong to single out one as if it alone were responsible. But the link between social Darwinism and the attempt to exterminate Jews, Roma, Sinti and the mentally and physically handicapped is unmistakable.[13] In *Mein Kampf*, Hitler had written:

A stronger race will supplant the weaker, since the drive for life in its final form will decimate every ridiculous fetter of the so-called humaneness of individuals, in order to make place for the humaneness of nature, which destroys the weak to make place for the strong.[14]

An unpublished note of 1928 shows his reliance on Darwinism to justify his programme of eugenics and infanticide:

While nature only allows the few most healthy and resistant out
of a large number of living organisms to survive in the struggle
for life, people restrict the number of births and then try to keep
alive what has been born, without consideration of its real value
and its inner merit. Humaneness is therefore only the slave of
weakness and thereby in truth the most cruel destroyer of human
existence.[15]

The point is not simply that Hitler imbibed these ideas, whether
through Nietzsche, Spencer, Haeckel or other writers. They were
widely shared among intellectuals of the time. The movement
for eugenics, the selective breeding of humans and the sterilisation of the mentally handicapped and those otherwise declared
unfit, was pioneered by Darwin's half-cousin Sir Francis Galton
and supported among others by H. G. Wells, George Bernard
Shaw, John Maynard Keynes, Woodrow Wilson and Theodore
Roosevelt. Compulsory sterilisation of certain classes of individuals was undertaken by thirty states in America between 1907
and 1963. Only the full realisation of the scale of the Nazi genocide finally rendered such programmes unacceptable.

In Germany the escalation was almost seamless, beginning
with the compulsory sterilisation of unwanted types, then the
killing of 'impaired children' in hospitals, then the killing of
'impaired' adults (the mentally and physically handicapped) in
special centres by carbon monoxide gas, then the extension of this
to the concentration and extermination camps. The programme
was carried out, throughout, by doctors and psychiatrists, only
a handful of whom objected. It was eventually halted in August
1941 because of protests, largely from the Churches.[16]

Reading the vast literature on what Claudia Koonz calls 'the
Nazi conscience', the rationalisations Nazis gave for what they
were doing, what is striking is not only the specific ideas of social
Darwinism – the strong eliminate the weak, the Aryan race must
be protected against pollution – but the overwhelming sense of
the *authority of science*, whatever the science. You had to say no

more than that the Jews (or the gypsies or the Poles) were a cancer in the body of Germany and therefore needed surgical removal, and consciences were stilled, as if science had taken the place of revelation and could not be questioned. Here, for example, is Konrad Lorenz, a Nazi Party member who subsequently received the Nobel Prize for his work on animal experimentation, writing in 1940:

> It must be the duty of racial hygiene to be attentive to a more severe elimination of morally inferior human beings than is the case today ... In prehistoric times of humanity, selection for endurance, heroism, social usefulness, etc. was made solely by *hostile* outside factors. This role must be assumed by a human organisation; otherwise, humanity would, for lack of selective factors, be annihilated by the degenerative phenomena that accompany domestication.[17]

The language is calm, unemotional, matter-of-fact. 'Hygiene', 'degenerative phenomena', a self-evident 'must', and the simple implication: we must annihilate or we will be annihilated (by mentally defective children and so on).

To survive at Auschwitz, Primo Levi had to pass a test qualifying him, as a scientist, to work at a nearby chemical factory. The examination was conducted by a Doktor Engineer Pannwitz. This is how Levi describes it:

> Pannwitz is tall, thin and blond, with the kind of hair, eyes and nose that every German is supposed to have. He is seated menacingly behind an elaborate desk. And I, Häftling 174517, I stand in his office, which is a real office, neat and clean, with everything in order, feeling as if I would soil anything I touched.
>
> When he finished writing, he raised his eyes and looked at me.
>
> Since that day, I have thought about Doktor Pannwitz many times and in many different ways. I have often wondered about the inner workings of this man. What did he do with his time when he was

not producing polymers in a chemistry lab, when he let his imagination wander beyond the reaches of Indo-Germanic consciousness? Above all, I wanted to meet him again, now that I was free, not out of revenge, but to satisfy my curiosity about the human soul.

Because the look he gave me was not the way one man looks at another. If I could fully explain the nature of that look – it was as if through the glass of an aquarium directed at some creature belonging to a different world – I would be able to explain the great madness of the Third Reich, down to its very core.

Everything we thought and said about the Germans took shape in that one moment. The brain commanding those blue eyes and manicured hands clearly said: 'This thing standing before me obviously belongs to a species that must be eliminated. But with this particular example, it is worth making sure that he has nothing we can use before we can get rid of him.'[18]

Knowing what happened in Russia under Stalin, in China under Mao and in Germany under Hitler is essential to moral literacy in the twenty-first century. These were programmes carried out under the influence of ideas produced by Western intellectuals in the nineteenth century to fill the vacuum left by a widespread loss of faith in God and religion.

My point is not to argue that secular schemes of salvation are worse than religious ones. Such arguments are unworthy of serious minds. Religions, including the Abrahamic monotheisms, have done harm, while science and technology have, on the whole, done immense good. The point of this chapter is simply to note how fragile is the concept of human dignity, and how easily it can be lost in the course of scientific thinking.

Demoralisation and Dangerous Ideas

To repeat: no blame can be levelled at Marx, Darwin and Freud for what others made of their ideas. Yet they were inherently dangerous ideas. Why?

First, there is something intrinsically dehumanising in the left-brain mentality. The scientific mind lives in detachment, analysis, the breaking down of wholes to their component parts. The focus is not on the particular – this man, that woman, this child – but on the universal. Science per se has no space for empathy or fellow feeling. None of this is to say that scientists are not compassionate and loving human beings: surely they are. But when science is worshipped and religion dethroned, then a certain decision has been made to set aside human feelings for the sake of something higher, nobler, larger. From there it is a short distance to hell.

Second, as Nietzsche rightly asked: '*Why morality at all*, when life, nature, history are "non-moral"?'[19] There is no morality in nature. No good, right, duty or obligation are written into the fabric of things. There is no way of inferring from how things are to how things ought to be. The Talmud says that had God not revealed the commandments, 'we could have learned modesty from the cat, industry from the ant, marital fidelity from the dove, and good manners from the rooster'.[20] But equally we could have learned savagery from the lion, pitilessness from the wolf and venom from the viper.

Every civilisation has a way of identifying and pre-empting disastrous patterns of behaviour, some way of establishing boundaries, of saying, 'Thou shalt not.' In mythological societies the work is done by the concept of taboo. In the Judeo-Christian heritage there is the divine command. There are certain things you do not do, whatever the consequences. That is what was lost in the modern age. Hayek called it 'the fatal conceit': that we know better than our ancestors, that we can calculate the consequences better than them, circumvent the prohibitions they observed, and achieve what they did not achieve.[21]

By undermining the classic conceptions of humanity, Marxist, Darwinian and Freudian accounts tragically removed the great constraints on human behaviour. They did this in different ways, but all three subverted the force of the 'Thou shalt not'. When nothing is sacred, then nothing is sacrilegious. When there is no

Judge, there is no justice. There is only effectiveness and the will to power.

There is a third point no less significant. *Science cannot, in and of itself, give an account of human dignity*, because dignity is based on human freedom. From the outset, the Hebrew Bible speaks of a free God, not constrained by nature, who, creating man in his own image, grants him that same freedom, commanding him, not programming him, to do good. The entire biblical project, from beginning to end, is about how to honour that freedom in personal relationships, families, communities and nations. Biblical morality is the morality of freedom, its politics are the politics of freedom, and its theology is the theology of freedom.

Freedom is a concept that lies outside the scope of science. Science cannot locate freedom, because its world is one of causal relationships. A stone is not free to fall or not to fall. Lightning does not choose when and where to strike. A scientific law is one that links one physical phenomenon to another without the intervention of will and choice. To the extent that there is a science of human behaviour, to that extent there is an implicit denial of the freedom of human behaviour. That is precisely what Spinoza, Marx and Freud were arguing, that freedom is an illusion. But if freedom is an illusion, then so is the human dignity based on that freedom. Science cannot but deconsecrate the human person, thereby opening the gate to a possible desecration.

We are free. We know that as surely as we know anything. We know what it is to choose between alternatives, weigh the options, calculate the consequences, consult our conscience, ask the advice of others and so on. Yet throughout history human beings have found almost endless ways of denying choice. It wasn't me, it was the will of the gods, or the influence of the stars, or malicious spirits, or *fortuna*, luck or happenstance. It was the way we were brought up, or the influence of friends, or economic circumstance, or genetic endowment. Denial of freedom goes all the way back to the first couple in the Garden of Eden. Confronted with their sin, Adam blamed Eve, and Eve blamed the serpent. Our excuses become more sophisticated over time, but they remain just that, excuses.

The problem of free will has existed for close to twenty-five centuries. Plato discussed it. So did Aristotle. Paul spoke about it with great feeling in the epistle to the Romans. One of the earliest statements occurs in the fourth chapter of Genesis. God senses that Cain is angry and is about to commit a great crime. He warns him, telling him that though he is in the grip of strong emotion, he can control it:

> Then the Lord said to Cain, 'Why are you angry? Why is your face downcast? If you do what is right, will you not be accepted? But if you do not do what is right, sin is crouching at your door. It desires to have you, but you must master it.' (Genesis 4:6–7)

We can rephrase this a little more technically nowadays. Cain is experiencing a rush of emotion to the amygdala, the so-called reptile brain with its fight or flight reactions, including anger. God is urging him to use his prefrontal cortex, more rational and deliberative, capable of thinking beyond the immediacy of me, here, now. Neuroscience has shown us where in the brain the battle for freedom is fought, but it has not shown us freedom itself, which we can know only introspectively from within.

The dangers implicit in the scientisation of the human person have not disappeared. They have reappeared in new forms. One is the intensive use of psychotropic drugs like Ritalin to control moods and behaviour. It is not that there is something inherently wrong in the use of drugs to treat conditions like attention deficit hyperactivity disorder (ADHD), but there should be general concern at the risk of viewing ever larger areas of the emotional life as conditions to be treated rather than responses to be cultivated as part of moral and ethical self-control.

To the extent that we medicalise human behaviour, to that extent we deny freedom and responsibility. One can foresee a time when the whole idea becomes problematic. When that happens, criminal justice – laws, courts, trials and punishment – will cease to make sense, and instead law-breakers will be treated as they were for a period in the 1940s and early 1950s through a form of brain surgery known as lobotomy: justice will disappear and in its place will come social control. A brave new world along the lines of Aldous Huxley's novel of that name, in which people no longer strive, aspire or love but are kept permanently pacified by mind-altering drugs and virtual experiences, is entirely possible even now. What holds us back is the conviction that we are free, that the happiness we make is worth more than a drug-induced serotonin-stimulated ecstasy.[22] But there is no guarantee that we will always feel this way.

If human beings are mere organisms like any other, with nothing to distinguish them from the animals, then there is nothing whatever to justify the idea that we should treat them as ends rather than as means. The supreme irony of contemporary secular ethics is that humans are treated as possessors of rights because they have autonomy, the ability to choose, while at the same time evolutionary psychology and neuroscience are undermining the very idea that we freely choose anything at all. The contradiction at the heart of this secularised view of humanity cannot be sustained for ever.[23]

It is no accident that freedom occupies a central place in the Hebrew Bible but only a tenuous place in the annals of science. The relationship of soul to body, or mind to brain, is precisely analogous to the relationship of God to the physical universe. If there is only a physical universe, there is only brain, not mind, and there is only the universe, not God. The non-existence of God and the non-existence of human freedom go hand in hand.

The assertion of freedom as against its ever-present, ever-changing denials is what marks Abrahamic monotheism as a distinctive philosophy. We are free. We are choosing animals. 'I have set before you life and death, the blessing and the curse. Therefore choose life' (Deuteronomy 30:19). Life is choice. In that fact lies our dignity. If we have no freedom, what makes us different from the animals we kill for our own ends, sometimes even for sport? What makes us persons, not things? *If we deny freedom in theory, eventually we will lose it in practice*, as happened in Nazi Germany and Stalinist Russia, and as may yet happen in new and unforeseeable ways.

For the sake of human dignity, science must be accompanied by another voice. Not in opposition to science, but as the humanising voice of what once we called the soul. There is no greater defence of human dignity than the phrase from the first chapter of the Bible that dared to call the human being 'the image of God'.

7

The Politics of Freedom

God who gave us life gave us liberty. And can the liberties of a nation be thought secure when we have removed their only firm basis, a conviction in the minds of the people that these liberties are of the Gift of God?

Thomas Jefferson, Notes on the State of Virginia, *Query XVIII, p. 237*

Those who deny freedom to others, deserve it not for themselves; and, under a just God, cannot long retain it.

Abraham Lincoln, Letter to Henry Pierce, *6 April 1859*

The rights of man come not from the generosity of the state but from the hand of God.

John F. Kennedy, Inaugural Address, *20 January 1961*

There is a received narrative, a conventional wisdom, about the politics of freedom. Democracy was born in Athens. It is an achievement of the Greeks. The Bible knows nothing about democracy, and if you are sincerely religious you must have qualms about it. Democracy is, after all, about the will of the people. Religion is about the will of God. It was only when European societies began to become secularised in the seventeenth century that the first fruits of freedom began to grow. Liberal democracy is a secular achievement, and the more religion there is in a society, the more its freedom is threatened.

There is only one thing wrong about this narrative. It is false, at best a partial truth. The politics of the West are a consequence of the religion of the West and of the God of Abraham, whose first great intervention in history was to liberate a nation of slaves and bring them out to freedom. Liberty of conscience, the peculiarly modern form of freedom that has no counterpart in antiquity, was born in the most intensely religious of ages, based on religious texts and driven by a religious vision.[1]

The seventeenth century was the century of the Hebrew Bible. Three factors made this so. The first was the Reformation, whose aftermath was a series of wars throughout Europe culminating in the Thirty Years War of 1618–48. The second was the cumulative effect of the invention of printing, the growth of literacy and the massive spread of books, suddenly affordable for wide swathes of the population. The third was the maxim of the Reformation, *Sola Scriptura*, 'by the Bible alone', meaning that the Bible, not the Church or tradition, was the sole authority in the religious life. These forces combined with explosive force, and they changed the face of Europe.[2]

Able for the first time to read the Bible for themselves in vernacular translation, people discovered what a subversive document it actually is. Outside Israel, all religion in the ancient world was essentially conservative. It canonised the status quo. It explained why kings are born to rule and why people have to obey. There is a hierarchy in society just as there is in heaven, among the sun, the moon and the stars, the 'great chain of being'. Without order, there is chaos; without power, there is no order. That is why the gods have given power to their representatives on Earth, and their authority cannot be challenged without provoking the potentially fatal anger of the gods themselves.

The Hebrew Bible inverts this entire way of seeing the world. God is *against* the established powers, chief of them Mesopotamia, satirised in the story of the Tower of Babel, and Egypt, the longest-lived and most powerful empire of the ancient world. Nothing amuses and angers God more in the Bible than people setting themselves up as demigods, as many ancient rulers did and as tyrants have continued to do ever since, among them, in the twentieth century, Stalin, Mao and President Kim Il-Sung of North Korea.

The story of the Exodus, with its plagues and the division of the Red Sea, is not just about freedom. If it had been, the story could have been told without any of the miracles. It is about God taking a stand against Pharaoh, and by implication all absolute rulers who claim to be god, child of the gods or chief intercessor with the gods. One of the key biblical projects is to demythologise and secularise power.

Here the revolutionary power of monotheism is expressed to the full. In polytheistic religions, a god or gods reign supreme over a certain area. There is a chief god of Egypt (Ra), of the Moabites (Chemosh), of the Babylonians (Marduk) and so on. They are part of the national myth. Their standing among the gods rises or falls with the fate of the nation.

For the first time monotheism introduces a radical split *between* God and the people. The God of the Israelites is not only the God of the Israelites but of everyone. His power extends not only over their territory but everywhere. Such a God cannot be identified with the power of this or that nation. The point of the plagues is not to hasten the freedom of the Israelites but to show Pharaoh that God's power extends even over Egypt. The story of the Israelites in Egypt is above all a religious critique of political power. Nothing could have been more counterintuitive to the ancient world than the idea that the supreme power intervenes in defence of the powerless.

Many centuries later, when Judea was captured and Jerusalem destroyed by the Babylonians, the prophet Jeremiah interpreted this not as the defeat of a people *and* its God, but as the defeat of a people *by* its God, using the Babylonians as his instrument. This is the great paradigm-shifting moment.[3] God endorses not might, but right. For the first time, religion becomes not a justification, but a critique of power.

Internalising this, a group of Swiss, Dutch and English political thinkers in the late sixteenth and early seventeenth centuries, among them Thomas Erastus, Richard Hooker, Hugo Grotius,

Peter Cunaeus and the English Hebraists Thomas Coleman, John Lightfoot and John Selden, laid the groundwork for modern politics. James Harrington, Thomas Hobbes, John Milton and John Locke built on the foundations they had laid. These were the people who argued for constitutional (i.e. limited) monarchy, the principle of toleration and that uniquely modern freedom, liberty of conscience. Their story has recently been told in Eric Nelson's *The Hebrew Republic*, subtitled 'Jewish Sources and the Transformation of European Political Thought'.[4]

His case, like mine, is that the received narrative of European politics is misleading. It says that in medieval and Renaissance Europe, political thought was fundamentally Christian and theological. Only with the rise of science did it become secular and thus tolerant. To the contrary, argues Nelson, Renaissance humanism, inspired by the pagan inheritance of Greece and Rome, developed a secular approach to politics. The founders of modern European politics, by contrast, were religious, and their key text was the Hebrew Bible.

Using it as their warrant, they developed three revolutionary principles. The first is that all legitimate constitutions are republican. Monarchy is at best a concession and derives its authority, by social covenant or contract, from the will of the people, or, as the American Declaration of Independence was to put it, 'the consent of the governed'. The second – in contrast to Hellenistic principles – is that one of the tasks of the state is to fight poverty, if need be by redistribution of income and the widening of land ownership. The third is the principle of toleration, that it is no business of the state to legislate in matters of religious belief.

All three propositions were based, not on Plato or Aristotle, but on Leviticus and Deuteronomy and the books of Samuel and Kings. Even Hobbes, an atheist, based his political philosophy on the Bible, which he quotes 657 times in *The Leviathan*. The one exception was Spinoza, who, though he spent much of his time analysing the Bible, based his political theory on philosophical

principles alone. How, then, do you get from Abrahamic monotheism to the free society?

Politics is about power, and at the heart of the Abrahamic vision
is a critique of power. Power is a fundamental assault on human
dignity. When I exercise power over you, I deny your freedom, and
that is dangerous for both of us. The opening chapters of Genesis
are about the abuse of power. Cain murders his brother Abel, and
two chapters later we read, 'The Earth was corrupt in God's sight
and it was full of violence' (Genesis 6:11).

Abrahamic monotheism is based on the idea that the free God
desires the free worship of free human beings. The historical
drama of the Bible turns on the question of how to translate *individual* freedom into *collective* freedom. How do you construct
a free society without the constant risk of the strong dominat-
ing and exploiting the weak? That is the issue articulated by the
prophets, and it was never completely solved. Politics is a problem
for the Bible, precisely because it believes that no human being
should exercise coercive force over another human being. Politics
is about power, and Abrahamic faith is a protest against power.

This is the point made by the profoundly religious historian
Lord Acton, who said, 'Power tends to corrupt and absolute
power corrupts absolutely.' People have always sought power as
the way of ensuring that their will predominates over others.
Hobbes, that cold-eyed analyst of the human condition, characterised the 'general inclination of all mankind' as 'a perpetual and
restless desire of power after power, that ceaseth only in death'.[5]
The politics of the Abrahamic tradition is only secondarily about
the use of power. Fundamentally it is about the limits of power.[6]

Can a political order exist *without* the use of power? As
Nietzsche and Hannah Arendt understood, there is only one
alternative, namely the act of promising.[7] Promising is the fundamental moral act. When I promise, I voluntarily agree to bind
myself. It is this ability of humans to commit themselves to do
or refrain from doing certain acts that generates order in the

relations between human beings without the use of coercive force. Nietzsche was the first thinker to say this clearly:

> To breed an animal with the prerogative to promise – is that not precisely the paradoxical task which nature has set herself with regard to humankind? Is it not the real problem *of* humankind? . . . [M]an himself will really have to become *reliable*, *regular*, *necessary*, even in his own self-image, so that he, as someone making a promise is, is answerable to his own *future*. That is precisely what constitutes the long history of the origins of *responsibility*.[8]

A free political order is possible only when *the fundamental political act is a mutual promise* between governor and governed. But no human being can be trusted to keep his or her word when he or she has access to power – a power not available to opponents. Sooner or later, if not in the lifetime of the ruler, then in that of his or her descendants, there is an inescapable risk of tyranny. Freedom can only be guaranteed in a political system where the constitutional sovereign is God himself, where he has sought and obtained the free consent of the governed, and where he has bound himself to respect human freedom. That is what happens in Exodus 19–20, the making of a covenant – a mutually binding promise – between God and the children of Israel.

Covenant is the most radical attempt ever undertaken to create a politics of freedom by taking all sovereignty out of human hands altogether. Whoever governs in Israel does so only under the authority delegated by God on the one hand, the people on the other, and can be criticised, and dethroned, for exceeding that authority. That is why, simultaneous with the birth of monarchy in biblical Israel, the prophet-as-social-critic with the right to criticise kings in the name of God, was born.[9] That right of opposition, first embodied in the prophet as the man or woman mandated to speak truth to power in the name of God, is fundamental to the free society.

*　　*　　*

Covenant was reborn as the key idea of the new politics of the sixteenth and seventeenth centuries, in Calvin's Geneva and the Dutch Republic, among the Scottish Covenanters and the English Puritans, and the Pilgrim Fathers of America. Though it faded as an idea as Europe became more secularised in the eighteenth century, it has remained part of the vocabulary of American politics to this day.[10]

Covenantal politics is a politics of new beginnings, of a people pledging themselves to one another and to the common good, a politics of 'we, the people'. It is a politics of moral principle and collective responsibility. This is what John F. Kennedy meant when he said, 'In your hands, my fellow citizens, more than in mine, will rest the final success or failure of our course,'[11] and Barack Obama when he said, 'For as much as government can do and must do, it is ultimately the faith and determination of the American people upon which this nation relies.'[12] Unlike hierarchical societies where rulers rule, a covenant society is always based on the mutual responsibility of citizens as a whole. The fate of the nation lies with the people, not with the rulers of the people.

A covenant always has a *narrative*. In the case of the Bible, it is the story of the Exodus. In the case of the United States, it is about a journey from oppression to freedom in the new world, the almost promised land. The narrative is retold at significant and symbolic moments – in the United States in presidential inaugural addresses – and they are accompanied by an explicit or implicit renewal of the covenant, a commitment to *keep faith* with the founders and their vision. The politics of covenant is about faith and hope, the faith that together we can build a gracious future and the hope that history can be redeemed from tragedy. A nation predicated on covenant can always renew itself.[13] It is highly doubtful whether other political formations can do so.

Covenant is politics scored for the right brain. It is based on story-telling, not abstract theory. It focuses on us-together-in-relationship, as opposed to the atomic individual of social contract theory – the citizen who works out that it is to his advantage to cede some of his powers to a central authority so that he can live in peace. It is a politics rooted in a religious vision of human dignity and equality.[14] It is a politics of 'one nation under God, indivisible, with liberty and justice for all'. It is a politics inconceivable *without* God, for only belief in the sovereignty of God is strong enough to set limits to human ambition and empower a population to overthrow those who overstep the bounds of 'liberty and justice for all'.

That is the irony as well as the strength of Abrahamic politics, that though its vision is religious, its conception of power is secular. Judaism expressed this by its principled distinction between kingship (government) and priesthood (religion). Priests must never hold political power. Christianity did so, somewhat differently, by its statement, 'Render unto Caesar the things that are Caesar's and to God the things that are God's' (Matthew 22:21). The vision that drives this secularisation is religious through and through. It says that power is not to be sacralised. Rulers, kings and emperors are not holy. They are there to serve, not to be served. All power is subject to the overarching imperatives of the right and the just. The moment it oversteps those limits, it is *ultra vires* and may rightly be opposed.

Politics, in the Abrahamic vision, is not the highest good. It is not where we meet God, not where we construct our deepest relationships, not where we exercise our highest virtues, not where we achieve individual and national glory. It is a means to an end, no more, no less. It is there to secure peace, security, safety and law-abidingness so that we can get on with our lives, serving God in work and worship, in family and community, arenas we do not entrust to politicians and the state because they require absolute liberty. It is the secondary nature of politics in the Judeo-Christian vision that is the surest guarantor against an intrusive state. Where politics is primary, politicians rule supreme; and where politicians rule, freedom is in danger.

That is the key difference between liberal democracy and Athenian democracy, the democracy Solon introduced into Athens some five centuries before the Christian era. In Greece, the citizen served the *polis*, the state. In liberal democracy, the state serves the citizen. In Athens and Sparta and later in Rome, the state was the vehicle of the people's highest ideals. *Dulce et decorum est pro patria mori*: 'It is sweet and right to die for your country.' The supreme virtue was to sacrifice everything for the glory and welfare of the city. Patriotism was the overarching value, and those who died in the course of war achieved the highest honour. The purpose of education, said Plato, is to make one 'desire and love to become a perfect citizen who knows how to rule and be ruled with justice'.[15]

The law of the state requires absolute obedience, but there is no higher law, no transcendental ethic, no divine norm, to which the state is answerable and in the light of which it can be criticised and if need be opposed. That is why Athenian democracy has within it the potential to become a tyranny, even if it is a tyranny of the majority. When politics is the highest value, it becomes a way in which the people worship the collective embodiment of themselves, and they can sacrifice many essential liberties to it, including the liberty of the minority.

Throughout the Hebrew Bible, by contrast, politics is seen as a necessary concession to reality, no more. Ideally the people should need no king, no government, no state. God was their sovereign; that should be enough. As the military hero Gideon said in the book of Judges (8:23) when the people offered to make him king, 'I will not rule over you, nor will my son rule over you. The Lord will rule over you.' The great ideals of justice and compassion, human dignity and social inclusion belonged to an arena where people related to one another not as citizens of the state but as neighbours and friends, covenantal partners. That is where we meet not as rulers and ruled but as co-creators of the good society.

Fundamental to Abrahamic politics is a distinction between the state on the one hand and civil society on the other. Civil society – the domain of families, communities, religious congregations, voluntary associations, charities, neighbourhood groups and the like – is where we relate to one another on the basis of friendship, reciprocity and a moral bond, without the use of power. Abrahamic politics depends on a strong civil society to counterbalance the power of the state, a power that has an inbuilt tendency to grow over time.

Few people said this better than Thomas Paine, the English radical and the only individual to have had a significant role in both the American and French revolutions. His pamphlet *Common Sense* was published in America in January 1776, and became an instant best-seller, selling 100,000 copies almost immediately. Its impact was huge, and because of it he became known as the father of the American Revolution. Here is how it begins:

> Some writers have so confounded society with government, as to leave little or no distinction between them; whereas they are not only different, but have different origins. Society is produced by our wants, and government by our wickedness; the former promotes our happiness positively by uniting our affections, the latter negatively by restraining our vices . . . Government, like dress, is the badge of lost innocence; the palaces of kings are built on the ruins of the bowers of paradise.[16]

Paine proceeds to justify this point on the basis of citations from the Hebrew Bible, especially those that criticise the institution of monarchy. This was all the more notable since Paine, as later became clear, was an atheist. You do not have to be religious to understand the force and logic of Abrahamic politics.

Which brings us to liberty of conscience. The idea that we should be free to hold the opinions we do was not born in Athens or Rome. It did not exist in the Bible. It did not figure anywhere in the ancient world. It appeared under very specific circumstances: a Europe which had suffered a debilitating series of wars of religion in the aftermath of the Reformation. It was the product of an intensely religious age in which religion had become a source of conflict.

There are three things that can happen in such circumstances. The first is that the victorious party imposes its view on its opponents, ruthlessly suppressing their rights if they persist in their views. That was the norm before the seventeenth century and it remains true in totalitarian states today. The second is to say: a plague on both your houses. Since religion is a source of conflict, let us ban it altogether, at least in public. If people must worship, let them do so in the privacy of their homes or places of worship but nowhere else. That was the view of Voltaire and the French revolutionaries: *Écrasez l'infâme*, 'Crush the infamy.' The second strategy denies liberty to all religions, the first to all but one.

The third view says this: today our side holds power. We can impose our views on our opponents. But tomorrow they may hold power, and they may do to us what we did to them. Under those circumstances we would not be free to practise our religion, and that is something we wish to avoid at all costs. Therefore we will grant religious liberty to all who are willing to undertake to keep the civic peace. We will guarantee our opponents the freedom to practise their faith, so long as they are loyal to the state. That is how liberty of conscience was born. It was born specifically at a time of strong religious passion, with the aim of preserving a space where liberty was protected as sacrosanct regardless of who held power.

So in England, and eventually in a different way in the United States, religious liberty came to be created by people for whom religion mattered a great deal, in a way that surprised and intrigued French observers. In the early eighteenth century, Montesquieu said that the English know 'better than any other people upon Earth how to value, at the same time, these three great advantages – religion, commerce, and liberty'.[17] In the nineteenth century Alexis de Tocqueville was likewise to say, 'I enjoyed, too, in England what I have long been deprived of – a union between the religious and the political world, between public and private virtue, between Christianity and liberty.'[18] That is what surprised the French: that religion can be a force for freedom.

It is often said that history provides us with no action replays. It is not given to controlled experiments. We only learn what can go wrong after it has already done so, and by then it is too late to put it right. In fact, though, the history of freedom in the modern world can be seen as a testing ground for different conceptions of politics.

It witnessed four revolutions: the English (1640), the American (1776), the French (1789) and the Russian (1917). They had very different trajectories. The English and American revolutions led to war, but they left in their wake stable societies with respect for human rights. The French and Russian led to reigns of terror. They began with dreams of utopia, but eventually they turned into nightmares of repression.

The difference between them was that the English and American revolutions were inspired by the Bible. They were led by Puritans who had a strong sense of covenant, a deep familiarity with the Hebrew Bible and its rabbinic commentaries, through the Christian Hebraists mentioned above. They were religious through and through. The French and Russian revolutions were based on philosophy – Rousseau and the *philosophes* in the case of France, Marx and Engels in the case of Russia.

Why did this make a difference? I would suggest three reasons. The first is that the Bible and philosophy have a different sense of time. The Hebrew Bible – the first work to see God in history, the first even to think in terms of history – understands that it takes time for human beings to change. The message of Exodus to Deuteronomy can be summed up simply: it took a few days for Moses to take the Israelites out of Egypt. It took forty years to take Egypt out of the Israelites. The road to freedom is long and hard, and you cannot force the pace. Even Moses, the man who led the Israelites out of slavery, was not the leader to take the next generation into the land.

Philosophy since Plato has found time a difficult idea. Time, said Plato, is a moving image of eternity. Philosophical truths are timeless. They belong to a heavenly realm in which nothing ever changes. Philosophy is about truth as system. The Bible is about truth as story. Systems are theoretical constructs, but stories are about people and the time it takes for them to change. Revolutions inspired by philosophy attempt the impossible: to create a new social order overnight.

The second, as already mentioned, is that biblical politics places a huge emphasis on civil society: on strong families, supportive communities, voluntary associations, philanthropic endeavours and the like. This was the great strength of Britain and America, as Burke and Alexis de Tocqueville saw and said. It was Burke's 'little platoons' and de Tocqueville's 'associations' that kept liberty alive by serving as a buffer between the individual and the state. That is why the French and Russian revolutionaries disliked them. Rousseau, Marx and Engels distrusted families and communities, *because* they got in the way of the direct relationship between the citizen and the state.

The third reason has to do with the different ways biblical and revolutionary politics understood the concept of rights. Two of the greatest writers on liberty in the mid-twentieth century, Friedrich Hayek in *The Constitution of Liberty* and J. L. Talmon in *The Origins of Totalitarian Democracy*, distinguished English and French approaches to liberty.[19] The English approach was gradual, evolutionary, mindful of history and respectful of tradition. The French approach was perfectionist, philosophical, even messianic in a secular way. For the French revolutionaries there is an ideal template of society that can be realised by the application of politics to all spheres of life. The English, by contrast, knew 'How small of all that human hearts endure / That part which laws or kings can cause or cure'.[20]

This leads to two different concepts of human rights. The English version saw rights as defining the space in which governments may not intervene. In the social contract, we hand over some of our liberties to government for the sake of law and order and defence against foreign powers. But there are certain liberties – life, liberty and the pursuit of happiness, as Thomas Jefferson put it – that are inalienable, meaning we do not and cannot sign them away. They define an area of freedom by setting limits to the power of the state.

The French approach was to see rights as an ideal description of humanity which it is the task of politics to enforce. Politics is about the transformation of society by the force of law. The French Revolution was undertaken in the name of rights, conceived as part of a scheme of social harmony that would reconcile personal good with the general good. Politics is about the use of power to bring about an ideal state of affairs. As Talmon writes, 'When a regime is by definition regarded as realizing rights and freedoms, the citizen becomes deprived of any right to complain that he is being deprived of his rights and liberties.'[21] Whereas English liberty set *limits* to the state, French liberty was to be *imposed by* the state. If need be, said Rousseau, we must force people to be free.

Hayek, writing in 1959, prophetically saw that the French tradition was everywhere displacing the English one. That has become suddenly, and unexpectedly, an issue in both Britain and the United States, where there has been an alarming erosion of religious liberties in recent years. The Attorney General of Massachusetts forced the Catholic Charities of Boston to close their adoption services because of their principled objection to same-sex adoptions. A similar situation occurred in Britain. In Britain also, an airport worker was forbidden to wear a crucifix in public, a teacher was dismissed for talking to a sick pupil about prayer, and an officer of the Royal Society was forced to resign for suggesting that teachers, if asked, should be prepared to discuss the idea of creation.

These are dangerous intrusions into the freedom of religion, codified in article 18 of the United Nations Universal Declaration of Human Rights (1948) which states, 'Everyone has the right to freedom of thought, conscience and religion; this right includes . . . freedom, either alone or in community with others and in public or private, to manifest his religion or belief in teaching, practice, worship and observance.' That religious rights are being curtailed in Britain and the United States, the two nations that led the world in religious liberty, is deeply disturbing.

This is French freedom, not English; philosophical freedom, not biblical. It is a step towards totalitarian democracy. When politics becomes the pursuit of abstract perfection by means of legislation, freedom is in danger. There has, historically, been only one counterforce strong enough to prevent the slide from democracy into tyranny, as happened in Athens in antiquity and in France during the Reign of Terror: that is the recognition of the limits of human authority under divine sovereignty.

That remains, even today, the difference between Abrahamic politics and ideological politics, between a minimalist and a maximalist state, between the idea that civil society is sacrosanct because it is not based on relationships of power, and the idea that it should be circumscribed as far as possible so that political power should prevail.

My argument has been that contrary to the received narrative, freedom has been better served in the modern world by a religious vision than by a secular one. The Abrahamic vision, with its insistence on the non-negotiable dignity of the human person and the importance of protected space – the families and communities that make up civil society – where relationships are not based on power, saved England and America from the worst excesses of revolutionary politics that cost tens of thousands of lives in France and tens of millions in Russia.

Revolutionary politics bears all the hallmarks of left-brain thinking, with its preference for abstractions over the concrete men and women, with their specific histories and loyalties, who make up society. Abrahamic politics, by contrast, is politics with a human face, the politics that knows the limits of power, as well as the transformative effect of free persons freely joining together to make social institutions worthy of being a home for the divine presence. Abrahamic politics never forgets that there are things more important than politics, and that is what makes it the best defence of liberty.

8

Morality

There is no significant example in history, before our time, of a society successfully maintaining moral life without the aid of religion.

Will and Ariel Durant[1]

Every ethos has its origin in a revelation, whether or not it is still aware of and obedient to it.

Martin Buber[2]

Dostoevsky is said to have commented, 'If God does not exist, all is permitted.' Was he right? Do you have to be religious to be good?

The short answer is, 'No.' You do not have to believe in God to save a drowning child, give food to the hungry or dedicate your life to fighting poverty in Africa. Some of those who risked their lives to save others in the Holocaust were religious, some were not. The most remarkable thing about such people is that they thought there was nothing remarkable in what they did.

The moral sense is prior to the religious sense. Long before they have begun to think about God or the human condition, young children understand concepts like fairness and injustice and can be quite forceful on the point. Adam Smith thought that (almost) all of us have the capacity for empathy. We are pained by other people's pain, moved by other people's plight. 'How selfish soever man may be supposed, there are evidently some principles in his nature, which interest him in the fortune of others, and render their happiness necessary to him, though he derives nothing from it, except the pleasure of seeing it.'[3]

We now know how this works. Our brain contains mirror neurons. These are brain cells that react not only when we perform actions but when we see others doing so.[4] These make us imaginatively identify with others. When we watch a high-wire artist we share his suspense. When we see someone being humiliated we share their embarrassment and shame. Emotions within a group are contagious. When one laughs, we all laugh. Mothers and children mimic one another in precisely synchronised body language. Astonishingly, even one-day-old children cry in response to another infant's cries of distress.[5] We are hard-wired for empathy. We are the 'moral animal'.[6]

Nor are we the only moral animal. The primate studies of Jane Goodall and Frans de Waal have shown us how widely distributed empathy can be. De Waal tells the story of a female bonobo named Kuni who found a wounded bird in her enclosure at Twycross Zoo in England. She picked up the bird and when the zookeeper signalled to her to let it go she climbed up a tree, unfolded the bird's wings and spread them wide, a gesture that made no sense for a bonobo but every sense when trying to help a bird. When the bird failed to fly, Kuni climbed down and guarded it until the end of the day when it finally flew to safety.[7]

In 1964 researchers discovered that rhesus monkeys would refuse to pull a chain to release food for themselves if they could see that doing so would deliver an electric shock to another member of the group. One monkey, after seeing another receive a shock, stopped pulling the chain for twelve days, risking starvation to avoid hurting a companion.[8]

I am going to argue in this chapter that religion is important to morality, vitally so. But the relationship between them is neither simple nor superficial. Religious people can easily slide into the belief that only we are good; the others, the unbelievers, are either immoral or amoral. That is arrogance, not humility, and it is, in any case, simply untrue. We are social animals, we have social intelligence, and we have the instincts and skills that allow us to survive as groups, often putting the welfare of others ahead of our own. We have a moral sense, and this has nothing to do with religion or faith.

That is the short answer. But there is a longer one. Voltaire was highly sceptical about conventional religious beliefs, but said, 'I want my attorney, my tailor, my servants, even my wife, to believe in God, for I think I shall then be robbed and cuckolded less often.'[9]

Rousseau thought that a nation needed a religion if it was to accept laws and policies directed at the long-term future. Without it, people would insist on immediate gain, to their eventual cost.[10]

George Washington in his farewell address said, 'Let us with caution indulge the supposition that morality can be maintained without religion ... Reason and experience both forbid us to expect that national morality can prevail in exclusion of religious principle.'[11]

What these views have in common is the belief that religion holds societies together as moral communities. The fear of God makes people think twice before defrauding or deceiving others. Conscience, the voice of God within the human heart, would, without religious faith, be more and more easily ignored. People would take advantage of one another whenever they thought they could avoid detection, and there would be a slow but inevitable breakdown of trust.

Tolstoy has a wonderful passage in which he offers an analogy:

> The instructions of a secular morality that is not based on religious doctrines are exactly what a person ignorant of music might do if he were made a conductor and started to wave his hands in front of musicians well-rehearsed in what they are performing. By virtue of its own momentum, and from what previous conductors had taught the musicians, the music might continue for a while, but obviously the gesticulations made with a stick by a person who knows nothing about music would be useless and eventually confuse the musicians and throw the orchestra off course.[12]

Tolstoy's point is subtle and substantive. When people begin to lose their religious convictions, often the first thing they stop doing is observing religious rituals. The last thing they lose is their moral beliefs. A whole generation of mid-Victorian English intellectuals, most famously George Eliot and Matthew Arnold, lost their Christian faith but held fast to their Christian ethics.[13] But that, implies Tolstoy, cannot last for ever. New generations appear for whom the old moral constraints no longer make sense, and they go. Moralities may be a long time dying but, absent the faith on which they are based, they die.

In 1959 the English philosopher Elizabeth Anscombe wrote a fascinating article in which, in effect, she said that what Tolstoy predicted had happened.[14] Morality had become incoherent because we had lost the foundation on which it was built. Words like 'obligation' and 'ought' belonged to a culture in which people believed that there was such a thing as a divine law: the belief shared by Jews, the Greek Stoics and Christians. Lose this and the words themselves lose their meaning. It was, she said, as if the word 'criminal' remained when the criminal law had been abolished and forgotten.

In 1981, in one of the classics of modern philosophy, *After Virtue*, Alasdair MacIntyre went further, and argued that our entire moral vocabulary had collapsed. All we are left with is fragments, half-remembered words like duty, virtue and honour, which no one understands any more. We speak without knowing what we are saying. We argue about morality without having any shared standards or beliefs. We are, he seemed to be saying, in a post-moral age.[15]

When I read these texts, my initial impression was that they were exaggerating. We all know certain moods in which the world as we knew it seems to be coming to an end, but somehow the heavens never fall. Yet as time passed, I began to realise how prophetic Anscombe and MacIntyre were. In public discourse, moral considerations became harder and harder to defend.

Almost any condemnation of any private behaviour was dismissed as 'judgemental', possibly the first time in history in which judgement – usually seen as a virtue akin to wisdom – has been regarded as a vice. To argue that one way of life is better than another is seen as prejudiced, intolerant or authoritarian. Moral relativism tells us that there are no absolutes in the moral life. Multiculturalism insists that every culture is equally entitled to respect. All else is a form of racism or phobia or authoritarianism. Allan Bloom, in *The Closing of the American Mind*, rewrote the Ten Commandments for the new age: 'I am the Lord your God who brought you out of the land of Egypt: Relax!'[16] We have in fact come very close to losing the traditional sense of right and wrong, meaning that there are certain things we may not do, and others that we must, even if no one is looking, even if we will not be found out, and even if no one else will be harmed.

That does not mean to say that we no longer have concerns. Manifestly we do. We care about things our grandparents hardly thought about: world poverty, economic inequality, global warming and the loss of biodiversity. But these issues have in common that they are vast, distant, global and remote. They are problems that require the coordinated action of millions, perhaps billions of people. They are, in essence, *political* rather than *moral*.

To be sure, we can each make a difference, and we can put pressure on governments, global corporations and other key players. But world poverty or the economics of equality are not about personal morality. They are not about prudence, justice, temperance and wisdom, or about faith, hope, charity and love. They are not about the choreography of interpersonal grace. The global economy and ecology are vital to our future. But they are not what previous generations would have thought of as moral issues. They are political ones.

When it comes to personal behaviour, we have come to believe that there is no right and wrong: there are only choices. The market facilitates those choices. The state deals with the consequences, picking up the pieces when they go wrong. The idea that there are choices we should not make, desires we should not satisfy, things we would like to do and can afford to do but which we ought not to do, because they are dishonourable, or a betrayal of trust, has come to seem outmoded.

To take an obvious example: there were some spectacular failures of business ethics as well as irresponsible behaviour on the part of banks and financial institutions that led to the Great Crash of 2008. Yet there was remarkably little remorse on the part of the people responsible. Few of those involved admitted that they had done wrong. They were in effect saying: It's legal, therefore it's moral. Besides which, everyone else is doing it, so why shouldn't I? But morality is based on the idea that there are things that are wrong *even though* they may be legal, and *even though* others are doing them.

This is a fundamental and historic shift. One of the first people to diagnose it was the American sociologist David Riesman, who argued in the 1950s that we were moving from an *inner*-directed society to an *other*-directed one. An inner-directed society is one where people have an internalised sense of right and wrong. An other-directed society is one in which people take their cues from what other people do. Only in the latter can you have a situation in which people say, 'If everyone else is doing it, it can't be wrong.'[17]

When social conformity becomes our only standard, concepts like duty, obligation, responsibility and honour come to seem antiquated and irrelevant. Emotions like guilt, shame, contrition and remorse are deleted from our vocabulary, for are we not all entitled to self-esteem? The still small voice of conscience is rarely heard these days. Conscience has been outsourced, delegated away.

So, in place of an inner code, we have regulatory authorities. Where once people believed that God sees all we do, now we have CCTVs and video surveillance. When self-imposed restraint disappears, external constraint must take its place. The result is that we have become the most regulated, intrusive society ever known. And still it fails, and will always fail, because without an internalised sense of responsibility to others, people will always find ways of outwitting the most sophisticated systems. In fact, it becomes a game to see how much and how often the system can be beaten.

That is what Voltaire was talking about, even if he was doing so with a measure of cynicism. To believe in God is to believe that we are known. God sees. Therefore we are seen. We can deceive others. Sometimes we can deceive ourselves. But we cannot deceive God. That forces on us a degree of honesty that is an essential part of moral integrity.

Plato in *The Republic* has one of his characters ask us to engage in a thought experiment. He tells the story of Gyges' ring, whose effect was to make its wearer invisible. What would prevent the possessor of the ring from committing any crime he felt like committing? He could never be caught. Would we not all be tempted, if we had such a ring, to do whatever our heart desired, knowing we would not, could not, be found out?[18]

The religious answer is that if God exists, the evil we do, even in secret, is nonetheless evil and is known. That does not mean, as some would caricature it, that God is a kind of cosmic police-man, patrolling the inner recesses of our mind like a member of the London constabulary on the beat. It means that we have a compelling psychological reason to take right and wrong seriously, even if those around us do not. That is what Riesman meant when he spoke about inner-directed individuals, people who do not get swayed by others, who have the moral courage to stand out against the crowd.

Edmund Burke once wrote, 'Men are qualified for civil liberty in exact proportion to their disposition to put moral chains on their own appetites. Society cannot exist unless a controlling power upon will and appetite be placed somewhere, and the less of it there is within, the more there is without.'[19] By that he meant that the less self-restraint we have, the more we will be forced to depend on police, surveillance and all the other intrusions we have had to introduce in the past half-century. That is what has happened. As we have become more convinced of each individual's right to do as they choose, we have lost the idea of a shared moral code voluntarily enforced, and come instead to rely on law enforcement agencies. Society has become manifestly less trusting and open than it was when doors could be left unlocked and people could walk the streets safely at night.

The trouble with humanity, Richard Weaver remarked, is that it forgets to read the minutes of the last meeting.[20] We can fall into the illusion of thinking that because scientifically and technologically we are far in advance of previous societies, we are morally so as well. We have left behind the superstitions and inhibitions of the past and are ready to face a brave new world.

That is not so. There is a case for saying that we have not moved forward but back. Two figures in particular held views very close to today's secular materialists, namely the third century BCE Greek thinker Epicurus (341–270 BCE) and his Roman disciple, two and a half centuries later, Lucretius (95–52 BCE).[21] They believed that the material world is all there is; that we are temporary concatenations of atoms which will split apart when we die. We have no souls. There is no life after death. The gods are uninterested in the affairs of human beings. We are here, we live, we die and cease to be. There is nothing to fear about death, because when we are here, death is not, and when death is here, we are not. Epicurus and Lucretius could be writing today. Their books would be best-sellers.

How did they believe we should live? Unsurprisingly, they had no interest in the concepts of right and wrong. Human life is governed by two considerations only, the pursuit of pleasure and the avoidance of pain. To pursue pleasure, it helps to have good food and good friends. To avoid pain, stay out of public life, which will only cause others to envy you. Do not marry or have children: the risk of emotional entanglement is too great. Sex is fine; love is best avoided. Keep your wants simple: that way you will not be troubled by the things you cannot afford. The end result will be *ataraxia*, 'tranquillity of mind', that absence of passion that the Greeks – Stoics, Cynics and Sceptics as well as Epicureans – seemed to see as the mark of a philosophical life. In a word: Chill!

As a way of insulating yourself from the heartaches of the world, Epicureanism cannot be faulted. But what a low-risk, uninspiring prospect it is, a Greek version of a self-help manual rather than a vision of the true, the good and the beautiful. Herschel Baker, in *The Image of Man*,[22] says about Epicurus' philosophy that it is 'clearly symptomatic of the slackening of Greek thought' and belongs to 'a crumbling society'. 'Wry, shallow', it is 'the last weary effort of the pagan world'. Even Bertrand Russell says that 'the age of Epicurus was a weary age, and extinction could appear as a welcome rest from travail of spirit'.[23]

When humanity loses faith in faith, as it did with Epicurus and Lucretius then and the scientific materialists now, the human ceiling suddenly seems lower and the horizons of possibility more foreshortened.

Something else linked the Greeks of the third century BCE with moral attitudes today. The Greeks had no concept of the sanctity of life. They practised abortion on a wide scale. They practised infanticide also.[24] Babies born with congenital defects were often simply left to die. That is how the story of Oedipus begins, with his father Laius pinning his ankles together and handing him over to a servant to abandon him on a nearby mountain. They had no qualms, either, about euthanasia. The word itself is Greek. It means 'a good death'.

It is astonishing how lightly the Greeks took the idea of suicide. It was, for the Stoics, Cynics, Sceptics and Epicureans, a perfectly legitimate assertion of human freedom. If life was distressing, end it. If living would force you to compromise your standards, choose dying. Epictetus, the former slave who became a Stoic philosopher, is reputed to have said that leaving life is no

more consequential than leaving a smoky room. It is even said
that Zeno, the first Stoic, tripped, broke his toe, and promptly
committed suicide.[25]

The contemporary West is headed in this direction, with abortion legalised, a strong movement for voluntary euthanasia and
assisted suicide, and a number of ethicists including Peter Singer
of Harvard arguing for the permissibility of infanticide.[26]

How shall we argue this case? We are faced here with two
incommensurable philosophies of life. For one, there is nothing
special about humanity, nothing that sets us qualitatively apart
from other life forms. We are bodies not souls, matter not spirit.
Nothing of us survives. Dust we are and to dust we return. What
conceivable reason could there be to deny people the choice to
die if, because of pain or incurable disease, they feel they have no
reason to live?

For the other, yes, we are dust of the Earth, but within us is the
breath of God. To be moral is to recognise that right and wrong are
not of our choosing. We are answerable to God, to the universe, to
life itself. To be morally mature is to recognise that there are limits
to what we may legitimately do. The world does not always yield
to our will. Sometimes our will must yield to the world. There are
certain things that are holy, sacrosanct, non-negotiable, lines drawn
in the sand. For the Judeo-Christian tradition the most significant
is life itself, which we see as belonging to God, not to us.

What makes this particular disagreement so interesting is that
it helps us see the larger issue at stake. For the Greeks in the third
pre-Christian century and secularists now, the fundamental value
is personal preference, autonomy, the choosing 'I'. For the Judeo-
Christian tradition, it is something infinitely larger than the 'I'
– the beyond-within that is the voice of God. Curiously enough,
it is just this connection between the self and the world beyond
the self that answers one question atheists tend not to ask. Why,
if Darwin is correct and survival over time is the test of fitness or
success, does religion survive so much better than atheism?

✳   ✳   ✳

It was none other than Darwin himself who gave us one of the great arguments for religion. He tells the story in *The Descent of Man.*

It began with a paradox Darwin noticed at the heart of his system. If evolution is the struggle to survive, if life is a competition for scarce resources, if the strong win and the weak die, then everywhere ruthlessness should prevail. But it does not. All societies value altruism. People esteem those who make sacrifices for the sake of others. This, in Darwinian terms, does not seem to make sense at all, and he was honest enough to admit it.

The bravest, most sacrificial people, he wrote, 'would on average perish in larger number than other men'. A noble man 'would often leave no offspring to inherit his noble nature'. It seems scarcely possible, he wrote, that virtue 'could be increased through natural selection, that is, by survival of the fittest'.[27]

It is a measure of Darwin's greatness that he acknowledged the answer, even though it contradicted his general thesis. Natural selection operates at the level of the individual. It is as individual men and women that we pass on our genes to the next generation. But civilisation works at the level of the group. As he put it:

> A tribe including many members who, from possessing in a high degree the spirit of patriotism, fidelity, obedience, courage, and sympathy, were always ready to give aid to each other and to sacrifice themselves for the common good, would be victorious over most other tribes; and this would be natural selection.[28]

How to get from the individual to the group was, he said, 'at present much too difficult to be solved'.

Technically, this is known as the 'free rider' problem. It is always in my interest to pay less or take more than my share in some public amenity: to travel on a bus, for example, without paying for a ticket if I can get away with it. Public goods – not just tangible ones like roads and transport systems, but intangibles like safety and trust – depend on everyone sharing the burden. If I can avoid paying, it will be to my advantage to do so; but if everyone did so, the system would collapse. So, for its own survival, every group has to devise ways of detecting and discouraging free riders, people who exploit the system.

One way of doing so, as we have seen, is to erect complex systems of law, regulation, inspection, detection, surveillance and prosecution. But these are costly and cumbersome and do not always work. The alternative is to create, within the minds of individuals, an identification with and concern for the group as a whole so strong that it defeats the constant temptation to become a free rider. This generates 'high trust' societies where enforcement costs are low and adaptability swift. Any group in which all the members can trust one another is at a massive advantage to others.

This, as evolutionary biologist David Sloan Wilson has argued, is what religion does more powerfully than any other system.[29] God is the voice of the other within the self. It is God who teaches us to love our neighbours as ourselves, to welcome the stranger, care for the poor, the widow and the orphan, heed the unheeded, feed the hungry, give shelter to the homeless, and temper justice with compassion. It was Nietzsche, Darwin's younger contemporary, who saw most clearly how unnatural these things are. Nature is the will to power. Faith, in the Judeo-Christian tradition, is care for the powerless. Religion is the prime example of how, for Homo sapiens, culture overrides nature.

Perhaps without fully realising what he had done, Darwin was pointing us to the central drama of civilisation. Biological evolution favours individuals, but cultural evolution favours groups. So, as Judaism and Christianity both knew, there is a war within each of us as to which will prevail: self-regard or concern for others, egoism or altruism. Selfishness benefits individuals, but it is disastrous to groups, and it is only as members of a group that individuals can survive at all. As Darwin himself put it, 'Selfish and contentious people will not cohere, and without coherence nothing can be effected.'[30]

There are three ways of getting individuals to act in a way that is beneficial to the group. One is power: we force them to. The second is wealth: we pay them to. The disadvantage of both these is that they leave selfishness untouched. They use external incentives. The danger is that strong individuals will outwit the system. They will use power or wealth for their own advantage.

The third alternative is to educate them to see that the welfare of others matters as much as their own. No system has done this more effectively than religion, for an obvious reason. Religion teaches us that we are part of the whole, a thread in the fabric of God's creation, a note in the symphony of life. Faith is the ability to see ourselves as joined to others by God's love.

Not only does it teach us this, through story and ritual, celebration and prayer, it weaves it into our personalities, affecting all parts of the almost infinitely complex labyrinth of the human brain. No wonder then that religion has survived, and that we need it if we are to survive. And it was Charles Darwin who pointed the way.

Religion binds people into groups. It creates altruism, the only force strong enough to defeat egoism. Selfishness is good for me and my genes, but bad for us and therefore bad for my descendants in the long run. In Homo sapiens a miracle of nature meets a miracle of culture: religion, which turns selfish genes into selfless people.

It does it because great religious texts have the power to inspire the moral imagination. Reading the Bible, we encounter God listening to the prayer of a childless woman and giving her a child; Moses confronting Pharaoh and demanding that he let his people go; the prophets fearlessly condemning kings and priests for their corruption. This is morality at its most dramatic and world-transforming.

Michael Walzer argues that a religious morality is likely to be more *interesting* than its secular equivalents. It comes to the prophet with the force of revelation. Often it overthrows long-standing beliefs. When Hannah sings a song to God on the birth of her son, she says:

> He raises the poor from the dust
> and lifts the needy from the ash heap;
> he seats them with princes
> and has them inherit a throne of honour.
>
> (1 Samuel 2:8)

We hear the power of hope expressed in those words. Perhaps the social structure is not immutable. Perhaps the low can become high. Perhaps there is justice after all. A secular morality, says Walzer, 'is likely to fall short of the radical newness and sharp specificity of divine revelation'. He asks us to consider, as an example, Thomas Nagel's 'objective moral principle' that we should not be indifferent to the suffering of other people. Walzer comments, 'I acknowledge the principle but miss the excitement of revelation. I knew that already.'[31]

Not only is secular moral philosophy often dull, flat and predictable, one of its least lovely features, as we saw in the previous chapter, is that its greatest thinkers embodied a 'hermeneutics of suspicion'. They reinterpreted human behaviour to give it the worst possible construction.

So for Marx the consolations of religion are simply the way by which the rich and powerful keep the poor and weak in their place. For Freud the voice of conscience is just the once repressed, now returned, voice of the father we wanted to kill and who now haunts us with guilt. For the neo-Darwinians every act of altruism is merely the work of selfish genes blindly seeking to replicate themselves. 'Scratch an altruist and watch a hypocrite bleed.'

No wonder that the more we believe these stories the more we are minded to think that morality is for wimps and that there is some truth in Michael Douglas's famous remark as Gordon Gekko in *Wall Street*: 'Greed, for lack of a better word, is good. Greed is right. Greed works. Greed captures the essence of the evolutionary spirit.' Of course it does not, not even for evolution-ists. But the combined impact of a century and a half of high-minded cynicism is to sap our moral energies and confuse the moral sense.

At the end of the day there is a difference between discover-ing morality and inventing it. Discovering it means that it exists independently of our will. It comes to us as a call from the heart of being. Love your neighbour. Love the stranger. Feed the hungry. Heal the sick. Stretch out your hand to the poor. Do not hate. Do not harbour a grudge. Do not take revenge. Do not stand idly by in the face of injustice. Forgive. I, the Lord, do these things. Go thou and do likewise. There is a power to these teachings that lifts the human spirit and mobilises moral energies.

No human substitute has had anything like that power. Yes, we should promote the greatest happiness for the greatest number, but what if the greatest number find the greatest happiness in things that are plain wrong, like prejudice in a racist society, or violence in a lynch mob? Utility can conflict with integrity and sometimes we have to do the right thing even though it makes people unhappy.

Yes, we should do our duty. But to whom? Our family, our friends, our neighbours, our fellow countrymen, humanity as a whole? What should we do if these things conflict? And does duty exhaust the moral life? As Bernard Williams was fond of pointing out, some-times a person who is nice because she feels it to be her duty is simply less nice than one who is so because it comes naturally.

Alasdair MacIntyre's point in *After Virtue* is that the Enlightenment project – a morality constructed on rational grounds with no reference to religion or tradition – simply failed, not because it came up with no answers but because it gave too many of them. Kant's ethics are incompatible with Hume's, which are irreconcilable with Bentham's, which are anathema to Schopenhauer. The philosopher's slide rule does more sliding than ruling, and we are left bewildered and confused.

*   *   *

I have not argued in this chapter that you need to be religious to be moral, or that you need to believe in God to believe in good. Manifestly that is not so. Goodness is widely distributed through our species. Whether it is Bill Gates and Warren Buffett giving away billions of dollars to charity, or the nurse whose gentle care and quiet smile ease the fear of a single sick patient, whether it is Nelson Mandela's ability to forgive those who imprisoned him and enslaved his people, or the teacher who by believing in her pupils brings out the best in them, the world is full of goodness, whether or not we call it God's grace.

This is important for religious believers to acknowledge. There is something profoundly self-serving and self-deceiving in thinking that 'we', us and our fellow believers, have a monopoly of virtue, that we alone find favour in God's eyes. It is not so, and faith should give us the humility to see that it is not so. The great religious teachers show us virtue and moral courage where we least expect it, among people the world ignores or takes for granted. They teach us that a stranger may be an angel, and there is moral beauty in a slum, a shanty town, Skid Row, if you have eyes to see and a listening heart.

Yet there is a connection between religion and morality nonetheless. The great religions are the most effective moral tutors the world has ever known. They begin by turning our gaze outwards, to the human other who is a reflection of the divine Other. They teach us habits of virtue by getting us to do ethically demanding things, visiting the sick, comforting the bereaved, helping the needy, giving time and money to charitable causes. There is hardly a religion that does not encourage its followers to do deeds such as these. And they are done in the context of community. For it is in community that we learn the habits of cooperation and mutual support that make us 'moral animals'. As Darwin showed us, without altruism there could be no community, and without community we could not survive.

Judaism and Christianity are used to being countercultural forces. Christianity began as a small and persecuted minority.

Judaism has spent the better part of four thousand years in that condition. So both know how to sustain identity and principle even when this means going against the flow. That is why they can keep alive values and institutions necessary to our survival, that are being lost in the wider world outside. Many Christians fought slavery.[32] Many Jews fought apartheid in South Africa. Those motivated by the opinions of others conform to the crowd, while inner-directed individuals listen to the still small voice of internalised conscience. We need religion to remind us of the importance of marriage and fidelity and loyalty; of the fact that success, fame, wealth, affluence, the siren songs of today's culture, are trivial in comparison with character and integrity. And we need communities in which the virtues live, are rehearsed and are valued. If it takes a village to raise a child, it takes a community to sustain the moral life.

Atheists like John Stuart Mill and Bertrand Russell fully understood this. Mill wrote about societies in general:

> Whenever and in proportion as the strictness of the restraining discipline was relaxed, the natural tendency of mankind to anarchy reasserted itself; the state became disorganized from within; mutual conflict for selfish ends neutralized the energies which were required to keep up the contest against natural causes of evil; and the nation, after a longer or briefer interval of progressive decline, became either the slave of a despotism or the prey of a foreign invader.[33]

Russell wrote that even the greatest civilisations like ancient Greece and Italy of the Renaissance eventually lost their 'traditional moral restraints', because people lost faith in the ideas that supported them. The result was that 'the liberation from fetters made individuals energetic and creative, producing a rare florescence of genius; but the anarchy and treachery which inevitably resulted from the decay of morals made Italians collectively impotent, and they fell, like the Greeks, under the domination of nations less civilized than themselves but not so destitute of social cohesion'.[34]

Social cohesion is precisely what religion sustains and much else undermines. When societies grow affluent, when the burden of law-abidingness falls on the state and its institutions, when people define right and wrong in terms of externalities – punishments and rewards – and in terms of what other people do and are seen to get away with, when people focus, as they naturally do, on immediate benefits not long-term sustainability, then society begins to erode from within and there is little anyone can do to halt it.

The signs are unmistakable:

People lose a sense of shame. Rudeness is taken as a sign of sophistication. People pursue the pleasure of the moment. They lose their respect for leaders. The young no longer defer to the old, and the old behave as if they were young. The difference between the sexes is blurred. People get irritated by the least touch of authority and they dislike any rules that inhibit their freedom to do as they like.

A Christian evangelical bemoaning the secularism of today? No: Plato speaking about the democracy of Athens.[35]

A law of entropy governs societies. They rise to power and affluence and then they begin to decline as individualism saps the collective spirit that brought them to greatness in the first place. When this happens, only a countercultural force can revive flagging energies, renew institutions, defeat cynicism, generate trust and restore altruism. The Abrahamic monotheisms are the most powerful countercultural forces the world has ever known because they speak to something indelible in the human spirit: the dignity of humanity as the image of God.

So Dostoevsky was wrong and Tolstoy right. Morality does not suddenly break down when people stop believing. People do not conclude: God does not exist, therefore everything is permitted.

But they do in the long run, like an orchestra without a conductor, lose the habits that sustain the virtues that create the trust that preserves the institutions that shape and drive a moral order. That is when you see the first signs of discontent with secularisation. People, even those who do not practise a faith, start sending their children to faith schools. Children, even if only a few, start becoming more religious than their parents. Religious voices begin to be listened to with respect, if only because so many other voices sound cynical or self-seeking. The moral sense is not a blazing fire but a flickering flame, and it seems to have been the fate of faith to have kept it burning even when the winds of individualism are strong.

God and good are connected after all.

9

Relationships

A Roman lady asked Rabbi Yose bar Halafta, 'What has God been doing since the six days of creation?' The rabbi replied, 'He has been sitting and arranging marriages.'

Midrash[1]

Said Rabbi Akiva, 'If a man and a woman are worthy, the Divine presence rests between them.'

Talmud[2]

As long as family feeling is kept alive, the opponent of oppression is never alone.

Alexis de Tocqueville[3]

Genesis begins with human relationships, a whole book of them. It is about husbands and wives, parents and children, and the tense rivalry between siblings, as if to say: This is the locus of the religious life. In the love that brings new life into the world. In marriage where love becomes a covenant of loyalty. In parenthood, the one thing that, this side of heaven, grants us an intimation of immortality. In the family as a bond between the generations. In the calibrated distance between individuals that allows them to be joined in responsibility and fidelity while at the same time left the space to be themselves – a modern theme to be sure, but at the heart of these biblical stories also.

Something of immense consequence is being asserted here. Genesis, the book of 'first things', is about matters that have not just chronological but also axiological priority. We are told about relationships first because they matter most. There are two aspects to God in the Bible, for which it uses different names. There is *Elohim*, the God of creation, Spinoza's and Einstein's God, the God of nature and nature's laws. But there is, holier still, *Hashem*, the God of relationships, the God who loves and is the ground of love, the God who brings the universe into being in love.

Ultimately, that is what the faith of Abraham is about: love as the supreme creative force within the universe. Not sex, passion, physical desire, though in The Song of Songs the Bible has a place for that too. Not procreation and the continuity of the species, though that is the first command God gives to humanity. Nor is it mere sentiment, though love as emotion is not missing from the Bible's stories. It is love as loyalty, love as a pledge of mutual responsibility, love as the commitment of two persons to share their lives and destinies, love as the redemption of solitude.

The faith of Abraham makes two monumental claims: first, that the relationship between God and humanity is a matter of love, not power; second, that you can build a society on the basis of love, love of neighbour and stranger, that leads us to care for their welfare as if it were our own. These remain, even now, astonishing ideas, and one would say that they were wildly utopian were it not for the fact that the faith of Abraham has lasted longer than any other known civilisation. Its adherents may have fallen short time and again, but they never quite lost their sense that there was something moving and humane about this ideal and the demand it makes of us.

There is a clear structure to the way the Bible tells its story. Genesis, which is about personal relationships, is the necessary prelude to Exodus, which is about politics and power, liberation and nation-building. We find the same pattern in the closely linked books of Ruth and Samuel. First comes the intensely moving story of Ruth, her loyalty to her mother-in-law Naomi and the kindness of Naomi's distant cousin Boaz. Then, at the end of the book, we discover that Ruth becomes the great-grandmother of David, Israel's greatest king. It is a prelude to the books of Samuel, which tell of the birth of Israelite monarchy.

Genesis-Exodus and Ruth-Samuel are the literary way of establishing *the primacy of the personal over the political*. It is as if the Bible were telling us that on the surface, history is driven by the pursuit of power; in reality, it is driven by the text and texture of interpersonal relationships. Power diminishes those who wield it no less than those they wield it against. We grow not through exercising power over one another but by kindness, attachment, compassion; by listening to one another and making space for one another. Politics makes the headlines. It always did, even if headlines in ancient times took the form of hieroglyphic testimonies on temple walls or inscriptions carved into triumphal arches. But what the world thinks large the Bible thinks small, and what the world dismisses as of minor account the Bible focuses on and frames with minute attention.

I am aware that in this chapter, more perhaps than in any other, I will be challenging strongly held stereotypes. I will be arguing for a radical re-reading of some famous biblical passages. I will be bypassing the note of asceticism that entered Abrahamic monotheism through Paul and the Church Fathers, that saw sex as somewhat sinful and the pleasures of the flesh as secondary to those of the spirit. There is in Judaism no place for monasticism and celibacy. Some of this came from the heritage of Greece: Socrates thought that carnal passion disturbed the rational mind, Plato that the family stood in the way of total identification with the *polis*, and Epicurus that love and marriage were simply too great an emotional risk. In any case, we inhabit a culture in which talk of a normative sexual ethic is as politically incorrect as it is possible to be. But this I know beyond doubt: that it was the strength of its families and its consecration of the love between husband and wife, parent and child, that made Judaism what it is and gave it the passion and resilience it has always had.

I believe that God lives in the grace of our dealings with others. Religion, for monotheism, is about relationships.

* * *

What is lost when religion declines? The standard answer is ecclesiastical power. God in the form of his official representatives, the clergy, comes to exercise less and less authority in government, in the mediation of knowledge through schools and universities, and eventually in culture as a whole. The standard definition of secularisation is the removal of more and more areas of life from ecclesiastical control.[4]

My suggestion is that we should think in a different way since, as I have argued, monotheism is not about power, but about the limits of power. Religion is really about relationships. Therefore when religion declines, we would expect the effect to be visible in relationships. To be sure, there will still be men, women, sex, reproduction, children and sibling rivalry. Those are biological phenomena. They exist among all higher life forms. They form the very pulse of Darwinian evolution. Subtract religion and culture from humanity, and you are left with biology. That will always remain.

But there is a dystopian nightmare that this is what we will indeed be left with: sex without love, promiscuity without limits, love without commitment, fatherhood without responsibility, predatory males, females often left to bear the burden of childcare alone; in short, the sexual habits of the higher primates. The faith of Abraham is about consecrating biological instinct and etching it with the charisma of moral beauty.

Today in the West we have a series of societies in which almost half of children are born outside marriage, where people are marrying later or not at all, where close to half of marriages end in divorce, and where the chances of a child growing to maturity in a stable relationship with its biological parents are slimmer than they have been for a long while. Why should this matter? Because children pay the price. When stable marriages cease to be the norm, children are more likely to live in poverty, and a significant minority to be abused, sexually assaulted, abandoned, intimidated or neglected.[5] We can trace the impact. Within the space of two generations, against a background of steadily increasing affluence, there has been an increase of between 300 and 1,000 per cent in the incidence of alcohol and drug abuse, eating disorders, stress-related syndromes, depression, violent crime, suicides and suicide attempts among the young.[6]

Children pay the price for the abdication of responsibility on the part of their parents, and it can be a high price. Two thousand years ago, the rabbis could no longer accept the literal truth of the phrase 'visiting the sins of the parents on the children'. It struck them as an injustice, and they reinterpreted every passage in which this phrase appeared (they held that it referred only to instances where children repeated the sins of the parents).[7] Today, in a sense, secular society *is* visiting the sins of the parents on the children.

What has happened to marriage is what happens when a right-brained, integrative culture gives way to a left-brained, atomistic one. What made marriage unique was the way it brought together in a single institution a whole series of essential human activities: sex, reproduction, companionship, love, responsibility for the welfare and nurture of those we have brought into being, and responsibility for their education. Marriage is to society what a unified field theory is to physics: a way of threading diverse phenomena together so that they radiate with a single light. When marriage breaks down, as it has done throughout the West from the 1960s onwards, human bonds splinter and fragment into a myriad component parts, so that we can have sex without reproduction (birth control) and reproduction without sex (techniques from artificial insemination to cloning). We can have both without love, love without companionship, and children without responsibility for their nurture.

Each of these can be further fragmented, so that even basic biological facts of parenthood become a complex set of options: genetic mother, host mother, commissioning mother, genetic father, mother's partner, same-sex partners and so on. The permutations are open-ended and bewildering. There is even a danger that children may become a commodity to which people have a right and that, with genetic interventions, they will be designed to order. In large swathes of contemporary society, single parenthood has become the norm and fatherhood hardly exists as a social reality. Already in the 1980s an elderly vicar told me that he could no longer talk to children about 'God the Father'. The word they did not understand was not 'God' but 'Father'.

What are in danger of being lost are the linked qualities of loyalty, fidelity, duty, trust and the sharing of a pledge by which both partners promised not to walk away, the very things that make love a glimpse of eternity in the midst of time, and parenthood the closest any of us can come to God: love bringing new life into the world. What is lost when faith is lost is marriage as the supreme moral commitment that lifts humanity from biology to poetry.

How does monotheism transform relationships? It begins by transforming religion itself. The religious literature of the ancient world was about politics and power, dominance and submission, struggle and victory. The race was to the swift and the battle to the strong. Ra, Marduk, Zeus and their counterparts ruled because they conquered their opponents. They were the divine equivalents of alpha males. The metaphysics of polytheism is largely about who rules what and how.

That is not the picture the Bible gives us. That God has total power is taken for granted at the outset. God speaks and the world is. The power of God is largely irrelevant to the religious life. Miracles in the Bible are usually for the sake of impressing people who believe in that sort of thing. So the ten plagues and the division of the Red Sea are performed against the Egyptians. God sends fire at Elijah's request to defeat the false prophets of Baal. Even the appearance of God at Mount Sinai – with thunder, lightning and the sound of the ram's horn – is intended to awe a people who until a few weeks earlier had been slaves. When God speaks at the same mountain centuries later to Elijah, he makes a point of showing him that God is not in the whirlwind, the Earthquake or the fire, but in the 'still small voice'.

God, in the Bible, has a monopoly of power in order to take power out of the equation. It is not at issue. It is not what the religious life is about. *Faith is about relationship sustained without the use of power.* If any relationship, whether between husband and wife, parent and child, siblings, neighbours, strangers and friends, is dependent on power, faith has broken down. God does not live in such relationships. So the first revolution of monotheism is to demythologise and thus secularise power.

The nature of the second revolution is best brought out by reflecting on a remarkable recent book by two distinguished American philosophers, Hubert Dreyfus and Sean Dorrance Kelly, *All Things Shining*.[8] The book, subtitled 'Reading the Western classics to find meaning in a secular age', is a candid acknowledgement of the nihilism that haunts our godless culture. The remedy the authors propose is not a return to monotheism. It is instead a return to polytheism, to the world of Homer.

The scene they choose to illustrate Homer's view of the world shows perfectly what is at stake. It is the dinner party Menelaus, king of Sparta, throws for his guest Telemachus. Menelaus' wife, the beautiful Helen, tells a story to entertain the company. She describes how, many years earlier, she abandoned Menelaus and their young child to run away with a young houseguest named Paris – the event that led to the Trojan War.

What we find shocking about the story, say Dreyfus and Kelly, is that no one is shocked. There is no moral outrage at this tale of betrayal and adultery. Homer admires Helen. So, in his account, does Menelaus himself. When she has finished, he says, 'An excellent tale, my dear, and most becoming.' Menelaus goes to sleep that night, says Homer, beside 'Helen of the light robes, shining among women'.

Clearly a culture in which someone can be admired for an act of adultery that led to a war in which thousands died is different from ours, and Dreyfus and Kelly do a fine job of explaining why, focusing on Homer's concept of the sacred. Homer did not think in terms of internalised conscience, a sense of duty, an inner voice saying, 'Thou shalt not.' He did not think of moral agency at all as we do now.

Instead, he and his contemporaries thought in terms of people being open to external forces, personified as gods, that call forth wonder and gratitude. What makes Helen great to Homer is 'her ability to live a life that is constantly responsive to golden Aphrodite, the shining example of the sacred erotic dimension of existence'. A god, in Homer's world, is 'a mood that attunes us to what matters most in a situation, allowing us to respond appropriately without thinking'.

Helen is 'the embodiment of Eros', and Eros for Homer is 'not just physical or sexual pleasure' but rather 'an entire way of being that draws the best kinds of people naturally to one another'. Clearly Dreyfus and Kelly do not mean 'the best kinds of people' in a moral sense. Their entire case is amoral or pre-moral. They mean people who shimmer, like the dancer Nureyev, with the charisma of beauty or physical grace. That Helen betrays her husband and child, that yielding to erotic passion is incompatible with loyalty, duty and fidelity, is irrelevant. That is precisely their point. Polytheism – which the authors advocate – actually means 'receptivity to a plurality of incompatible gods'.

By reviving the ancient idea of polytheism the authors allow us to see with fresh eyes what is at stake in monotheism. At its heart is *the moralisation of love*. Once we step back from the minority Christian interpretation of Adam and Eve as a story about the sinfulness of sexuality, there is nothing anti-erotic in the Hebrew Bible. What the Bible is against is not Eros but adultery, not sex but infidelity, not beauty but betrayal.

The key narrative of Genesis is the story of Abraham and Sarah, a married couple who embark on a journey together, suffer trials and disappointments and grow old together, but who stay faithful to one another and to God. Dreyfus and

Kelly's candid polytheism helps us understand why Genesis consistently portrays the world outside the covenantal family as a place of sexual anomie. Abraham and Isaac both fear that they will be killed so that their attractive wives can be taken into the royal harem. The people of Sodom attempt to commit an act of homosexual rape on two strangers. Shechem, a local prince, abducts and rapes Jacob's daughter Dinah. In Egypt, Potiphar's wife attempts to seduce Joseph. Failing, she accuses him of rape.

Genesis does not contrast monotheism with idolatry. That comes later in the Bible. Instead it contrasts it with a world of sexual free-for-all. Many gods means many commitments, or rather no commitment at all, just the mood of the moment, deified, sacralised, stripped bare of any moral content, with no qualms for whom one may be betraying or what the consequences may be. It is not surprising that when Dreyfus and Kelly seek contemporary examples of the sacred they choose sport (the baseball hero Lou Gehrig, Roger Federer the tennis master) or art (Nureyev, the ballet dancer). Sport and art are for us safe space, time out, where we experience emotions that would be devastating if we were to live by them in the real world.

There is a reason why the world of Homer exists no more. A world of beautiful heroines and noble warriors is also a world where the unbeautiful are inconsequential, where battlefields are strewn with corpses, where moral commitments mean nothing and where life, when it loses its vividness, is a bore. The Hebrew Bible achieved something no other literature, sacred or secular, has ever done: made love a moral adventure and invested marriage with metaphysical grandeur. Comparing the fidelity of husband and wife to the ideal of faithfulness between humanity and God, it turned marriage into a sacred covenant.

Consider the metaphors for God in the Bible. There are, to be sure, times when God is seen as a king, a sovereign. That is a political image and it is used for the social, legislative and judicial aspects of religion. But overwhelmingly the imagery is drawn from the family. God is a husband and we are his wife. God is a parent and we are his children.

It is in those relationships, between marriage partners, or between parents and children, that we find the love, responsibility, steadfastness, kindness and care that are the essence of covenantal relationships. Yes, there are times in the Bible where God is portrayed as majestic, royal, all-powerful, sustaining all life and watching over the affairs of humanity. But the most powerful images are of God the caring father (and, in the last chapters of Isaiah, a comforting mother) and the loving partner:

> 'Though the mountains be shaken
> and the hills be removed,
> yet my unfailing love for you will not be shaken
> nor my covenant of peace be removed,'
> says the Lord, who has compassion on you.
>
> (Isaiah 54:10)

Faith is the moralisation of love. It is not a cognitive act. *Emunah*, the biblical word for faith, really means 'covenant loyalty'. It means being true to the bond you have made with another, honouring your word and trusting them to honour theirs. God makes promises to us. We make promises to God. At the deepest level of metaphor and meaning, faith is a marriage, a bond entered into in love and honoured in life.

Faith lives, breathes and has its being in the world of relationships, in the respect we pay our marriage partner, the steadfastness with which we bring up our children, and the way we extend the feeling of family to embrace neighbours and strangers in acts of hospitality and kindness. 'Love your neighbour as yourself.' 'Love the stranger.' The familiarity of these commands should not blind us to their strangeness. The Greeks would have found them unintelligible. Strangers, to them, were barbarians. Every morality contains a principle of justice. Unique to Abrahamic faith is the centrality of love.[9]

Here, though, the possibility of misunderstanding is great, and I need to revisit the two most misunderstood of all biblical passages: Adam and Eve in the Garden of Eden, and the binding of Isaac. The former is about the relationship of husband and wife, the latter about that between parent and child. I will argue that neither means what it has been taken to mean.

The story of Adam and Eve has been read, outside Judaism, as a story about original sin, by which we are all tainted. There are good grounds for not reading it this way. First, the concept of original sin is not mentioned anywhere in the Hebrew Bible.[10] Second, it offends against justice. As Jeremiah and Ezekiel both say, guilt attaches only to the sinner, not to his or her descendants.[11] Third, God explicitly forgives humanity after the Flood: 'Never again will I curse the ground because of man, *even though every inclination of his heart is evil from childhood*' (Genesis 8:21). Fourth, there is a partial return to Eden through the covenant of Sinai. The ark the Israelites carried with them in the wilderness was adorned by cherubim, angelic figures mentioned elsewhere only in the context of Eden.[12] The Torah is described in the book of Proverbs (3:18) as 'the tree of life'. The sanctuary in space, the Sabbath in time, symbolise paradise regained, Eden re-entered.[13]

The key to the story of the first humans lies in a sequence of three sentences at the end, whose juxtaposition seems to make no sense at all. They begin with Adam's curse for having eaten the forbidden fruit:

'By the sweat of your brow you will eat your food until you return to the ground, since from it you were taken; for dust you are and to dust you will return.'
    The man named his wife Eve, because she would become the mother of all the living.
    The Lord God made garments of skin for Adam and his wife and clothed them. (Genesis 3:19–21)

What is the connection between mortality ('to dust you will return') and the man giving a new name to his wife? And what is the connection between that and God making the couple garments of skin, as if he were giving them a gift as they left the garden?

To understand the passage we have first to realise that it is not a myth but a philosophical parable about language and relationships, the difference between species and individuals, nouns and names, and about what lifts the relationship between husband and wife from the biological to the anthropological, from animal reproduction to human relationship and love.[14]

The story of the first humans in Genesis 2 begins with God giving Adam the ability to use language to classify things. He names the animals: 'Whatever the man called each living creature, that was its name.' He sorts and labels them as species. But human beings do not function at the level of species. They are conscious of themselves as unique individuals. They are not merely alone, a physical state. They can also feel lonely, a psychological state. So, 'for the man no suitable helper was found'. He is not alone, but he is lonely. Animals form species; humans are individuals.

God then creates a partner for the man. But if we listen carefully to the poem he speaks on seeing her for the first time, we note something odd: 'She shall be called *woman*, for she was taken out of man.' He names the woman as he named the animals. He uses a generic noun. She is 'woman', not a person but a type. She is 'taken out of man', 'helper to man', but not an individual with her own fears and feelings. Adam does not understand her otherness. She is, for him, merely his mirror image: 'bone of my bones, flesh of my flesh'.

Eve rebels against this by striking out on her own. The conversation she has with the serpent is the first conversation she has. Adam has spoken about her but not to her. She eats the forbidden fruit. She gives some to her husband, who also eats. She has become the prime mover in the relationship, but still they have not spoken.

Then comes the discovery of their sin. God confronts them both. Each responds by denying responsibility. Adam blames the woman. The woman blames the serpent. Still they are talking about self and other as if they are not free and choosing individuals, but mere things caught up in the forces that operate on things.

Then Adam hears that he is mortal. Dust he is, and to dust he will return. Suddenly Adam understands the difference between individual and species. Species live on; individuals die. There was a world before we were born, there will be a world after we die, but we will not be here to see it. In the knowledge of our mortality we discover our individuality.

But if Adam is an individual, so is the woman. And God has just said to the woman, 'With pain you will give birth to children.' Within the curse is a blessing. Humans may be mortal, but something of them survives their death, namely children. But children are born only when man and woman are joined in a bond of love. That is when Adam gives his wife the name *Chavah*, Eve, meaning 'mother of all life'. The point is not which name, but the fact that it is a name, not a noun. Species have nouns, individuals have names. The woman is now, for the man, not 'woman', but Eve. Adam has discovered personhood, uniqueness, individuality, and thus the difference between biology and anthropology. Animals form species, humans are individuals. Animals mate, humans relate. Animals reproduce, humans beget. Animals have sex, humans have love.

The rabbis said that Adam became the first penitent and was forgiven.[15] God then shows kindness to the couple by making them garments of skin. The rabbis said that they were made of snakeskin,[16] as if to say: The very thing that led you to sin (the serpent) will now protect you. Your physicality, which first caused you embarrassment, can be made holy when transmuted into love and sanctified by a bond of trust. Far from ending on a note of condemnation, it ends on a note of divine grace.

The story teaches us about language and love, and about the difference between biological reproduction – a property of the species – and the human family, which is always made up of individuals who are more and other than their similarities. Even clothing, which God endorses with his gift, signals that we are not naked and transparent to one another. There is a part of each of us that always remains hidden. In Hebrew the word *chavah*, Eve, also has the meaning of 'hidden'.[17]

There are two subtle hints in the narrative that this is what the story is about. The first, often confused in translation, is that the text speaks throughout of *ha-adam*, 'the man', not *adam*, 'Adam', which is, like Eve, a proper name. 'The man' becomes Adam only when 'the woman' becomes Eve.

The second is that the name of God changes too. In Genesis 1, God is called *Elohim*, a noun meaning roughly 'the totality of forces operative in the universe'. In Genesis 2 – 3, he is called *Hashem-Elokim*, and in Genesis 4, immediately after the Adam-Eve story, he is called *Hashem* alone. *Hashem* is God's proper name, just as Adam is Adam's and Eve, Eve's. Our experience of God mirrors our experience of other people. When we relate to other people as persons, we relate to God as a person. Or, to put it differently, God as *Hashem* is the transcendental reality of interpersonal relations. We love God through loving other people. That is the only way.

The story of the forbidden fruit and the Garden of Eden is less a story about sin, guilt and punishment and more about the essential connection between mortality, individuality and personhood. In one sense it is a pre-emptive refutation of the neo-Darwinian argument that we are all just animals, selfish replicators. We are precisely *not* animals, not because we are biologically unique – they and we are mere dust of the Earth; nor because we have immortal souls – we may, but they are wholly absent from the narrative. We are not animals because we are self-conscious, because we are aware of ourselves as individuals, and because we are capable of forming relationships of trust. We have culture, not just nature; anthropology, not just biology.

It is also a parable about otherness. Adam's poem about 'bone of my bones, flesh of my flesh' sounds beautiful, but it leads to moral failure because it fails to acknowledge the otherness of the other. Until Eve is Eve, not merely 'woman', the man does not know who she is.

The biblical word *da'at*, 'knowledge', does not mean in Hebrew what it is normally taken to mean in the West, namely knowledge of facts, theories, systems and truths. It means interpersonal knowledge, intimacy, empathy. The 'tree of knowledge' is about this kind of knowledge. True knowledge that the other is not a mirror image of me, that he or she has wants and needs of her own that may clash with mine, is the source of all love and all pain. To know that I am known makes me want to hide: that is the couple's first response after eating the fruit. The turning point comes when the man gives Eve a proper name. Love is born when we recognise the integrity of otherness. That is the meaning of love between people. It is the meaning of love between us and God. Only when we make space for the human other do we make space for the divine Other.

God created the world to make space for the otherness that is us.

The second narrative is the binding of Isaac. The traditional interpretation of this passage, for Jews and Christians alike, is that the point of the story is to show that Abraham is willing to sacrifice his child for the sake of his love of God.

There is one difficulty with this interpretation, namely that child sacrifice is consistently singled out in the Bible as the most heinous of all sins. According to the Bible itself, there is nothing noble, honourable or worthy of admiration about the willingness to sacrifice your child. That is what the pagans do. It is what the king of Moab did, and was rewarded by victory in war (2 Kings 3:27).

Abraham, whose original name Abram means 'mighty father', is chosen 'so that he will teach his children and his household after him to keep the way of the Lord by doing what is right and just' (Genesis 18:19). Abraham was chosen to become the role model of father-as-teacher. To portray him as a man willing to sacrifice his child is at odds with everything else we know about the Bible's moral vision of parenthood and child sacrifice. So there must be another interpretation.

The answer is given by context. God consistently promises Abraham, Isaac and Jacob two things: children and a land. Seven times God promises the land to Abraham, once to Isaac, three times to Jacob. They are promised children: as many as the dust of the Earth, the sand on the seashore, the stars of the sky.

Repeatedly, both promises are delayed and sidetracked. Abraham and Sarah have to wait until they are old before they have a single child. Sarah is infertile. So is Rebecca. So is Rachel. Repeatedly, too, they are forced to leave the land, through famine or family conflict. The land does not become theirs or their children's throughout the whole of the Mosaic books. Abraham has to haggle to buy a cave in which to bury Sarah. Isaac is challenged by the locals for using the wells his father dug. Jacob has to pay a hundred pieces of silver to buy the right to pitch his tent.

Something very strange is being intimated here. Children and a land are the most natural of all endowments. Almost everyone has them. What makes the patriarchs and matriarchs different? Only this: that *what everyone else has naturally, they only have as the gift of God*. Most couples have children. The matriarchs, except Leah, were all infertile. Their children were seen as the gift of God.

Likewise with the land. Most people have a land. What made Abraham different was that he was told at the beginning of his mission to 'leave' his land, his birthplace and his father's house. The patriarchs were nomads, Hebrews, travellers, outsiders. Israel becomes the people who have a land only by the grace of God. From this fact, the Bible draws a remarkable legal conclusion. 'The land must not be sold permanently,' says God, '*because the land is mine* and you are but strangers and sojourners with me' (Leviticus 25:23).

The Israelites do not own the land. They merely inhabit it, and their right to do so is conditional on their recognition that it does not belong to them but to God. And what applies to the land applies to children likewise. Abraham, whose name means 'mighty father', is to live out an experience that will establish, once and for all time, that *our children do not belong to us but to God.* Isaac, the first child of the covenant, is the child who belongs to God. Only thus is parenthood to be conceived in the life of the covenant.

The trial of the binding of Isaac is ultimately about whether Abraham is *willing to renounce ownership in his child by handing him back to God.* That is what the angel means when he tells Abraham to stop, saying, 'Now I know that you fear God, because you *have not withheld from me* your son, your only son.'

The story of the binding of Isaac is opaque to us because we take it for granted that children have their own legal identity and rights. But this is a very modern proposition indeed. Throughout the Victorian era, social activists had to work hard to mitigate the brutalities of child labour – children being sent down mines or working long hours in factories. In Roman law, the principle of *patria potestas* meant that children were the property of their fathers, who had the legal right to do with them what they chose, including kill them.

Only when we take this background into account can we begin to understand that the binding of Isaac is God's way of teaching Abraham that *patria potestas* has no place in Judaism. The Bible is saying to the people of the covenant: Just as you do not own your land, you do not own your children. Thus is born the biblical idea of parent-as-educator as opposed to parent-as-owner.

This is also what the Bible means when it speaks of God as a parent. God is a non-interventionist parent. During the early years of his people's history he intervened to deliver them from slavery, but increasingly as they matured he too moved from parent-as-owner to parent-as-educator. God does not do our work for us. He teaches us how to do it for him. For God himself abides by the laws he gives us.

*   *   *

This is not how either story has been understood in the past. I have offered these interpretations to show that they can, and I believe should, be understood differently. If my readings make sense, they show that the presence of God within a relationship prevents it becoming a struggle for dominance between two wills. Husband and wife must acknowledge the otherness of the other rather than seeing the other as a mirror image of themselves. Parents, despite the fact that they have brought a child into the world and nurtured and protected it in its early years, do not own the child. The presence of God in a relationship forces us to make space for the other.

All this, of course, is mere abstraction compared to the way it takes on vividness and colour, energy and passion, in the actual life of faith. Once, while making a television documentary about the state of the family in Britain, I took Penelope Leach, Britain's leading childcare expert, to see what happens in a Jewish school on Friday morning. The children, as usual, were performing their 'mock Shabbat', role-playing what would happen that night at home. Penelope watched fascinated as the five-year-old parents blessed the five-year-old children and welcomed the five-year-old guests. When it was over, she asked one five-year-old boy what he liked most about the Sabbath. 'I like it', he said, 'because it's the only time *Daddy doesn't have to rush off*.' It was a revealing insight into how the Sabbath preserves time and space for the family against the pressures of the world outside. As we walked away from the school, Penelope turned to me and said, 'That Sabbath of yours is saving their parents' marriages.'

Of course you do not have to be religious to have a happy marriage or be a caring parent. No one would suggest otherwise. But marriage has ceased to be supported by the wider culture.

One of the turning points in my life was listening to the Cambridge anthropologist Edmund Leach deliver the Reith Lectures in 1967. I was just starting my second year at university, and I was shaken by his statement, 'Far from being the basis of the good society, the family with its narrow privacy and tawdry secrets is the source of all discontents.'[18]

That, for me, was the moment I knew that our academic role models were making a mistake, and that I had to set out on a journey of my own, into the faith of my ancestors. 'Narrow privacy' and 'tawdry secrets' spoke to nothing in my experience. For me and most of my friends, family was our source of at-homeness in the world, the only place we could turn to for unconditional love. 'Home', said Robert Frost, 'is the place where, when you have to go there, they have to let you in.'[19] I sensed a great betrayal. None of us could have known then how high a price successive generations of children would pay for this high-minded abdication of responsibility.

If all faith did was show us how to sustain a marriage and a family in love and loyalty, making space for one another, I would count it as God's great and sufficient gift. Religion sacralises relationship, which is why those who care about relationship will seek ways of investing it with holiness.

Faith, for the prophets, was a kind of marriage. Marriage is an act of faith.

IO

A Meaningful Life

It is as if
We had come to an end of the imagination,
Inanimate in an inert savoir.

Wallace Stevens[1]

The sad sight of human life untouched by transcendence.
Rebecca Goldstein[2]

Max Ostro was a young Jew living in Poland when the Nazis came. He and his family were rounded up. Together with one of his brothers and his father, he was herded into a cattle truck in a train bound for Treblinka. No one came back from Treblinka. It was an extermination camp. There, many of Poland's three million Jews were gassed, burned and turned to ash.

In the train, barely able to breathe, his father held his two sons. He said to them, '*Mein kinder*, if you stay on the train you will die. It belongs to *malach hamoves*, the angel of death. I want you to *davven maariv* – pray the evening prayer. Then I want the two of you, when the opportunity presents itself, to jump. The Nazis will shoot. But one of you will survive. This I promise you: one of you will survive.'

The sons prayed. Both jumped from the train. The Nazis saw the movement and started firing. Max's brother was killed instantly. Max, under cover of darkness, survived.

The family had hidden a sum of money which Max was able to recover, and with it he paid a farmer to hide him in his hay barn. Max survived this way for some time. Then came November 1944. The Nazi effort to round up and exterminate all remaining

Jews intensified. Max later told his son that he had a dream at that time. In it he saw the Rebbe, the holy teacher his father had admired. The Rebbe told him, 'It is no longer safe for you in the barn.'

So Max came to an arrangement with the farmer. He had himself buried in a grave in the ground with only a narrow space open to the sky. Through it Max was able to breathe. Once a week the farmer would come and bring something for Max to eat and drink. He survived like that, buried alive, for two months until the war came to an end.

Max eventually came to Britain, built a business, married and had two children. He went to the synagogue regularly, prayed every day, lived his life as an Orthodox Jew and gave much of the money he made to charity. He never spoke bitterly about the Holocaust, and though he sometimes wept for the family he had lost – he was the only survivor – he and the other survivors in Britain became a kind of extended family to one another.

I did not know Max well – I saw him from time to time at gatherings of Holocaust survivors. I knew his face, but not his story. While I was writing this book, he died and I went to comfort his son Maurice, whom I knew. That was when I heard his story. A book has been written about it.

Louis S. was not a Holocaust survivor. His family had left Poland long before, after a succession of pogroms and a wave of antisemitic incidents. He came to Britain when he was six. The family were poor. Louis had to leave school at the age of fourteen and work to help support his parents and siblings.

Eventually he was able to open a shop selling remnants of cloth, *schmatters* as they were known, to local tailors. It was not a successful business. Days would pass without a customer. Louis would listen to the radio and read. Eventually he too married and had children.

Louis went to synagogue every day. He did not understand much Hebrew, but this he knew: he was a Jew, he believed in God, and his fate was in God's hands. That was enough for him. Louis walked tall.

Towards the end of his life, in his eighties, he had to undergo five major operations. Each sapped his strength and he grew progressively weaker. In the hospital he had with him his *tallit* and *tefillin* – his prayer shawl and phylacteries – and he would put them on as best he could, and pray. At other times he would read from a little Hebrew copy of the book of Psalms. God was watching over him, and Louis trusted him. He knew his days on Earth were nearing their end and God was about to take him to himself.

He died peacefully, one of his sons holding his hand. He told me later that he had been saying the morning prayers and had just reached the passage, 'The soul you gave me is pure . . .' when Louis died.

Louis was my father.

I tell these stories because Max and Louis were ordinary people – Max who, through no choice of his own, had a quiet greatness thrust upon him by surviving the darkest night in history, and Louis who remained ordinary and yet whose life had a dignity and thankfulness to which I, his son, could barely aspire.

They believed in God and they lived their lives in his presence. That fact gave their lives meaning. They were here through God's love, they lived on God's Earth, they breathed God's breath, what they had they owed to God, and therefore whatever they could they shared with others, they came to God's house, the synagogue, and thanked him for their lives, their families and the freedom to thank him.

Their lives had a kind of radiance and gravitas, a belongingness. Neither Max nor my father suffered existential angst. They lived each day as God's blessing and saw no need to philosophise beyond that point. When asked, 'How are you?' they would reply, as Jews of their kind always did, *Barukh Hashem*, 'Thank God.' They did good to others unostentatiously, because that is what you do, that is why we are here. They did not trouble heaven with their bootless cries, desiring this man's art and that man's scope, with what they most enjoyed, contented least. What they had they gave thanks for, and what they lacked did not trouble them. God knew what was best, and they trusted him. They accepted fate. They made a blessing over life. They were a blessing while they lived.

Their faith did not rest on the principled belief that God created the world in six days, or that the ontological argument was true. They had not read Kierkegaard and made a reason-defying leap into commitment. In fact, had you wanted to discuss any of these things with them, they would probably have poured you a whisky and said, *Zog a lechayim*, 'Drink to life.'

They were religious because that was the commitment their ancestors had made and stayed true to for more than a hundred generations, because that is how a Jew lives, and because people who live that way are somehow more real, more honest, than those who pursue the idols of fame or wealth or success, which always have a habit of coming back and biting you.

Nu, their lives seemed to say. God exists. The universe exists. We exist. What more do you want? There is a simplicity in that faith I respect.

Not everyone consciously raises the question of the meaning of life. Max was too busy trying to stay alive. My father was too busy trying to make a living. It takes a certain freedom and spaciousness, a reflective calm, to ask whether life has meaning. Ironically, life has to be quite good for people to think it is quite bad. But so it is. Everything that exists has a drive to go on existing, said Spinoza. So it is only relatively rarely that people ask, at a level both philosophical and existential, both abstract and real: Why, given the nature of life as such, should I go on living? Three people who famously did so were the biblical author of the book of Ecclesiastes, Lev Nikolayevich Tolstoy and Albert Camus.

Let's begin with Tolstoy. The year is 1879. Tolstoy is fifty-one. He has published two of the greatest novels ever written, *War and Peace* and *Anna Karenina*. He has, in his own words, 'a good, loving and beloved wife, good children and a large estate'. He has wealth, partly inherited, partly earned by the success of his writing. He has not the slightest doubt about his genius or his place in history. He writes, 'Well, fine, so you will be more famous than Gogol, Pushkin, Shakespeare, Moliere, more famous than all the writers in the world.' One question, though, obsesses him: 'So what?' So I have everything, wealth, fame, work, love, the recognition and respect of others. But what does it all add up to? Why should I carry on living? 'I had', he writes about his mood at the time, 'absolutely no answer.'[3]

Tolstoy's *Confession*, the book he eventually wrote about his inner search, is by any standards an extraordinary document. Most people would have found satisfaction in any of the myriad ways he occupied his time, writing, bringing up a family, pursuing experiments in education, running his vast estates, caring for the peasants under his aegis. Yet we can sense something of what Tolstoy is speaking about. When we are young we say, 'If only I had X, or achieved Y, or did Z.' We locate the meaning of life in our aspirations. If we are lucky or work hard or both, eventually we acquire X and achieve Y and do Z. Yet we can find that *still the question remains*. 'Is that it? Is that all? Why, with all the success and acclaim, do I still feel empty, unfulfilled?'

Few put it with the drama Tolstoy did. He tells the following story. Once there was a traveller who, wandering in the steppe, sees coming towards him a ravening beast. To save himself he climbs into a waterless well, but he looks down and sees at the bottom a dragon, its jaws open, waiting to eat him. He dare not climb out and he dare not fall. So he clutches hold of a wild bush growing in a cleft in the wall of the well. This alone suspends him between the death awaiting him above and below. But his hands grow tired. He feels he must soon let go. Then he sees two mice, one white, one black, gnawing at the roots of the bush. Soon, even if he manages to keep hold of the bush, it will break off and he will fall into the mouth of the dragon. At that moment he sees some drops of honey on the bush's leaves and he reaches out to lick them. That, says Tolstoy, is life. The dragon is death, the white and black mice, our days and nights, and all our pleasures are no more than drops of honey on a bush that will soon give way.[4]

Tolstoy searches in science, philosophy, wisdom and reason and finds no answer to convince him that life is worth living. Science answers many questions, but not the one that obsesses him. He sees too that meaning does not lie in something superadded to life: possessions, achievements, honours, awards. Those are externalities, gift-wrapping, not life itself. The answer that eventually came to Tolstoy was religious faith. 'No matter what answers faith may give, its every answer gives to the finite existence of man the sense of the infinite – a sense which is not destroyed by suffering, privation or death.' Faith, he said, is the force of life. 'If a man lives, then he must believe in something.' If that something is finite, it will not ultimately satisfy him, since everything finite eventually perishes. The only thing worth believing in is the infinite. And, 'Without faith it is impossible to live.'[5]

The faith that Tolstoy arrived at was not a conventional religiosity. He was highly critical of the Church. He believed it had not kept faith with its original mandate. He developed his own idiosyncratic Christianity. But he became a changed person, a *Homo religiosus*, a man of faith. He discovered truth not among the aristocrats and intellectuals he met in the capital cities of Europe, who, he said, were living lives of self-deception, 'grabbing hold of everything they could' yet secretly afraid of suffering and death. He found it in the strength and endurance of ordinary people. I think that was the genius of Rembrandt too: the ability to show the radiant light that shone from the faces of people who were neither beautiful nor specially favoured by fortune. The meaning of life is not so obscure that it needs advanced degrees in physics or metaphysics, nor so rare that it is the possession of only the few.

Tolstoy did not give precise definition to the faith he found, other than the divine call to 'love one another in unity', but I

suspect it was something like this. The meaning of life is the realisation that you are held in the arms of a vast presence; that you
are not abandoned; that you are here because you were meant to
be. It is the sense that life is something you have been given, so
that you live with a feeling of gratitude and you seek to give back,
to 'pay it forward', to be a blessing to others. This presence in
which you live knows you better than you know yourself, so it is
no use pretending to be what you are not, or denying your short-
comings, or justifying your mistakes, or engaging in self-pity, or
blaming others. It is a loving, forgiving but challenging presence,
demanding much but never more than you can do. It asks you to
give your best, not for the sake of reward, but because that is what
you are here on Earth to do.

This is not a testable proposition. There is no scientific
experiment that would establish it to be true or false. It is more
and other than a belief, a creed. It is an attitude to life, what
Wittgenstein called 'a trusting'.[6] It is the opposite of the mood
that runs through ancient myth and contemporary atheism, that
of a universe at best uncaring, at worst hostile, to our existence:
'As flies to wanton boys, are we to the gods. They kill us for their
sport.'[7] Instead, in the love of the Infinite for us we find eternity
in the here and now.

> Though lovers be lost, love shall not;
> And death shall have no dominion.[8]

Tolstoy knew that he had essentially undergone the same journey
of radical doubt travelled by the author of the biblical book of
Ecclesiastes, in Hebrew, *Kohelet*, meaning 'Teacher' or 'Preacher',
traditionally identified with King Solomon. Ecclesiastes is the
most unexpected, even subversive, book in the Bible. Tolstoy
quotes it repeatedly in *A Confession*. Its author is the man who
had everything – palaces, vineyards, gardens, parks, pools, servants, the entire entourage of wealth and success – and finds that
they mean nothing:

> 'Meaningless! Meaningless!' says the Teacher.
> 'Utterly meaningless! Everything is meaningless.'
>
> (Ecclesiastes 1:2)

Ecclesiastes is obsessed by mortality, to a degree understated by most translations. The key word of the book – it figures thirty-eight times – is *hevel*, usually translated as 'vain', 'pointless' or 'meaningless'. In fact, though, it means 'a breath'. As in many other ancient languages, the Hebrew words for soul or life are all forms of respiration. *Nefesh*, 'life', comes from the verb meaning 'to breathe deeply'. *Neshamah*, 'soul', means 'to inhale'. *Ruach*, 'spirit', also means 'wind'. *Hevel* is a part of this family of words. It means specifically 'a shallow breath'.

What Kohelet means in the opening chapters of the book is that seeking refuge in wealth and possessions, or even in books and wisdom, is futile since life is no more than a fleeting breath. Ecclesiastes is a sustained meditation on the vulnerability of life. It speaks of *hevel* in a way that recalls King Lear at the end of Shakespeare's play as he holds dead Cordelia in his arms and says, 'Why should a dog, a horse, a rat, have life / And thou no breath at all?'

Hevel, a shallow breath, is all that separates the living from the dead. We live, we die, and it is as if we had never been. We build, and others occupy. We accumulate possessions, but others enjoy them. The good we do is soon forgotten. The wisdom we acquire is useless, for it merely brings us back to a recognition of our mortality. To seek happiness in objects that endure is a kind of self-deception: they last, we do not. This leads Kohelet to a dark and almost heretical conclusion:

> Man's fate is like that of the animals; the same fate awaits them both. As one dies, so dies the other. All have the same breath; man has no advantage over animal. Everything is but a fleeting breath. All go to the same place; all come from dust, and to dust all return. (Ecclesiastes 3:19–20)

What is extraordinary about Ecclesiastes, given our conventional understanding of religion, is that it makes no reference to an afterlife. There is no moralisation of fate. There is no argument that virtue is its own reward. There is no alleviation of the stark fact of mortality.

Yet Kohelet refuses to let disillusion have the final word. Once we acknowledge that only God is eternal and human happiness must be sought within the limits of our all-too-brief span of years, then we can find it in the now-ness of time:

> A man can do nothing better than to eat and drink and find satis-
> faction in his work. This too, I see, is from the hand of God.
> (2:24)

> I know that there is nothing better for men than to be happy and
> do good while they live. (3:12)

> The sleep of a labourer is sweet, whether he eats little or much.
> (5:12)

> Enjoy life with your wife, whom you love, all the days of this
> fleeting life that God has given you under the sun. (9:9)

Ecclesiastes, a man of untold wealth and sophistication, like Tolstoy eventually finds meaning in simple things, love and work, eating and drinking, doing good to others and knowing that there is a time for all things: to be born and to die, to weep and to laugh, to acknowledge the eternity of God and to accept the limits of a human life.

This is the happiness of the great wisdom traditions, not a million miles from the Stoics and Epicureans, or even Sigmund Freud and Bertrand Russell. Yet Ecclesiastes is ultimately a religious book: 'Remember your Creator in the days of your youth,' the author says at the start of his great poem about creeping old age (12:1–8). He is a man trying to find meaning in what God has given us, not in a godless world. What he discovers at the end of his journey is not what the Stoics and Epicureans found. Their form of happiness was *ataraxia*, a kind of affectless calm that is indifferent to triumph and disaster, Kipling's 'twin imposters', alike. Ecclesiastes' happiness – another key word of the book, as it is of the Hebrew Bible generally – is *simchah*, which means 'joy, celebration, exuberance'. More about *simchah* anon, but suffice it to say that Ecclesiastes' vision of the good life is simply happier than that of the Greeks of the third pre-Christian century, and this too has something to do with a basic attitude of trust.

The third great explorer of the human desert was Albert Camus (1913–60) who, like Tolstoy explicitly and Ecclesiastes implicitly, identified as the central existential question, 'Why should I not commit suicide?'[9] What makes Camus emblematic for the subject of this book is that he refused to take refuge in religious faith. He is the prime example – the only other serious competitors are Nietzsche and Schopenhauer – of the Western intellectual for whom the God of Abraham is not an option and who refuses to see this as a superficial fact. Rightly he recognises that it changes everything. The conclusion to which he is driven is that life is absurd:

> The absurd man thus catches sight of a burning and frigid, transparent and limited universe in which nothing is possible but everything is given, and beyond which all is collapse and nothingness. He can then decide to accept such a universe and draw from it his strength, his refusal to hope, and the unyielding evidence of a life without consolation.[10]

How then are we to characterise such a life? Camus's answer is the Greek myth of Sisyphus. Sisyphus was the king who stole the secrets of the gods, in return for which he was condemned by Zeus to spend his life laboriously rolling an immense boulder up a hill, only to watch it roll down again and having to repeat the labour endlessly, never achieving either the final goal or rest from it. That, says Camus, is life as 'the absurd'. And that is what we are condemned to. We can either be defeated by it, or we can refuse to be defeated. That refusal, tragic, heroic, defiant, is what gives life its glory and even its brief fragments of happiness.

I have mentioned this view of life before. Give or take a detail here and there, it is, I think, what my teacher Bernard Williams believed. It is quintessentially Greek. It is the lifeblood of Greek tragedy, of Aeschylus and Sophocles. It believes in fate rather than freedom. In the deepest sense it is bereft of hope. It is coherent, consistent, lucid, perfectly rational within its own terms of reference, and yet hardly compelling as the only possible way of interpreting the universe and our place in it. These are Camus's closing words about Sisyphus's life in a godless world:

> This universe henceforth without a master seems to him neither sterile nor futile. Each atom of that stone, each mineral flake of that night-filled mountain, in itself forms a world. The struggle itself toward the heights is enough to fill a man's heart. One must imagine Sisyphus happy.[11]

Must one? Really? If that is happiness, what is misery? What is despair? Where is Tolstoy's or Ecclesiastes' joy? They too peered into the abyss with no less honesty. But they returned with an affirmation that led them back into a world of relationships, of love and kindness to others, a willingness to accept their vulnerability but rest secure within it, knowing that they were held in the vast embrace of Being-as-love. Camus rightly says, 'There is no fate that cannot be surmounted by scorn.'[12] But scorn is not the only possible response to a life that one knows must end. The atheist is no more sure of the godlessness of the universe than the believer is of his or her God-filled vision. So why choose that way rather than this? There may be no fate that cannot be surmounted by scorn, but there is none either than cannot be transfigured by a sense of dimly discerned significance, and transmuted by a principled and fearless hope.

What then is meaning? What would help us understand what is truly at stake between Camus and Tolstoy, or my late father and today's non-believers? Here I come back to the deep question Bernard Williams asked me – the only one he asked me – about my faith. 'Don't you believe that there is an obligation to live within one's time?' What he meant, I think, was that you cannot live as if history had not happened, as if there had been no Enlightenment, no Hume, no Kant, no Darwin, no challenge to a literalist understanding of certain biblical passages, no shaking of the foundations of the medieval worldview. Unless we are prepared to live, like the Amish or certain ultra-traditionalist Jews, in complete segregation from the wider world, we are creatures of our time. We live, in the deep sense given by Charles Taylor in his masterwork of that title, in 'a secular age'. We live in the world of Camus, the absurd, and the meaningless. Meaning in the old, traditional sense simply is not available to us. So, I think, he implied.

Well, yes and no. Certainly a naive, pre-modern traditionalism is not available to us. But what if tradition was never as naive as we thought it was? There is, to be sure, a certain naiveté as well as an undeniable beauty to the Greek rationalist tradition, the tradition Nietzsche associated with Apollo as against Dionysus, of order, harmony, time as the moving image of eternity, reason as the lens of truth, and the compatibility of all true ideals and virtues, the orderliness of Greek architecture and formal gardens and the music of Bach. Much of that today lies in ruins, enchanting and enchanted ruins to be sure, but not a structure within which we can live.

We postmoderns know the darker truth about the bestiality within man that Darwin charted biologically and Nietzsche philosophically. We know about *eros* and *thanatos* and the will to power. We know that progress, modernity's masterword, is neither limitless nor guaranteed. We have moved beyond the

193

touching faith of Mandeville and Adam Smith and Montesquieu, that you can devise economic and political systems that will turn vice into virtue and greed into the common good. Vice remains vicious and greed rapacious, despite all the control mechanisms built into liberalism, democracy and market economics. The 'dream of reason' can all too readily turn into a nightmare when, under stress, people elbow reason aside in pursuit of their more destructive passions.

But I for one never read the Hebrew Bible as that kind of document, infused with that kind of naive optimism. To the contrary, it tells us that the first inhabitants of paradise, instead of enjoying all they had, longed for the one thing they could not legitimately have. The first recorded act of worship – the offerings made by Cain and Abel – leads to the first act of murder. The world by the time of Noah is filled with violence, and even in the mind of Isaiah, the poet laureate of hope, a war-free universe is only a distant utopia. God creates order, but man creates chaos, and within his world as opposed to the world of nature, truth, beauty and goodness are won only by constant effort against perennial temptation. The world we live in now is the world the children of mortals never left, and the illusions we have lost are ones Moses and Amos and Jeremiah never had.

So how does time affect the meaning of meaning and the possibility of a meaningful life? One suggestive set of concepts was set out by the strange, unclassifiable critic of what he called our 'therapeutic' culture, the late Philip Rieff (1922–2006). In *My Life among the Deathworks* he spoke about the history of civilisation as a move from *fate* to *faith* to *fiction*.[13]

It is a difficult work, and the interpretation I give of it is almost certainly not quite what he intended, but this is how I see it. In an age of *fate*, everything was in the hands of the gods. Meaning is a given. It is out there, written in the fabric of the cosmos. Our lives are shaped by forces beyond our control and the best we can do is placate the gods, or at least not offend them, for if we do we will die. Meaning is inexorable, and it tells a story of birth, growth, decline and death in which only nature – the rule of power over the powerless – is eternal.

In the age of *fiction* – what has come to be called the postmodern condition – everything people once thought was true is now seen as merely constructed, invented, a fiction. There is no truth any more, only the various stories humans devise to make sense of their lives. Usually they are stories told by the strong to keep the weak in their place. They are 'colonialist' or 'imperialist' or 'hegemonic' narratives, and behind them is a history of oppression. Of course, we can liberate ourselves from these narratives, but there is nothing to put in their place because we are now too sophisticated, too *knowing*, to believe that there is such a thing as truth. We no longer take meaning seriously. Our attitude to the world becomes *ironic*, detached, amused. In short, we are back with the Cynics and Sceptics of third-century BCE Greece.[14]

Between these two is the age of *faith*, the axial age that saw the appearance of Israelite monotheism, Greek philosophy and the classic traditions of India and China. It was an age of great thinkers and a dawning sense of human dignity. The individual was no longer powerless in the face of blind forces. Humans began to understand the universe of which they were a part. They learned how to control their environment. They built cities, devised systems of agriculture, invented writing, accumulated knowledge, substituted the rule of law for the operation of vengeance, and began to tame the wilderness of untrammelled nature. They were neither helpless in the presence of the gods, nor godless in a world of their own devising. That was the age of faith.

It is precisely here, in the middle of Philip Rieff's scheme of things, that the concept of covenant – the central concept of the Hebrew Bible – belongs. Covenant is about *the meanings we make together*, as opposed to the meanings people found written in the stars in an age of fate, or the meanings we individually invent in an age of fiction.

The Bible does not deny that there are ultimate meanings in the universe. There are. Human life is sacred, is one of them. But it

195

does not help, so God found. We will always be blind to the truths we do not like, that cramp our style, circumscribe our power or stand in the way of the fulfilment of our desires. So the Bible turns to covenants – the agreements God makes with Noah, then Abraham, then the Israelites at Sinai. These are meanings that have ceased to be mere facts and become instead morally binding commitments. Do not murder, do not rob, do not commit adultery, do not bear false witness. These are part of a total system of meanings, that include the historical memory of liberation from slavery in Egypt, by which a people agreed to bind itself and its descendants, taking on themselves the collective vocation of aspiring to be 'a kingdom of priests and a holy nation'.

This is *meaning as moral identity*, something I acquire by being born into a specific community with a distinctive history, when I recognise a duty of loyalty to a past and responsibility for a future by living faith and handing it on to those who come after me. It is what Edmund Burke thought society was: 'a partnership not only between those who are living, but between those who are living, those who are dead, and those who are to be born'. It is not meaning *discovered* or meaning *invented*, but meaning collectively *made and renewed* in the conscious presence of God – that is to say, an authority beyond ourselves and our merely human devices and desires.

If that is what meaning is, then it is *not* lost in a postmodern, anti-traditional, aggressively secular age. It is never lost, because it can always be remade whenever a group of people decide to make or renew a covenant with God, as did the Jews in Jerusalem after the Babylonian exile in the days of Ezra and Nehemiah, or as did the Puritans aboard the *Arabella* in 1630 on their way to the New World, there to build 'a city upon a hill'. The very idea of covenant means that certain types of meaning can always be renewed, because they are not 'out there' as fate, nor 'in here' as fiction. They may lie dormant, like seeds frozen into inactivity by cold or drought, but ready to burst into life with the sun and the rain. Covenants can be renewed, which is why I could not agree

with Bernard Williams, because although he was the most rigor-
ous and subtle thinker I ever met, he did not seem to have come
across the concept of covenant as it exists in Judaism – one of
those elements that was lost when it was translated into Greek.

So meaning is made, not just discovered. That is what religion
for the most part is: the constant making and remaking of meaning, by the stories we tell, the rituals we perform and the prayers
we say. The stories are sacred, the rituals divine commands, and
prayer a genuine dialogue with the divine. Religion is an authentic response to a real Presence, but it is also a way of making
that presence real by constantly living in response to it. It is truth
translated into deed.

By the stories we tell: When I take part in a seder service on
Passover, telling the story of the book of Exodus, I am not engaged
in a cultural act like watching a film or reading a book about it.
I am enacting it, making it part of me. On Passover the Exodus
ceases to be mere history and becomes memory: not something
that happened somewhere else to someone else long ago, but
something that is happening to me, here, now. It defines me as
part of that story, linking me to a community of others in different places and times. It changes me, for I now know what it feels
and tastes like to be oppressed, and I can no longer walk by when
others are oppressed. People who have lived the seder service are
different for having done so, and the world is different because of
them. It is why there were so many Jews (Joe Slovo, Albie Sachs,
Joel Joffe, Helen Suzman, Nadine Gordimer and others) in the
fight against apartheid, and why Rabbi Abraham Joshua Heschel
marched with Martin Luther King.

By the rituals we perform: The American anthropologist Roy
A. Rappaport (1926–97) understood more than most that ritual
is an act of meaning-making. Societies, like nature, suffer from
entropy, a breakdown of order over time. Religion is the great
counter-entropic force that prevents the decay or disintegration of
order by performative acts that renew the collective order of the

group. A ritual is an *enactment of meaning*. That is what makes a house of worship not a theatre, and a congregation something other than an audience. A congregation participates in a ritual; an audience merely watches and listens. A congregation lives the reality encoded by the ritual; an audience merely suspends its disbelief while the play is going on, knowing that what it is seeing is a fiction. A ritual is an act in the world; a drama is not, it is a mere imitation of one. Rappaport calls ritual 'the primary social act', because it makes meanings.[15]

By the prayers we say: Prayer is a way of seeing, not unlike the account Iris Murdoch gives of the aesthetic sense:

> I am looking out of my window in an anxious and resentful frame of mind, oblivious of my surroundings, brooding perhaps on some damage done to my prestige. Then suddenly I observe a hovering kestrel. In a moment, everything is altered. The brooding self with its hurt vanity has disappeared. There is nothing now but kestrel. And when I return to the thinking of the other matter it seems less important.[16]

She calls this 'unselfing', and sees as it essential to the moral life. This is what happens, or ought to happen, when we pray. The relentless first-person singular, the 'I', falls silent and we become aware that we are not the centre of the universe. There is a reality outside. That is a moment of transformation. We hear the universe singing a song to its Creator. We join our ancestors as they sang psalms in the Temple, or lifted their voices in thanksgiving as they passed through the divided waters of the Red Sea. For a moment we still the clamour of desire and experience instead:

> that serene and blessed mood,
> In which the affections gently lead us on,
> Until, the breath of this corporeal frame,
> And even the motion of our human blood
> Almost suspended, we are laid asleep

In body, and become a living soul:
While with an eye made quiet by the power
Of harmony, and the deep power of joy,
We see into the life of things.[17]

Religion is a sustained process of using the deep power of joy to see into the life of things. No Jew, knowing history, can be a naive optimist. Like Tolstoy and Camus, we have stared into the abyss. Jews are not strangers to the valley of the shadow of death. But people like Max Ostro and my father never gave up hope, because they never conceded the loss of meaning.

The Greeks thought of knowledge as a kind of seeing. And modern science tells us that we can no longer see meaning when we look at nature. On this, the atheists are right. Galaxies are born. Stars explode. Planets form. Species emerge, spread and become extinct. There is nothing meaningful about this whatsoever, so long as we stay in the world of subject and object, seeing and testing, theorising and experimenting, the left-brain world that takes things apart to see how they work.

But meaning-as-covenant never was seen; it is heard as the voice of God. It is not found, but made. It belongs to the intersubjective world of persons in relation to one another. Meanings are socially constructed. They exist in the form of words, stories, constitutive narratives. They belong to the shared life of communities. They involve a living connection to a past to which we feel ourselves to belong, and a future for which we hold ourselves responsible. They are always particular – to this group, that nation, this faith, that tradition. Science may be universal. Meaning never is. *Sacred* meanings are those we make when we covenant with God, listening to his voice, heeding his call. Because one of the covenant partners is God, sacred covenants never die, because God never abandons humanity however much humanity abandons him.

People who are not religious, and even some who are, often do not fully understand this. They think faith is about seeing meaning on the surface of things, as if God's existence or his presence or involvement in history should be *obvious*, and if it is not, it does not exist. The Bible tells a completely different story. Even when plague after plague strikes Egypt, Pharaoh still does not believe. Every miracle, says Maimonides, can be doubted. When, in the first century, the Israelites lost their Temple, their holy city and their land, there was nothing left to proclaim the presence of God in their midst except what the rabbis call a *bat kol*, an echo. Jews have long known precisely what Isaiah meant when he said, 'Truly, You are a God who hides himself.'

Faith, Abrahamic faith, is about God and human beings *making meaning in covenant together*. Giambattista Vico, that strange genius of the late seventeenth century, was the first in the modern age to understand this when he distinguished between the two kinds of truth: the partial truth we discover through science, and *verum-factum*, the moral truth we make through human, especially religious, action.[18]

Happiness has proved elusive in the contemporary world.[19] By any conceivable measure of the good life, we are better off than any previous generation since the birth of time. We are more afflu-ent. We have more choices. We can travel farther and more easily. We have more access to education and information. Our health is better. We live longer. We keep ourselves fit. We have leisure. We are freer. There are fewer constraints on our lifestyles. We are living, compared to any previous generation, as close to paradise as people have ever lived.

Yet by indexes of self-reported life satisfaction, we are no happier than people were two generations ago. In some respects our lack of happiness is palpable. We take more anti-depressants. People suffer from more stress-related syndromes. They are less optimistic than they used to be. They no longer think their chil-dren will have better lives than they did. There has been a palpa-ble breakdown of trust. These facts are all well known. They are among the clichés of our time. But it is still worth asking why things have gone wrong.

Some attribute it to our consumerist culture. Economic growth, even economic stability, depends on continuing consumption, but there are just so many televisions, cars, smart phones and watches we can have at any given moment. To keep demand flowing, we have to be made dissatisfied with what we have and desirous for what we do not yet have. But within days of a new acquisition, the epiphany fades, and the hidden and not so hidden persuaders are telling us that there is something else we do not have, or if we do, then we need the new model or the upgrade. It is hard work, this 'hedonic treadmill'. Wordsworth said so more than two centuries ago:

> The world is too much with us; late and soon,
> Getting and spending, we lay waste our powers.[20]

Tony Judt spoke for many when, at the beginning of *Ill Fares the Land*, the book he published shortly before his death in 2010, he wrote, 'Something is profoundly wrong with the way we live today.' He continued, 'For thirty years we have made a virtue out of the pursuit of material self-interest: indeed, this very pursuit now constitutes whatever remains of our sense of collective purpose. We know what things cost but have no idea what they are worth.'[21]

Consumerism has self-defeat written all over it, because of the nature of positional goods. Positional goods are ones whose goodness depends on their scarcity. An attractive house is a good; the most attractive house in town is a positional good. The more our basic needs and desires are satisfied, the more we turn to positional goods, and there are never enough of these to go round, however affluent a society is.

The same is true generally about wealth and poverty. Most people in the West tend to rate their wellbeing not on an absolute scale, but relative to others. Given the choice between earning $50,000 a year in a society where the average wage is $30,000, or earning $100,000 a year in a society in which the average wage is $200,000, most prefer the former. This is symptomatic of the force driving consumerism, namely envy, whose strange logic consists of letting someone else's happiness spoil mine. Envy is the art of counting other people's blessings. The fastest route to happiness is precisely the opposite: not thinking of what others have and we do not, but instead thanking God for what we do have, and sharing some of that with others.

Happiness is a state of being, not having, and still today, as it always did, it depends on strong and stable personal relationships and a sense of meaning and purpose in life.

As we saw in the last chapter, relationships are more fragile than they were. Marriage is in disarray. In its place have come serial relationships with no formal act of commitment. They last on average just two years.[22] The same applies to work. The expectation of a job for life has disappeared. Work colleagues are no longer expected to become lifelong friends, but rather temporary associates. All our relationships have become provisional. That means that we invest less emotion in them, and they give us less emotional satisfaction in return.

In general there has been a substitution of mediated relationships – through mobile phones, social networking sites, virtual reality, chat rooms, Second Life and the like – instead of face-to-face encounters. But it is only in face-to-face encounters that we engage in empathic relationship, much of which has to do with personal presence, body language, facial gestures, touching and so on. Second Life is not real life. Virtual communities are not real communities. You can substitute electronic objects like e-books for their physical counterparts, but you cannot substitute e-people for living, breathing family and friends.

Which brings me back to Ecclesiastes, his search for happiness, and mine. I spoke in chapter 4 about my first meeting, as a student, with Rabbi Menachem Mendel Schneersohn, the Lubavitcher Rebbe. As I was waiting to go in, one of his disciples told me the following story. A man had recently written to the Rebbe on something of these lines: 'I need the Rebbe's help. I am deeply depressed. I pray and find no comfort. I perform the commands but feel nothing. I find it hard to carry on.'

The Rebbe, so I was told, sent a compelling reply without writing a single word. He simply ringed the first word in every sentence of the letter: the word 'I'. It was, he was hinting, the man's self-preoccupation that was at the root of his depression. It was as if the Rebbe were saying, as Viktor Frankl used to say in the name of Kierkegaard, 'The door to happiness opens outward.'[23]

It was this insight that helped me solve the riddle of Ecclesiastes. The word 'I' does not appear very often in the Hebrew Bible, but it dominates Ecclesiastes' opening chapters.

> I enlarged my works: I built houses for myself, I planted vineyards for myself; I made gardens and parks for myself and I planted in them all kinds of fruit trees; I made ponds of water for myself from which to irrigate a forest of growing trees. I bought male and female slaves and I had homeborn slaves. Also I possessed flocks and herds larger than all who preceded me in Jerusalem. Also, I collected for myself silver and gold and the treasure of kings and provinces. (Ecclesiastes 2:4–8)

Nowhere else in the Bible is the first-person singular used so relentlessly and repetitively. In the original Hebrew the effect is doubled because of the chiming of the verbal suffix and the pronoun: *Baniti li, asiti li, kaniti li*, 'I built for myself, I made for myself, I bought for myself.' The source of Ecclesiastes' unhappiness is obvious and was spelled out many centuries later by the great sage Hillel: 'If I am not for myself, who will be? But if I am only for myself, what am I?'[24]

Happiness in the Bible is not something we find in self-gratification.

Hence the significance of the word *simchah*. I translated it earlier as 'joy', but really it has no precise translation into English, since all our emotion words refer to states of mind we can experience alone. *Simchah* is something we cannot experience alone. *Simchah* is joy shared.

So I come back to Max Ostro and my late father and the religious people – Jews, Christians, Muslims, Hindus, Sikhs, Buddhists and others – I have come to know. They had not necessarily undergone the kind of deep soul-searching in which Tolstoy and Camus engaged, but instinctively, it seems to me, they knew that Tolstoy's life made sense in a way that Camus's did not, admirable though it may have been in its relentless refusal to be consoled. They told stories and practised rituals and prayed and thus made real the things worth making real: love and loyalty and marriage and parenthood and membership in a community and doing acts of kindness to others. They created oases of meaning in the wilderness, places where others could rest and find shade and shelter, friendship, help and hope.

And though such simple things have always had their cultured despisers, the truly great minds, even those who did not believe, recognised the connection between faith and meaning. Here is Albert Einstein: 'To know an answer to the question, "What is the meaning of life?" means to be religious.'[25] And here, Sigmund Freud: 'The idea of life having a meaning stands or falls with the religious system.'[26] And here, Wittgenstein: 'To believe in God means to see that life has a meaning.'[27] And lastly, Nietzsche, who said of a purely 'scientific' interpretation of life that it would understand 'nothing, really nothing, of what is "music" in it'.[28]

I have argued in these five chapters what we stand to lose if we lose faith: the dignity and sanctity of life, the politics of covenant and hope, the morality of personal responsibility, marriage as a sacred bond, and, in this chapter, the meaningfulness of life. Faith is not magical. It reveals meanings because we work at making them real in our lives and in the communities we build.

It makes a difference. It made a difference to Max Ostro, to my late father, and to all those who follow Abraham and Sarah, the first to hear meaning as a call, the idea Viktor Frankl defined as 'man's search for meaning'. To those who live by faith, it sustains relationships even when they are fraying everywhere else. It gives us a sense of continuity even in an age of destabilising change.

I believe in a personal God, because religion in the Abrahamic tradition is the consecration of the personal. It lives in interpersonal relationships: in love and revelation and vulnerability and trust, all those things in which we put our faith when we commit ourselves to one another in a covenantal bond of loyalty and mutuality. Love is what redeems us from the prison cell of the self and all the sickness to which the narcissistic self is prone – from empty pride to deep depression to a sense of nihilism and the abyss.

So in the silence of the soul I listen for the still small voice, which is God's call to each of us to engage in the work of love and creativity, to bring new life into the world, and to care for it and nurture it during its years of vulnerability. And whenever I see people engaged in that work of love, I sense the divine presence brushing us with a touch so gentle you can miss it, and yet know beyond all possibility of doubt that this is what we are called on to live for, to ease the pain of those who suffer and become an agent of hope in the world.

That is a meaningful life. That is what life is when lived in the light of God's presence, in answer to his call.

PART THREE

Faith and Its Challenges

II

Darwin

To claim the world as creation is not to denounce evolution and debunk science. To the contrary, it is to join in covenant with science in acknowledging creation's integrity, as well as its giftedness and worth. To see the world as creation is to re-commit ourselves to its care, not as the fittest, most powerful creatures on the animal planet but as a species held uniquely responsible for creation's flourishing.

William P. Brown[1]

We are intelligent beings: intelligent beings cannot have been formed by a crude, blind, insensible being . . . Newton's intelligence, therefore, comes from another intelligence.

Voltaire[2]

So far as we know, the tiny fragments of the universe embodied in man are the only centres of thought and responsibility in the visible world. If that be so, the appearance of the human mind has been so far the ultimate stage in the awakening of the world.

Michael Polanyi[3]

Science cannot solve the ultimate mystery of nature. And that is because, in the last analysis, we ourselves are part of nature and therefore part of the mystery that we are trying to solve.

Max Planck[4]

There are three major challenges to religion. The first and deepest, addressed in the next chapter, arises from the very heart of monotheism itself and was first uttered by Abraham: 'Shall the judge of all the Earth not do justice?' (Genesis 18:25). How can the goodness of God coexist with the presence of evil and the suffering of the innocent? The second is a kind of mirror image of the first. It is, as it were, not our question of God but God's question of us: How can religious people commit evil in the name of God? That is the subject of chapter 13. The third challenge – call it the clash between religion and science – varies from age to age, but it usually has the same form, first set out in the Bible in the story of the Tower of Babel.

Human beings discover a new science or technology: in the case of Babel, the art of making bricks. Breaking free from the limitations of the past, they feel as if they have become gods and they set about storming the heavens. Every new accession of knowledge or power has tempted humans into hubris. 'Must we ourselves not become gods?' asked Nietzsche.[5]

Perhaps Freud was right in a way he did not anticipate. He argued that the myth of Oedipus explained much of human behaviour including religion. We, especially sons, have a desire to murder our parents, especially fathers. We then feel guilty for this – Freud called it 'the return of the repressed' – and this guilt becomes the source of religion: the demanding, unEarthly voice of the murdered father.[6]

As a theory of religion, this may work for Greek myth; it cannot work for Abrahamic monotheism. In Greek myth the gods were hostile to humans. In Abrahamic monotheism, God loves humans, sets his image on them and creates space for them to exercise their freedom. The myth of Oedipus works much better as an explanation not of religious belief but of its opposite: atheism. People feel the need to pursue knowledge uninterruptedly and without constraint, and they can experience religion – the Church's attitude to Galileo then, or to evolutionary theory now – as a constraint on that freedom. They can then feel the need to murder the beliefs and traditions of the past to create space for a future that is both human and free.[7] Hence the anger of atheism and the intense desire to displace the Father-God. It can be atheism, not religion, that becomes a comforting illusion. We are free because there is no one to tell us what we may or may not do.

The idea that there is a conflict between religion and science draws heavily on Greek myth, specifically the myth of Prometheus. Prometheus was a figure unique among Greek deities, a god who liked human beings. For their sake he stole the secret of fire from Zeus and gave it to mortals. For this he was punished by Zeus. He was chained to a rock where each day an eagle ate his liver, which grew back each night so that it could be eaten again.

Embedded in this myth is a profound conviction that the universe is hostile to humankind, that knowledge and its pursuit are dangerous, even sinful, and that it is a zero-sum conflict in which either the gods or humankind win. Hence *either* religion *or* science, but not both. A trace of the myth of Prometheus survives in the form of one Christian reading of the first humans eating from the tree of knowledge, a sin for which they were exiled from paradise. On this reading, God does not want us to know.

But that is not the only way of understanding the story. Maimonides, for example, says that the tree of knowledge represented the wrong kind of knowledge: aesthetics, not physics or metaphysics. The fruit of the tree was 'pleasing to the eye'. It represented appearance, not reality.[8] Recall that when Adam and Eve ate it they did not suddenly understand a set of truths. Instead, they saw they were naked and they felt shame. Their sensibility shifted from the ear to the eye. They became more concerned with how things seemed than with the voice of God within the mind that we call the moral sense.

In Jewish tradition God *wants* us to pursue knowledge. The first thing Solomon asked for, and the first thing we ask for in our three-times-daily prayers, is wisdom, understanding and knowledge, and that includes science. Recall that the rabbis instituted a blessing over scientists, whether they shared Jewish faith or not. They also told a story precisely designed to negate the myth of Prometheus.

In Judaism, each week the Sabbath ends and secular time begins with a ceremony known as *havdalah*, literally 'making distinctions'. It includes the lighting of a special candle. Explaining this candle, the rabbis said that Adam and Eve were created, and sinned, on the sixth day, Friday. They were sentenced to exile, but God deferred the punishment by twenty-four hours so that they could stay one full day – Sabbath – in paradise. As the Sabbath ended and night fell, they were afraid of their journey into the dark. So God taught them how to make fire and kindle a light.[9] It is in memory of this that we light the havdalah candle. This is the counternarrative to Prometheus. We do not have to steal secrets from God. God wants us to know, and to use that knowledge responsibly.

The process of displacing God in the modern age began in 1796 with Laplace and his statement, in reply to Napoleon's question as to where God was in his scientific system, *Je n'ai pas besoin de cette hypothèse*, 'I have no need for that hypothesis.' The mechanistic universe needed no ongoing interventions on the part of God; it seemed indeed to rule them out. Hence the attraction of Deism, the idea that, as it were, God designed the machine and set it in motion, and then retired from the scene. As a graffito I saw in my undergraduate years said, 'God exists, it's just that he doesn't want to get involved.'

The challenge of Darwinism has seemed altogether deeper than this because it suggested that, at least as far as biology is concerned, life has not been mechanistic and thus designed. It has emerged as the result of a process that is random, fortuitous and blind. The existence of life, sentience, consciousness and Homo sapiens itself are all purely accidental. 'Man', wrote George Gaylord Simpson in *The Meaning of Evolution*, 'is the result of a purposeless and natural process that did not have him in mind.'[10]

If my argument in chapter 1 is correct, it becomes immediately clear why Darwinism has proved to be the single greatest challenge to religious faith, more unsettling to believers than, say, the assault of Marx or Freud or plain common-or-garden atheism. For I have argued that the fundamental issue of religious faith, specifically of Abrahamic monotheism, is the meaningfulness or meaninglessness of the human condition.

Darwinism, or at least the use made of Darwin by his latter-day followers, the new atheists, seemed to provide a compelling scientific demonstration of the meaninglessness of life. It happened by chance. No one planned it. There was no design, no purpose, no intended and foreseen outcome. There was no intentional act of creation, at least not of life. We are here because we are here, because that is how the random operations of chance and necessity – genetic mutation and natural selection – happened to occur. We might not have been. No wonder that Richard Dawkins said that Darwin for the first time made it possible to be an intellectually fulfilled atheist.[11] Darwinism seems to be proof of the meaninglessness of life.

But if my argument is correct, then the new atheists must also be wrong, for I have argued that the presence or absence of meaning is not, in and of itself, something that can be established by science. Meaning or meaninglessness is in the eye of the beholder. To give two obvious examples, the first Impressionist exhibition in 1874, including works by Monet and Cézanne, created outrage among many traditionalists. This was not art as they knew it. So did the first performance of Stravinsky's *Rite of Spring*, which led to a riot. This was not music or dance as it had been before. But there was nothing chaotic or meaningless about either the paintings or the rhythms. They were precisely planned to achieve specific ends. It simply took time before people learned to see and hear in new ways.

So it is with Darwinism at many levels. At first it seemed to render life meaningless. This was not creation, design or, for that matter, Homo sapiens as people had been accustomed to thinking about them. It was shocking, unsettling, paradigm-shifting. To some, it still is. But it may just be that we have to think about creation, design and the emergence of order in new ways, not that they no longer exist.

The literature about Darwinism and creationism is vast, and overwhelmingly it consists of scientists arguing against religion and religious believers arguing against this or that finding of science. But again, if I am right, both literatures are misconceived. Science is not religion; religion is not science. Each has its own logic, its own way of asking questions and searching for the answers. The way of testing a scientific hypothesis is to do science, not read Scripture. The way of testing religion is to do religion – to ask, in total honesty and full understanding, is this really what God wants of us? It is not to make assertions about the truth or falsity of some scientific theory.

This is not an argument for *compartmentalisation*, seeing science and religion as did Steven J. Gould as 'non-overlapping magisteria', two entirely separate worlds.[12] They do indeed overlap because they are about the same world within which we live, breathe and have our being. It is instead an argument for *conversation*, hopefully even integration. For if science is about the world that is, and religion about the world that ought to be, then religion needs science because *we cannot apply God's will to the world if we do not understand the world*. If we try to, the result will be magic or misplaced supernaturalism. We will rely on miracles – and the rabbis ruled, '*Don't* rely on miracles.'[13]

By the same token, science needs religion, or at the very least some philosophical understanding of the human condition and our place within the universe, for each fresh item of knowledge and each new accession of power raises the question of how it should be used, and for that we need another way of thinking. As Einstein put it:

> For science can only ascertain what is, but not what should be, and outside of its domain value judgments of all kinds remain necessary ... representatives of science have often made an attempt to arrive at fundamental judgments with respect to values and ends on the basis of scientific method, and in this way have set themselves in opposition to religion. These conflicts have all sprung from fatal errors.[14]

It is precisely the space between the world that is and the world that ought to be that is, or should be, the arena of conversation between science and religion, and each should be open to the perceptions of the other. The question is neither, 'Does Darwinism refute religion?' nor, 'Does religion refute Darwinism?' Rather: 'How does each shed light on the other?' and, 'What new insights does Darwinism offer religion?' and, 'What insights does religion offer to Darwinism?' Those are the questions to which I want briefly to offer some thoughts.

Darwinism has immense religious implications.

First, it tells us that *God delights in diversity*. There are, for example, forty thousand different varieties of beetle, an impressive number by any standards. The God who created life in its staggering variety is clearly not a Platonist, uninterested in particulars. The rabbis sensed it better when they said, 'Even those creatures you hold superfluous in the world, such as the flies and fleas and gnats, they too are part of the creation of the world. Through all does the Holy One, blessed be he, make manifest his mission, even through the serpent, even through the gnat, even through the frog.'[15] Biodiversity is a source of wonder to the psalmist:

> How many are your works, O God.
> You have made them all in wisdom.
> The Earth is full of your creatures.
> There is the sea, vast and wide.
> There the creeping things beyond count,
> Living things great and small.
> (Psalm 104:24–5)

God loves diversity, not uniformity. That is a fact of theological as well as ecological significance. Every attempt to impose uniformity on diversity is, in some sense, a betrayal of God's purposes. One definition of fundamentalism, and an explanation of why it is religiously wrong, is that it is the attempt to impose a single truth on a diverse world.

Second, and this is Darwin's wondrous discovery: *the Creator made creation creative*. We already knew that he made man creative. Now, thanks to Darwin, we know that this applies to nature too. He did not make a static universe, a mere machine endlessly revolving through cycles of birth, growth, decline and death. He introduced into the very mechanism by which life reproduces itself, the genome, the tiny possibility of copying errors that results in variety and new biological possibilities. The God who chose to create our universe is one who delights in creativity. A universe in which life evolves is more creative than one in which life forms never change.

God as we see him in Genesis 2 is a gardener, not a mechanic, one who plants systems that grow. The constantly evolving, ever-changing nature of life revealed by biology after Darwin fits the theological vision far more than did the controlled, predictable, mechanical universe of eighteenth-century science.

The science writer Timothy Ferris argues that what we know scientifically suggests 'that God created the universe out of an interest in spontaneous creativity'. What would such a universe look like? It would be a universe impossible to predict in detail, just as ours is. It would give rise to agencies that are themselves creative. 'There is in our universe such an agency, spectacularly successful in reversing the dreary slide of entropy and making surprising things happen. We call it life.'[16]

There is even a hint of this in the biblical narrative of creation. The Hebrew text of Genesis 1:1 – 2:3 has a remarkable feature. It is precisely structured around the number seven, in ways not apparent in translation. The narrative speaks of creation in seven days. But the text itself is precisely patterned on this number. So the word 'good' appears seven times. The word 'God' appears thirty-five times. The words 'heaven' and 'Earth' each appear twenty-one times. The words 'light' and 'day' occur seven times in the first paragraph. The first verse contains seven words, the second fourteen words. The paragraph describing the seventh day contains thirty-five words, and so on. The passage as a whole contains 67x7 words. The entire passage is constructed like a fractal, so that the sevenfold motif of the text as a whole is mirrored at lower levels of magnitude.

When a text is written in this way, apparently superfluous words become highly conspicuous. There is one obviously superfluous word: the last of the entire passage. The verse says, 'God sanctified the seventh day for on it he rested from all the work he had created' (2:3). The sentence should finish there. In fact, though, there is one extra word in the Hebrew, *la'asot*, which means 'to do, to make, to function'. What is its significance?

Two classic commentators, Ibn Ezra and Abrabanel, interpret it to mean, '[he had created it] in such a way that it would continue to create itself.' Without stretching the text too far, we might say that *la'asot* means, quite simply, 'to evolve'. Evolution would then be hinted at in the very last word of the Genesis creation story.

It was this creative potential of creation that moved Darwin, in the last sentence of *The Origin of Species*, to almost religious awe:

> There is grandeur in this view of life, with its several powers, having been originally breathed by the Creator into a few forms or into one; and that, whilst this planet has gone cycling on according to the fixed law of gravity, from so simple a beginning endless forms most beautiful and most wonderful have been, and are being, evolved.

The twin operations of genetic mutation and natural selection are the simplest way of creating diversity out of unity, breathtaking simplicity resulting in almost unimaginable diversity.

Third, we now know that *all life derives from a single source*. That is the remarkable, unexpected fact. Here is Matt Ridley on the subject:

> The three-letter words of the genetic code are the same in every creature. CGA means arginine and GCG means alanine – in bats,

in beetles, in bacteria. They even mean the same in the mislead-
ingly named archaebacteria living at boiling temperatures in
sulphurous springs thousands of feet beneath the surface of the
Atlantic ocean or in those microscopic capsules of deviousness
called viruses. Wherever you go in the world, whatever animal,
plant, bug or blob you look at, if it is alive, it will use the same
dictionary and know the same code. All life is one. The genetic
code, bar a few tiny local aberrations, mostly for unexplained
reasons in the ciliate protozoa, is the same in every creature. We
all use exactly the same language. This means – and religious
people might find this a useful argument – that there was only
one creation, one single event when life was born.[17]

Again, unity in heaven creates diversity on Earth.

Fourth, science and Genesis have now converged, in an utterly
unexpected way, on the same metaphor. *Life is linguistic.* 'And God
said, Let there be . . . and there was.' The Jewish mystics held that all
life was the result of different permutations of the letters of God's
name. To be sure, this is mere metaphor. It is poetry, not science. But
it is nonetheless remarkable that life has a structure no one expected
prior to Crick's and Watson's discovery of DNA. It has hardware
and software. The cell is an information-processing system. Was
this even conceivable before the invention of the computer?

Recall that Crick and Watson were working in Cambridge
in the 1950s where, barely a decade before, Alan Turing had
been setting out his pioneering thoughts on the possibility of an
information-processing machine. Recall too that Francis Collins,
leader of one of the two projects to decode the human genome,
was moved by that experience to religious belief, and called the
book he wrote *The Language of God.*[18] That life is both intelligent and linguistic breathes new fire into the idea that the Source
of life is both intelligent and a user of language, and that nature,
no less than the Bible, is not a machine to be disassembled but a
book to be decoded. It took the discovery of artificial intelligence
to give us an insight into divine intelligence.

Fifth, the *interconnectedness* of all life – the fact that plants, animals and humans have a common origin – helps us understand in new depth the Bible's phrasing, 'Let the Earth bring forth . . .' and its generic name for Homo sapiens, Adam (from *adamah*, meaning 'the Earth'). Rabbi Joseph Soloveitchik took this as one of the central insights of Darwinian biology, echoing key biblical verses[19]:

All flesh is grass. (Isaiah 40:6)

Man has no pre-eminence over a beast: for all is mere breath. All go unto one place; all are of the dust, and all turn to dust again. (Ecclesiastes 3:19–20)

We are responsible for the preservation of nature and the animal kingdom, for we and they are part of the same continuum of life. Here is how the rabbis put it:

When the Holy One created the first man, he took him and led him around all the trees of the Garden of Eden, and said to him: Behold my works, how beautiful, how splendid they are. All that I have created, I created for you. Take care that you do not become corrupt and thus destroy my world. For if you become corrupt, there will be no one after you to repair it.[20]

The idea that in some sense the findings of science in the past two hundred years – whether in cosmology, quantum physics, the theory of relativity, Darwinian evolution, genetics and the mapping of the genome, or PET scans and the working of the brain – challenge our religious understanding of the universe is absurd.

The Jewish theologians of the Middle Ages faced a far more serious challenge: the Aristotelian belief in the eternity of matter, which implied that one of the fundamentals of Abrahamic faith, that God created the universe, was false. All of them, not just the rationalist Moses Maimonides, but also the critic of rationalism, Judah Halevi, agreed that if Aristotle had proven his point, they would simply reinterpret Genesis 1. In chapter 3 I gave two examples – planetary motion and the ensoulment of the foetus – where the religious sages were happy to acknowledge that they were wrong and the Greeks right. As it happens, on the first the Greeks were wrong, and on the second we have no way of knowing. But they recognised that within its own domain science has its own integrity and that faith must be compatible with the facts as we know them. This itself follows from the conviction that the God of creation and the God of redemption are one.

If an eternal universe was conceivable to the theologians of the Middle Ages, so should one 13.7 billion years old be to us. When a questioner troubled by Darwinism wrote to the famous Rabbi Abraham Kook, the rabbi replied (in 1905) by quoting an ancient rabbinic teaching that at the dawn of time, God 'kept creating universes and destroying them until he created this one, and said, This one pleases me; those did not please me.'[21] The idea that there were ages and extinct species before ours is one that should not trouble the theistic imagination.

Of course it was not this that represented the fundamental challenge of Darwinism to Abrahamic faith. It was the fact that it seemed to prove, beyond doubt, that the emergence of life and the appearance of humanity were unscripted, unplanned, the result of blind processes iterated over billions of years. We are here as the result of a 'purposeless and natural process' that did not have us in mind.

It is precisely here that the Bible tells a subtle story about stories in general, and what it is to see events as random on the one hand, designed on the other. Consider, as one example, the following episode from the Joseph narrative in Genesis. Joseph is envied and hated by his brothers. They resent the fact that their father loves him more than them. They are provoked by the sight of his many-coloured coat. They are angered by his dreams in which he sees them bowing down to him.

In swift strokes as the story unfolds we sense their anger build to dangerous levels. Then comes the critical moment. The brothers are away from home, at Shechem, tending the flocks. Jacob sends Joseph to see how they are doing. We sense it will be a critical encounter, and so it is. The brothers see him at a distance, plan to kill him, and eventually sell him into slavery. Ironically, it is this act that begins the sequence of events that leads to Joseph's dreams coming true.

Between Joseph setting out and his meeting up with the brothers, however, we read the following:

> When Joseph arrived at Shechem, a man found him wandering around in the fields and asked him, 'What are you looking for?'
>
> He replied, 'I'm looking for my brothers. Can you tell me where they are grazing their flocks?'
>
> 'They have moved on from here,' the man answered. 'I heard them say, "Let's go to Dothan."' So Joseph went after his brothers and found them near Dothan. (Genesis 37:14–17)

Joseph arrives at the place where the brothers are supposed to be and finds that they are not there. A stranger appears who is able to guide Joseph to them. This is an extraordinary piece of biblical prose. The Joseph story is one of the most tightly scripted in the whole of the Bible. Every detail is significant and we are told nothing we do not need to know. Why then are we told this utterly irrelevant detail that at first Joseph could not find his brothers and needed a stranger to point the way?

The story of Joseph is carefully constructed to be read on at least two levels. On the one hand, it is a story of chance human interactions. It is a tale of parental favouritism and sibling rivalry. People speak, have emotions and make decisions that have consequences. It might have been otherwise.

Read at another level, it is a story of divine providence in which the end is foretold at the beginning – one of the very few such stories in the Bible. The outcome is announced through the dreams. Joseph will become a leader. His brothers will bow down to him. As in a Greek tragedy, every act, whatever its intention, has the effect of leading towards the predestined end.

On the one hand, the Joseph story can be read as pure chance. At the key moment, he might not have found his brothers. He might have wandered around looking for them and then returned home. The entire drama of Joseph's fall and rise might never have happened.

On the other hand, divine providence is active at every stage. That is what this curious detail of the unnamed stranger is there to signal. At just the right moment a man appears to set Joseph on his way for the fateful meeting with the brothers. Not surprisingly, Jewish tradition identified the stranger who meets Joseph when he is lost as an angel – an 'angel who did not know he was an angel', in the fine phrase of the thirteenth-century scholar Nahmanides.[22]

In case we miss the point, the Bible later puts it explicitly in Joseph's mouth. Many years later, by now the viceroy of Egypt, Joseph tells his brothers, 'And now, do not be distressed and do not be angry with yourselves for selling me here, because it was to save lives that God sent me ahead of you . . . So then, *it was not you who sent me here, but God*' (Genesis 45:5–8).

In case we still miss the point, Joseph repeats it in a second scene, years and chapters later: '*You intended to harm me, but God intended it for good* to accomplish what is now being done, the saving of many lives' (Genesis 50:20).

The Bible is making, here and elsewhere, a philosophical point of some delicacy and power. It is rejecting the Aristotelian principle of the law of contradiction: either p or not-p. It is rejecting what William Blake called 'single vision'. It is telling us that there may be no unequivocal answer to the question, 'Was event X a chance event, or was it intended by divine design?' It may be both. From one perspective, the story of Joseph is a series of random events, driven by a series of human decisions that might have been otherwise. From another perspective, it is the working out of a providential pattern whose end was announced (in Joseph's dreams) at the beginning.

That is why a sentence like 'Man is the result of a purposeless and natural process that did not have him in mind' may be true and false in equal measure. Let us now give some substance to this proposition without invoking divine providence.

It is often said that Darwin refuted a famous argument for the existence of God, the 'argument from design'. Indeed, he believed this himself. Darwin did in fact refute something, but it was not the argument from design; it was one particular and faulty version of it.

In 1802 William Paley published a book called *Natural Theology* that had wide circulation in Victorian Britain and exercised a deep influence on the young Charles Darwin in particular. In it, Paley offers an early nineteenth-century updating of one of the classic arguments (dating back to Cicero before the birth of Christianity) for the existence of God, the 'argument from design'.

Imagine, says Paley, that we are walking across a heath. In our path is a stone. Seeing it, we are not moved to ask who put it there or why. It is just there. But suppose in our path we see a watch. That could not have been there since the beginning of time. The fact that it is fashioned from many different materials, precisely engineered and put together with integrated complexity, tells us that it was designed. It is a thing made. It bears the evidence of deliberate construction. Therefore it had a designer. The universe, says Paley, is more like a watch than a stone. Therefore it too had a designer.

The power of Darwin's theory of the origin of species is that it shows, with great simplicity and elegance, how design might emerge without a designer, through the simple processes of variation and natural selection, repeated in generation after generation over huge expanses of time. Within any given life form, there will be variations. They will compete for the scarce resources necessary for their survival. Those best adapted to their environment will commandeer what they need to live long enough to breed a new generation. Those less well adapted may die. This will account for variations within a species, as different environments favour different adaptations. Over time, those variations may be great enough to constitute a new species. The dual operation of chance (genetic mutation) and necessity (the competition for scarce resources) will generate design without a designer. So, says Darwin in his *Autobiographies*:

> The old argument of design in nature, as given by Paley, which formerly seemed to me so conclusive, fails, now that the law of natural selection has been discovered. We can no longer argue that, for instance, the beautiful hinge of a bivalve shell must have been made by an intelligent being, like the hinge of a door by man. There seems to be no more design in the variability of organic beings and in the action of natural selection, than in the course in which the wind blows.[23]

Darwin is careful to register a qualification. He says he has refuted the old argument of design in nature *as given by Paley*. Life turns out not to be like a watch after all. But who says that is the only way to design a system?

One of the great influences on Darwin was the economist Thomas Malthus, and Malthus himself was a disciple of the first great economist Adam Smith. In *The Wealth of Nations*, Smith put forward a famous argument about the working of the market economy. The division of labour leads to economic growth. The more people specialise, the more they are able to produce, and through market exchange they are able to sell their goods and acquire what they need. The paradox is that this process, which benefits (almost) everyone, is driven throughout not by empathy and altruism but by the pursuit of personal gain. 'It is not from the benevolence of the butcher the brewer or the baker that we expect our dinner, but from their regard to their own interest.'[24]

The system as a whole – the free market – has a property shared by none of its constituent parts, namely the men and women and their myriad transactions that make the system work. It results in the *common* good, but the people within the system intend only their private, individual good. Smith described this paradox in almost mystical terms: 'by directing that industry in such a manner as its produce may be of the greatest value, he intends only his own gain, and he is in this, as in many other cases, led by an *invisible hand* to promote an end which was no part of his intention'.[25]

By 'invisible hand' Smith meant that the system has a logic visible only when seen as a whole. Macro-economics is different from micro-economics. The result of many individuals seeking personal benefit is that collectively they produce general benefit, 'the wealth of nations'. The 'end', the consequence and effect of the system, is no part of the 'intention' of the millions who take part in it. To them it is 'invisible'.

This is a general feature of systems. From ant colonies to cities, individuals come together to form highly structured patterns of behaviour without anyone or anything ordering the process. The name given to this process is 'emergence', and the result, 'organised complexity'.[26]

What makes emergence distinctive is that it works through a highly distributed, bottom-up intelligence rather than a top-down centrally imposed one. Ant colonies function because individual ants follow simple rules of pattern recognition, tracking the pheromone trails left by fellow ants. The result is a kind of collective intelligence represented by the colony as a whole.

That is how natural selection works. Out of a seemingly blind process of life forms replicating and passing on their genes to the next generation, variants are produced. Natural selection operates, sifting out the best from the worst adapted, and out of this apparently blind process there emerges an evolving biodiversity that produces life forms of ever-increasing complexity until it arrives at us. Like the market economy with its billions of transactions, no one within the system intends the outcome, but it is not random. It was precisely to produce such an outcome that the system as a whole was designed.

So powerful is natural selection that since the 1980s it has been used in computing to develop artificial intelligence. Inspired by Richard Dawkins's book *The Selfish Gene*, David Jefferson and Chuck Taylor of UCLA devised a computer programme that reproduced itself with minor random changes as in natural reproduction, and then tested the resulting programmes against one another, jettisoning those that failed, keeping those that succeeded, letting them reproduce and so on.[27] The result is a computer that designs its own programmes to solve problems by mimicking the process of natural selection.

The implication of this is simple and momentous: *You can design a system that works on Darwinian lines.* There is nothing random or accidental about such a system, even though every component part of it seems to be functioning blindly. Out of a myriad local operations, none of which has the end point in mind, an order emerges at the level of the system as a whole.

What might make us think of evolution as part of a larger system of order like the market economy? The answer, suggests the Cambridge biologist Simon Conway Morris, is *convergence*. Biological systems are not random. Often, by taking different routes, they arrive at similar destinations. So, for example, cephalopods like the octopus developed a camera eye very similar to that of vertebrates like the blue whale. The development of intelligence in different phyla shows similar convergence. The paths taken by different life forms have not been random. They are constrained by the conditions in which they function and the problems they have needed to solve. Life forms begin from different starting points and take different routes, but they land up at the same destination with very similar soft- and hardware.

The direction of evolution is not open-ended. It tells a cumulative story of organisms of ever-growing complexity, able to thrive in different ecological niches, often in symbiotic relationship with other life forms. Steven J. Gould famously said that if the tape of evolution were replayed there is no guarantee that Homo sapiens would have emerged at all. Yet if convergence is a feature of evolution, then sooner or later something like Homo sapiens – a being with intelligence and self-consciousness – would have appeared. As Conway Morris himself puts it, 'What we know of evolution suggests the exact reverse [of Steven J. Gould's view]: convergence is ubiquitous and the constraints of life make the emergence of the various biological properties [e.g. intelligence] very probable if not inevitable.'[28] In short, you can design a universe that will eventually give rise to something very much like Homo sapiens, even when the process is built of steps none of which has this outcome in mind.

Darwinian biology does not entail the absence of design. What Darwin refuted was not the argument from design but Paley's version of it. The natural universe is not like a watch. It is not mechanical, a predetermined arrangement of interlocking parts. *But who thought the universe was like a watch to begin with?* Not the theologians, but the natural scientists and philosophers of the seventeenth and eighteenth centuries: Newton, Leibniz, Laplace and Auguste Comte. They believed that all physical phenomena were determined by, and could be predicted on the basis of, simple laws like those of Newton. What was wrong with Paley's argument was not the theology but the science. Good science refutes bad science. It tells us nothing at all about God.

What might make us think that this is the way God designed the universe? Because that is the way the Bible portrays him acting in relation to humans. The early experiments fail. God gives Adam and Eve paradise, but they sin. God tries to warn Cain against violence, but Cain does not listen. Seeing a world 'full of violence', God brings a flood, saves Noah and begins again, allowing him things, like eating meat, he forbade to the first humans. Again the plan fails. Noah gets drunk. Humanity starts building Babel.

God tries again, this time with a single human, Abraham. This too does not achieve the intended result. Within three generations Jacob's children are selling one of their brothers into slavery. God then exposes their descendants to slavery so that they will learn what it feels like and thus be motivated to create a society of freedom. Liberating them, God then gives them a command, the Sabbath, on which even slaves are free, so that they will eventually learn that no human should enslave another. Even this takes more than three thousand years.

The complex interaction between God and humanity in the Bible is more in the spirit of Darwinian evolution than in that of the God of Plato or Aristotle, the unmoved mover contemplating the unchanging, abstract forms of things. God, like evolution, operates in and through time. Humans act, God reacts, humans respond to divine response, and so on in ways that are often surprising and unpredictable. How this dovetails with Divine foreknowledge is a classic problem in Jewish theology (in the Middle Ages, Gersonides thought that God's foreknowledge was limited by human freedom, Crescas that human freedom was limited by God's foreknowledge, and Maimonides that human and divine knowledge were so unalike that we can know only that we will never know how God knows).[29] God, like evolution, is oriented to a not-yet-realised future: hence his name, 'I will be what I will be', which might equally serve as a Darwinian definition of life itself. God, like evolution, works on the basis of convergence, that distant vision of an end of days in which nation will no longer lift up sword against nation and the world will be in a state of *shalom*, the integrated diversity that constitutes peace.

What Darwinian science represents is not the refutation of the God of Abraham but the final overthrow of Aristotelian science, the idea that purposes are unequivocally discernible within nature. The Bible tells us, as in the narrative of Joseph, that at one level the story of life may seem like an entirely random sequence of events.

There is nothing obvious about divine design. It is oblique, subtle and sometimes non-linear. It needs much intelligence and depth to perceive it, and it is arrived at not by the left-brain process of analysing microscopic detail, but by the right-brain capacity to step back and see the picture as a whole.

Why would a Creator choose to operate this way, allowing species and eventually humankind to emerge obliquely rather than directly? For the same reason that the planned economies of the Soviet Union and Communist China failed and the market economies of the West succeeded. A planned economy fails to liberate energies. It does not grant freedom. It does not generate creativity. It is predictable, ungenerous, dictatorial, precisely the things the God of Abraham is not.

Darwinian evolution precisely fits the model I argued for in chapter 1, in the case of Abrahamic monotheism and the meaningfulness of life. *The meaning of the system lies outside the system.* That, I argued there, applied to systems in general and to the universe as a whole. Any system is made up of rules that govern events within the system. Those rules explain how the system works, but not why it was created or evolved. That is why Darwinism fulfils an important function for Abrahamic monotheism. It tells us that God, having created the conditions for life, transcends life as he transcends the universe. The idea that we should look for God in nature is essentially pagan and constitutes a pagan residue even within the great Aristotle himself. Faith says, all that breathes praises God. It does not say, all that breathes proves the existence of God.

The Hebrew Bible is simply uninterested in *Homo sapiens* the biological species. It is even relatively uninterested in *Homo faber*, the tool-making, environment-changing life-form. It passes over, in short order, Jabal, 'father of those who live in tents and raise livestock', Jubal, the first to 'play the harp and flute', and Tubal-Cain who 'forged all kinds of tools out of bronze and iron'. It is interested exclusively in *Homo religiosus*, the first humans to hear and respond to the Divine voice.

Ecclesiastes says that biologically, 'Man has no pre-eminence over the animals.' We are creatures of Earth, physical beings with physical drives. We live, we eat, we sleep, we reproduce, we age and die. But humans remain unique. We are culture-producing animals. There are other social animals, but none that produce – except at the most rudimentary level – cultures, symbols, systems of meaning. It is this that gives us our unique adaptability. Other animals are genetically conditioned to act in certain ways under certain conditions. We have something more powerful than genetically encoded instinct. We are culture-producing, information-sharing, meaning-learning animals. Nature built us for culture.[30]

No animal painted the bonobo equivalent of the Sistine Chapel ceiling. No animal said, 'To be or not to be.' No animal philosophised that he or she might be nothing more than a hairy human. No animal was even an atheist, as far as I know. We may share many of our genes with the primates, as we do with fruit flies, bananas and yeast. The stones of an ancient cottage have mineral similarities to those out of which Chartres Cathedral was built. But there the resemblance ends.

The Bible is interested not in *physis*, but in *nomos*: not in the laws that govern nature, but in the moral laws that should govern humankind. The Greek translation of *Torah*, the Jewish name for the Mosaic books, is *Nomos*, 'law'. Hence the Bible does not begin with the birth of Homo sapiens, a biological species, hundreds of thousands of years ago, but much later, with the discovery of monotheism some six thousand years ago. The critical moment seems to have been the dawn of individual self-consciousness.

Bruno Snell argues, in *The Discovery of the Mind*, that the Greeks discovered the human person as a person sometime between Homer and Aristophanes, that is, between the ninth and fifth centuries BCE.[31] The Bible dates it several thousand years earlier, at the dawn of civilisation. Adam and Eve are typological representations of the first monotheists. Finding God singular and alone, they found the human person singular and alone.

Because virtually all human activity is culturally mediated, and because humans are the only culture-producing animals (if we exclude such modest behaviours as chimpanzees learning how to wash potatoes), it follows that the biological similarities between humans and animals are irrelevant to most of human behaviour. The comparisons are interesting, but what makes humans human is the way basic drives – eating, reproducing, hierarchies of dominance – are transformed by culture into elaborately choreographed minuets that are forms of enacted meaning.

Evolutionary psychology tells us that we may have genetically encoded instincts, some of which date back to our pre-human history, our 'reptile brain'. Religious thinkers knew this long ago. The Jewish mystics spoke about our 'animal soul' which has to be overcome by our 'godly soul'. Even the most committed scientific materialists concede that genetically encoded instinct has nothing to do with ethics. Richard Dawkins himself says in *The Selfish Gene*, 'We have the power to defy the selfish genes of our birth . . . We alone on Earth can rebel against the tyranny of the selfish replicators.'[32] Steven Pinker writes that we can act against genetic predisposition, 'and if my genes don't like it they can go jump in the lake'.[33] Katharine Hepburn said it best. 'Nature', she says majestically to Humphrey Bogart in *The African Queen*, 'is what we are put in this world to rise above.'

The biblical story begins at that moment at which humans developed sufficient self-consciousness to become aware of themselves as deliberating, choosing, free and responsible moral agents, the point at which they were first able to understand that 'nature is what we were put on Earth to rise above'. The Bible is interested not in Homo sapiens the biological species, but in the moral animal who, communing with the source of his and all being, discovers for the first time that although, like everything that lives, we have desires, like nothing else that lives, we are able to pass judgement on our desires. That is when humans first heard the voice of God.

The story told by modern cosmology and Darwinian biology is wondrous almost beyond belief. It tells of a universe astonishingly precisely calibrated for the emergence, first of stars, then of second-, third- and fourth-generation stars, then of the formation of planets, one of which met exactly the conditions for the possibility of life. Then, in a way that still remains utterly mysterious, life emerged and evolved, through billions of years, yielding self-organising systems of ever-increasing complexity, until finally one life form appeared, capable of standing outside its biological drives for long enough to become self-conscious of itself and the sheer improbability of its own existence, and sensing in all of this a vast intelligence that set it in motion, and a caring presence that brought it into being in love. It took 13.7 billion years before the first human turned his or her thoughts beyond the physical universe and, searching for God, found God searching for us.

How it happened, we will never know for sure. But it suggests a story of almost infinite divine patience consistent with everything we know from the Bible yet on a scale only mystics hitherto imagined. So I am not surprised that the rabbis formulated a blessing to be said over scientists, for it remains the most unlikely and beautiful story ever told.

12

The Problem of Evil

The Bible is not the best book for putting us at ease with the world.

Herbert N. Schneidau[1]

A too confident sense of justice always leads to injustice.

Reinhold Niebuhr[2]

How can God allow unjust suffering in the world? How can he allow his creatures to use, abuse, manipulate, dominate, injure and kill one another? How can he allow an Earthquake, a flood, a drought, a famine to cause thousands, even millions, of deaths? How can he allow one innocent child to die?

No question so lacerates the heart of faith as does this. How, if God is good, is there so much evil in the world?

After the tsunami in the Indian Ocean in 2004 that killed 230,000 people and left more than a million homeless, I went to visit one young woman who had been in Thailand at the time and only narrowly escaped. She was in a state of extreme anguish. This was her story. She was in her hotel room when the wave struck. She was able to swim through the window, but then she found the surface of the water blocked with debris. She could only raise an arm above the surface and wave for help.

A local Thai man saw her waving, swam over to her and brought her to safety. Without this she would have died. Hours later, when the water had receded, she saw among the wreckage the dead body of the man who had rescued her. 'How', she asked me, 'could God have allowed him to die? He saved my life. Of all people, he should have earned the right to live.'

233

This question, or something like it, causes more people to lose faith than any other. There is none deeper. To fail to take it seriously is to fail to be serious at all. It is the question of questions, and it calls for nothing less than total honesty.

To give it its most famous philosophical expression: either God cannot prevent evil, or he can but chooses not to. If he cannot, then he is not all-powerful. If he can but chooses not to, then he is not all-good. How does a good God permit evil to deface and defile his creation?

No sooner have we asked the question than we realise something strange about the Bible. The later response of theologians, long after the biblical canon was closed, is familiar to us. We cannot fathom the workings of providence. If we could understand God, we would be God. Who are we to know what is for the best *sub specie aeternitatis*, from the perspective of eternity? What we cannot understand we must accept.

It is this view that we do *not* find in the Bible. Instead we find Moses saying to God, 'Why have you done evil to this people? Why did you send me?' (Exodus 5:22).

Here is Jeremiah, challenging God:

> You are always righteous, O Lord,
> when I bring a case before you.
> Yet I would speak with you about your justice:
> Why does the way of the wicked prosper?
> Why do all the faithless live at ease?
>
> (Jeremiah 12:1)

And here is Habakkuk:

> How long, O Lord, must I call for help, but you do not listen?
>   Or cry out to you, 'Violence!' but you do not save?
> Why do you make me look at injustice? Why do you tolerate
>   wrong?

Destruction and violence are before me; there is strife, and
  conflict abounds.
Therefore the law is paralysed, and justice never prevails.
  The wicked hem in the righteous, so that justice is perverted.

(Habakkuk 1:2–4)

Far from attempting to minimise the problem, the Bible maxim-
ises it, seemingly at every opportunity. The people who challenge
divine justice are not heretics, sceptics, deniers of the faith. They
are the supreme heroes of the faith: Moses and the prophets, the
people who carry God's word to the world. This cries out for
explanation.

So does the book of Job. The book sets up the following scenario.
Satan – not in Judaism an evil force, simply the prosecuting attorney
– challenges God on the faith he had in creating humanity. Show
me one person who is truly righteous, he says. Job, God answers.
Job is righteous, Satan replies, because you never tested him. He
has all he wants: a happy marriage, children, wealth. It is easy for
him to believe. He has no reason not to believe. But take away his
good fortune and you will see that he no longer believes.

In swift, successive blows, Job loses everything. His wealth.
His children. His wife loses faith. 'Curse God and die,' she says.
Job replies, in words Jews have used ever since, 'God has given.
God has taken away. May the name of God be blessed.' There is
a momentous acceptance in those words, and logically the book
should have ended there.

But it does not. Satan challenges God again and persuades him
to send Job one more affliction. It is a relatively minor one, but
this time Job breaks and curses the day he was born. From then
to almost the end of the book, for more than thirty chapters, Job
challenges God to show him how and why he deserves his fate.

His three companions – later they are joined by a fourth,
younger and surer of himself – give Job the conventional answers.
God is just. Therefore if Job has suffered, he must have sinned. He
is being punished for some wrong he did.

Yet we the readers know something Job's comforters do not. Job has not sinned. That was how the story was introduced in the first place. Job is the only person in the entire Hebrew Bible to be called sinless. There is therefore a massive irony throughout. Job's comforters, who defend God's justice, are in fact slandering Job, accusing him of a wrong he did not commit.

As the book rises to a crescendo, God, who has been absent throughout, finally reveals himself to Job. Now, we expect, we will hear the answer to the question of questions. Instead, for a full four chapters, God simply asks questions of his own – unanswerable questions. 'Where were you when I laid the Earth's foundation? Have you journeyed to the springs of the sea or walked in the recesses of the deep? Have the gates of death been shown to you?' And so on.

Job is silenced. Then, in an astonishing reversal, God tells Job that he, who challenged God's justice, is right and his comforters, who defended God, are wrong. Job is then blessed with a restoration of his wealth and with more children.

It is as bewildering a book as you will ever find. It raises questions without ever answering them. It bars the way to theodicy – explanations of why God permits evil in the world – since that is what Job's comforters do and they, in the book, are condemned as wrong. It is a book of questions without answers, the last thing we would expect to find in a canon of sacred scriptures.

There is a left-brain and a right-brain way of asking the question of why there is unjustified evil in the world. The left-brain, philosophical, analytical way is to ask it hypothetically. 'What would we expect the world to be like if . . . there were an omnipotent, omniscient, all-good God?' No child would die. Perhaps no adult would die. Animals would not hunt one another for food. There would be no sickness, no poverty and no hunger. No one would be homeless or without access to pure water and medical treatment. There would be no Earthquakes, no tsunamis, or if there were, they would cause no loss of life.

The world is not like that. Therefore there is no God. That is a philosophical way.

It is not the way an Abraham or a Sarah ask the question.

The religious mind begins not with the world there might hypothetically be, but with the world that is. There is suffering and injustice. There is sickness and premature death. There are natural disasters. That is the world we inhabit and for the time being there is no other. The religious mind starts with the world that is, not with the world that might have been.

Within this world, it seeks meaning. It does not seek explanation. Explanation is something else. Through explanation we learn how tsunamis happen, how populations suffer from sickle-cell anaemia or become infected by AIDS. The religious question is about meaning.

Suffering tears our world apart. Something in our life that once rooted us is taken from us. Where there was once wholeness there is now a gaping hole. Suffering threatens to render life meaningless. How can I live with this pain? How can I want to continue to live in such a world? In extremis we cry with the words of the Psalm, 'My God, my God, why have you forsaken me?' (Psalm 22:1).

In the Bible there is a whole literature of lament, grief, protest. Much of it is written in tears. There can be a darkness so dark that it extinguishes any attempt to light a light. The Bible does not hide from this. It is an honest book.

In the face of unbearable, inexplicable or unjustifiable suffering, there are three responses. The first says: This life is not all there is. There is another world, after death. There is heaven. There is peace and eternal life. All the evil of this world is banished in the world to come. It is there that we find justice, truth and God. God is good; the world is bad; therefore God is not to be found in this world but in another, the world we enter when we die.

This is an important belief. It was shared by the Greek philosophers. It makes sense in terms of the logic of divine goodness. Most importantly, it brings comfort, and that is no small thing.

But it cannot be the whole answer, for it is never given as such in the Hebrew Bible. God does not say to the Israelites suffering in slavery: My children, relax, endure, bliss awaits you in another life. God does not tell Moses to preach them a sermon on the delights of paradise. Nothing could be further from the spirit of the Hebrew Bible.

Yes, there is life after death. It is spoken of in the Bible. It is a fundamental of faith. But it occupies a surprisingly marginal part of the book of God's word.[3] There is an unEarthly, vivid description of a vision by the prophet Ezekiel in which he sees the Israelites as a valley of dry bones, which come together and grow flesh and come back to life. But this is not a vision of heaven. It is a glimpse into a future national renaissance on Earth.

All this is part of what makes people say of the Hebrew Bible that it is a this-worldly book, meaning that it is here, in the world God created and seven times pronounced 'good', that the drama takes place, the tragedies occur, the questions arise. Faith takes comfort, but not refuge, in the world to come.

The second response is to see, as did John Keats, that this world is 'a vale of soul-making'.[4] We suffer so that we can grow. Others suffer so that we can practise charity or kindness. The bad in our lives is an invitation to the good. For that is how we become morally responsible agents, by living in a world of trial and temptation, torment and tears. A world without suffering would be one in which we never needed to come to anyone's aid, never needed to make sacrifices of our own for the sake of someone else. Without pain, there is no gain.

Here too there is truth, but not enough. Maimonides, in his famous list of the eight levels of charity, says that the highest is to help someone start a business or find a job so that he or she does not need charity any more.[5] Had we offered Maimonides the argument above, he would surely have replied: Better a world in which no one needs charity than one in which there is charity because there is need. To say that Alan suffers so that Brian can give help is to treat Alan as a means to an end, which is not how we are supposed to treat people.

As a response to suffering, the argument makes sense, but as a justification for it, it makes no sense at all.

The third response, therefore, is to say: There is evil, therefore there is no God. There is no justice, therefore there is no judge. The world is as it is. *Homo hominis lupus est*, man is wolf to man. The world is a restless searching for power after power that ceaseth only in death, as Hobbes said, a struggle for survival in a world of scarce resources as Darwin argued, and there is no reason to expect otherwise. Life is absurd. Human beings are cruel. Epicurus was right. Pursue pleasure, avoid pain, endure such suffering as is endurable and when it ceases to be, then is the moment to cease to be.

I personally cannot accept such a world, though many can and do. A world in which there is no God is one in which there are no limits to hubris, no principled constraints to the will to power. In a godless world some, no doubt, will choose the way of Epicurus and live quietly among friends and innocent pleasures. But not all, and there's the rub.

As so often elsewhere, Nietzsche spells out the consequences. With an honesty not always shared by those who followed him, he insisted that the death of the Christian God would be the death of Christian morality, with its emphasis on kindness, compassion, forgiveness and all the rest, which he despised as the morality of slaves. 'When one gives up Christian belief one thereby deprives oneself of the right to Christian morality . . . Christian morality is a command: its origin is transcendental . . . it possesses truth only if God is truth – it stands or falls with the belief in God.'[6]

Nietzsche relentlessly draws the conclusion:

To talk of just and unjust in themselves has no sense whatsoever – it's obvious that in themselves harming, oppressing, exploiting, destroying cannot be 'unjust', inasmuch as life essentially works that way, that is, in its basic functions it harms, oppresses, exploits, and destroys – and cannot be conceived at all without these characteristics.[7]

If there is no Judge, there is no reason to expect justice. If there is no God, there is no transcendental 'Thou shalt not'. These were not theoretical propositions. In Nazi Germany, the Soviet Union and Communist China they were put into practice, and tens of millions died.

It is an optical illusion to believe that, under pressure of perceived injustice, we can abandon belief in God *and leave nothing unchanged*. The whole of the second section of this book was dedicated to arguing otherwise. If we give up belief in the God of justice, we relinquish belief in the objective reality and categorical imperative of justice also. In such a world there is no comfort for the sufferer, no rebuke for the oppressor, no hope, just the stoic endurance of hopelessness. 'The mass of men', said Thoreau, 'lead lives of quiet desperation.'[8] That is what the third response offers us: resignation to a world we have no reason to suppose could be other than unjust.

Three responses, the first religious and other-worldly, the second religious and this-worldly, and the third non- or anti-religious. What they have in common is that they are all, ultimately, *philosophies of acceptance*. Abrahamic monotheism is not a religion of acceptance. It is a religion of protest. It does not *try* to vindicate the suffering of the world. That is the way of Job's comforters, not Job.

Why did people think otherwise? There is, after all, a whole discipline of theology, known as *theodicy*, defined as 'the vindication of God's goodness and justice in the face of the existence of evil'. How can I claim – as I do here – that this entire discipline is inapplicable to the Hebrew Bible and the original form of Abrahamic spirituality?

Throughout this book my argument has been that Hebraic religious beliefs only imperfectly translate into the language of ancient Greece. Fundamental to Aristotelian logic is the law of the excluded middle: either a proposition is true, or its negation is true. It is this principle that frames the existence of evil as a theological problem. Either God exists, or evil exists. If God exists, then evil does not exist. It is either a prelude to, or a preparation for, the good. Seen in full context, it is not evil after all. Alternatively, evil exists, therefore God does not exist. This is a philosophical, detached, disengaged, analytical, left-brained way of thinking about facts.

But faith does not operate by the logic of the left brain and the law of the excluded middle. It feels both sides of the contradiction. God exists *and* evil exists. The more powerfully I feel the existence of God, the more strongly I protest the existence of evil. That is why in the Abrahamic faith it is the giants of faith, not the sceptics or cynics, who cry aloud, as Moses and Jeremiah and Habakkuk cried aloud, with a cry that echoes through the ages. That is why Job refuses to be comforted and why he would not let go of God.

There is a difference between a contradiction and a cry.

You can solve a contradiction by sitting quietly in a room, thinking, using conceptual ingenuity, reframing. Philosophy, said Wittgenstein, leaves the world unchanged. But faith does not leave the world unchanged. You cannot solve a cry by thinking. Moses, weeping for his people, is not consoled by Leibniz's admittedly brilliant proof that all is for the best in the best of all possible worlds.

Theodicy, the attempt to vindicate God's justice in a world of evil, is compelling evidence that in the translation of Abrahamic spirituality into the language of Plato and Aristotle, something is lost. What is lost is the cry.

At this stage we need a close reading of a biblical text. We are in the tent of Jacob at one of the most fraught moments of an unquiet life. He has sent his beloved Joseph to see how the other brothers are faring, tending the sheep far away. The brothers, inflamed beyond measure by jealousy at Jacob's favouritism, briefly contemplate killing Joseph, but eventually decide on a less drastic strategy. They sell him into slavery.

Now they are faced with the problem of how to explain his disappearance to Jacob. They take his distinctive many-coloured cloak, kill a goat and smear the cloak with its blood. This they take back with them, forcing Jacob to conclude that 'a wild animal has torn him'. Jacob concedes that the evidence is decisive.

The text then says, 'All his sons and daughters came to comfort him, but *he refused to be comforted*' (Genesis 37:35).

The sages asked: Why did Jacob refuse to be comforted? There are laws of mourning in Judaism, and they go back to its earliest days. There is the week of mourning; there is the first month; in some cases it takes a year. But there is a limit. Excessive mourning is seen in Judaism as a rebellion against reality. We are mortal. No one and nothing lives for ever. Why then did Jacob refuse to be comforted?

The traditional answer is surely the right one. Jacob refused to be comforted because he refused to give up hope that Joseph was still alive – as, indeed, he was.[9]

Hope is not costless in the way that optimism is. It carries with it a considerable price. Those who hope *refuse to be comforted* while the hoped-for outcome is not yet reached. Given their history of suffering, Jews were rarely optimists. But they never gave up hope. That is why, when the prophets saw evil in the world, they refused to be comforted. For that is what theodicy is: a comfort bought too cheaply.

Among the most remarkable words ever to have been included in a sacred text are the words of protest uttered by Abraham when he hears, from God himself, that he is about to destroy the cities of the plain. Abraham says: How is that possible?

> Will you sweep away the righteous with the wicked? What if there are fifty righteous people in the city? Will you really sweep

it away and not spare the place for the sake of the fifty righteous people in it? Far be it from you to do such a thing – to kill the righteous with the wicked, treating the righteous and the wicked alike. Far be it from you! Will not the Judge of all the Earth do justly? (Genesis 18:23–5)

The passage is so well known that we can forget to reflect on how strange it is. Does Abraham seriously suspect God of injustice? Does he believe that there are in fact fifty innocent people in the city and that God has somehow overlooked this fact? Does he believe that he is more righteous than God? How does 'the knight of faith', as Kierkegaard called him, challenge God himself?

The Bible leaves us in no doubt. The reason Abraham challenges God is that God has challenged him to do so. Immediately before this, we read the following:

Then the Lord said, 'Shall I hide from Abraham what I am about to do? Abraham will surely become a great and powerful nation, and all nations on Earth will be blessed through him. For I have chosen him, so that he will direct his children and his household after him to keep the way of the Lord by doing what is right and just, so that the Lord will bring about for Abraham what he has promised him.' (Genesis 18:17–19)

'Shall I hide from Abraham?' This, overheard by Abraham, is his cue. God is inviting Abraham to respond. 'For I have chosen him . . . to keep the way of the Lord by doing what is right and just.' This sets the terms of the challenge. Abraham is to be the voice of the right (*tzedakah*) and the just (*mishpat*). These then become precisely the words he uses in his challenge: 'righteous' (*tzadikim*) and 'Judge/justice' (*ha-shofet/mishpat*). Abraham challenges God because God invites him to challenge God.

Do not accept injustice even if you hear it in my name. That is what God is telling Abraham. As it happens, the next day the inhabitants of the city attempt to commit homosexual rape on two innocent visitors, which is enough to answer Abraham's doubt. There are no fifty righteous. There are none. But what we have here is a radical proposition, especially when compared to the story of Noah and the Flood.

The sages noted that while Noah was making the ark, he registered no protest against the fact that God was about to destroy most of life through the Flood. That is what made Abraham, not Noah, the hero of faith. Noah accepted. Abraham protested. The religion of Abraham is a religion of protest against evil, in the name of God.

Why then is there suffering in the world? The answer given by Maimonides still seems to be the best.[10] There are, he said, three kinds of evil. First is the evil that follows from the fact that we are physical beings in a physical world. There are tsunamis because the land mass of the Earth rests on tectonic plates which sometimes shift, creating Earthquakes and giant waves. Had the surface of the Earth not rested on tectonic plates, the conditions would not have existed for the emergence of life.

We are unique and complex creatures because of the nature of the human genome, which contains copying errors, which sometimes lead to genetic illnesses. But without those errors, there would not be the mutations that gave rise to species in the first place, Homo sapiens among them.

We know now far better than Maimonides could have done how slender are the limits within which a universe could emerge, let alone life, let alone us. To seek a world without floods and droughts, diseases and deaths is to seek a world that could not be. Contemporary science has shown us why it could not be.

The second kind of evil is that which humans commit against other humans. The third – by far the largest, says Maimonides – is the evil we commit against ourselves: the smoker who complains to God that he has developed cancer; the workaholic who rails against the high blood pressure that caused the heart attack.

These last two evils exist because of human free will. This

explanation is often criticised. Could God not have created human beings who – freely and with no divine coercion – only ever did good, not harm? And if the answer is 'No', then could God not have created humans *without* freedom, if freedom comes at so high a price?

The answer to the first is 'No'. Freedom means the freedom to do evil. Hence Adam and Eve, hence Cain, hence God's regret that he had created humanity in the first place. But freedom is not a minor, negotiable element of the human condition. Abrahamic faith is the religion of freedom as responsible self-restraint. God could have created billions of computers programmed to do nothing but sing his praises. Would such a God be worthy of worship? Is such a God conceivable except as a philosophical joke?

So evil exists because we exist as free beings in a physical world with all the accidents of matter and the pain of mortality. What difference, then, does it make whether our attitude to evil is one of acceptance or of protest?

It makes all the difference. Abraham's protest, and Moses' and Jeremiah's, were not mere cries wasted in the wind. They were cries born in the cognitive dissonance between the world that is and the world that ought to be. The only way of resolving this dissonance is a deed. That is the difference between faith-as-acceptance and faith-as-protest. The only way to deal with slavery is to lead the people to freedom. The only way to confront the evils of the *polis* is to build a more just social order, with special emphasis on loving the stranger.

God, in Abraham's faith, is not the solution to a contradiction but the call to a journey that will eventually change the world by showing that there is another way to live, an alternative to the will to power. It is no accident that those raised in this faith are disproportionately to be found among lawyers fighting injustice, economists fighting poverty, doctors and medical researchers fighting disease, and teachers and academics fighting ignorance. Philosophy does not change the world, but faith does.

To be sure, there is an objection to this way of seeing things. It was well put by the Russian writer Nikolai Berdyaev.[11] He believed that Jews had committed a fundamental mistake when they thought that justice could be sought within the human condition, this side of heaven. He speaks of 'this intense Jewish striving after truth, justice and happiness on Earth', seeing in it 'an unwarrantable principle of conflict with God, an unwillingness to accept the will of God. There is a resistance to God, an arbitrary assertion of a purely human justice and truth and their fulfilment on Earth against that destiny of all mankind revealed in the life and history of the world according to God's inscrutable will and design.'

According to Berdyaev, there is no ultimate justice and truth on Earth. These things can exist only in heaven. They are encountered after death, when the human soul is freed of its entrapment within the body and the physical world. Perhaps he was right. Jews staked their lives on the alternative conviction, that redemption is to be sought this side of heaven. That is why they consistently refused to believe that the Messiah has come in a world still filled with injustice and violence, terror and the pursuit of power.

My own view is that if God did *not* want us to seek justice in this world, why did he create it and why did he pronounce it good? If he did not believe that physical existence is a blessing, why are we here? As punishment? For what crime? Berdyaev wrote in 1923. Would he still have maintained his thesis once the full extent of the Final Solution had become clear: that suffering is to be accepted as 'God's inscrutable will and design'? There are such views in Judaism as well as Christianity, but I, for one, prefer the theology of protest. We must accept only that which we cannot change.

The philosopher John Cottingham, rejecting the view that religious faith is an inference from the balance of good over evil in the world, says something moving:

The most profoundly spiritual and passionately religious people in the world's history, the people who produced Moses and the prophets and Jesus and Paul, were a people whose history was conspicuous by the most terrible suffering, the cataclysmic traumas of slavery, wanderings in the desert, a homeland marked by the ever-present threat of war and annihilation, brutal captivity, exile, ruthless suppression and control by a series of imperial subjugators. This is the people who reflected endlessly on *chesed*, the loving kindness of God, who produced the immortal lines, *ach tov va'chesed yirdefuni kol yemei chayai* – 'surely thy goodness and loving kindness shall follow me all the days of my life'.[12]

Belief in God is an assertion of human dignity in the face of humiliation, and of hope in the midst of the dark night of despair. It is a refusal to accept evil as inevitable, but at the same time an acknowledgement that we cannot leave redemption entirely to God. He rescued Noah, but Noah had to build the ark. He dwelt among the Israelites in the wilderness, but they had to build the sanctuary. The very fact that the Bible devotes some fifteen times as much space to the Israelites' constructing the sanctuary as it does to God creating the universe tells us that our deeds are precious to God. God is not the solution of a contradiction, but a call to become his partners in the work of redemption.

If I did not believe in God, what would persuade me to fight against an injustice that, according to Nietzsche, is written into the basic biological structure of life itself? There were two major secular forms of social hope in the twentieth century. One was the Marxist vision of the proletarian revolution. The other was the Western dream of peace, market economics and technological progress. The former led to the loss of freedom, the latter to large and growing inequalities: hope for the few, not the many. The risk is that in the twenty-first century people will increasingly turn to pessimism, resignation, endurance and ataraxia. They are what the Greeks found refuge in when they lost faith in faith. Lose belief in God, and sooner or later you *may* lose belief in the possibility and necessity of justice.

Herbert Schneidau used the phrase 'sacred discontent' to describe the Hebrew Bible's contribution to Western civilisation. The historian Christopher Dawson argued similarly that, alone among the civilisations of the world, Europe 'has been continually shaken and transformed by an energy of spiritual unrest'. He attributed this to the fact that 'its religious ideal has not been the worship of timeless and changeless perfection but a spirit that strives to incorporate itself in humanity and to change the world'.[13] I have argued in this chapter that this energy is driven by the cognitive dissonance of a faith that sees the world as it is while refusing to let go of its vision of the world as it ought to be. In that world, contradiction is to be resolved not by philosophical thought but by redemptive deed.

There is a Jewish joke, a tragic one. The time, 1938, the place, a travel agency in Germany. A Jew has entered. He tells the woman at the desk that he would like to buy a ticket for a foreign journey.

'Where to?' asks the travel agent.

'What are you offering?' asks the Jew.

The travel agent passes him a globe. He turns the globe slowly, looking at country after country, knowing that each has closed its doors to people of his faith. He pushes the globe back to the travel agent with the words, 'Don't you have another world?'

Perhaps this is not the world we would have chosen, but it is the only one we have. Either we resign ourselves to the evil it contains, or we register a protest against it. It begins with a cry that is only stilled when we hear the Judge of all the Earth calling on us to help bring justice into the human world we make together.

I3

When Religion Goes Wrong

Both read the Bible day and night,
But thou read'st black where I read white.

William Blake[1]

Then I saw that there was a way to hell, even from the gates of heaven.

John Bunyan, The Pilgrim's Progress

On one point, and it is a substantial one, the critics of religion are right. Religion has done harm. It has led to crusades, jihads, inquisitions, autos-da-fé and pogroms. It has shed the blood of human sacrifice in the name of high ideals. People have hated in the name of the God of love, practised cruelty in the name of the God of compassion, waged war in the name of the God of peace, and killed in the name of the God of life. Those are undeniable facts and they are terrifying.

The great believers have always known this. Blaise Pascal said, 'Men never do evil so completely and cheerfully as when they do it from a religious conviction.'[2] Jonathan Swift said, 'We have just enough religion to make us hate, but not enough to make us love, one another.'[3] 'I think we must fully face the fact', wrote C. S. Lewis, 'that when Christianity does not make a man very much better, it makes him very much worse.'[4]

This happens not because religion is religion, but because human beings are human beings, not angels and certainly not God. Religion has power. It bonds people as a group. It moves people to act. It changes lives. And whatever has power can be used, misused or abused. Religion is like fire: it warms, but it also burns. And we are the guardians of the flame.

The same is true of every high ideal, secular no less than religious. Steven Weinberg was wrong when he said, 'With or without religion, you would have good people doing good things and evil people doing evil things. But for good people to do evil things, that takes religion.' The supporters, fellow travellers and 'willing executioners' of Lenin, Stalin, Hitler, Goebbels, Himmler, Eichmann, Mussolini, Mao, Pol Pot, Idi Amin, Robert Mugabe, Radovan Karadzic, Slobodan Milosevic, Saddam Hussein and Kim Jong Il prove otherwise. A reading of Jonathan Glover's *Humanity*, a history of secular evil in the past hundred years, should cure all thoughts that it takes religion to move people to do wrong in the belief that they are doing right.[5]

Science and technology can also be misused with devastating consequences. The twentieth century gave rise to social Darwinism, the so-called scientific study of race, Zyklon B, the extermination camp, Marxist economic ideology, the Gulag, social engineering, B. F. Skinner and his vision of a world 'beyond freedom and dignity', lobotomy, the use of brain surgery to pacify criminals, eugenics, forced sterilisation, euthanasia, abortion on demand, and the various other horrors of a technological age, including modern methods of torture and mind control.[6]

The problem is not science or religion, but us: 'The heart is deceitful above all things and beyond cure' (Jeremiah 17:9). Some humans hate. Some envy. Some seek power over others. Some want revenge for real or imagined humiliation. The human mind is almost infinite in its capacity to rationalise and justify evil, especially when driven by hate. There is religious hatred, ethnic hatred and ideological hatred: Christians versus Muslims, Serbs against Croats, and the cold war stand-off between capitalism and Communism. The methods used for inciting hatred, demonising the other, making people feel threatened and thus defensive-aggressive, are essentially the same in all cases.

It is sometimes said nowadays that religions can do what secular systems cannot do, namely persuade people to become suicide bombers for the sake of eternal life in heaven, but that is not

so. The first suicide bombing in recent history was the assassi-
nation of Tsar Alexander II of Russia in 1881 by an anarchist.
The Tamil Tigers of Sri Lanka, the first to use suicide bombing
as a systematic tactic, were not a religious group, nor were the
Japanese kamikaze pilots on their suicide missions in the Second
World War. As Eric Hoffer wrote in *The True Believer*, ideological terrorists merge their identity with that of the group. They
are willing to give up their lives not for the sake of their share in
heaven, but for the sake of the collective with which they identify on Earth.[7] Scott Atran's recent book *Talking to the Enemy*
documents this in vivid detail.[8] Suicide bombers, he discovers
through spending time with them, kill not for the cause, but for
one another: because of friendship and group loyalty. Atran is
particularly critical of the new atheists for using terror as an argument against religion.

Religion is no more likely than secularism to lead good people
to do bad, and sometimes evil, things. But merely saying this is
not enough. If we are honest, whether we are religious or secular,
we must ask why the ideals in which we believe can, in certain
circumstances, do harm. Failure to do this led too many Western
intellectuals not to acknowledge the crimes of Soviet Communism
– the 'god that failed' – until tens of millions of people had died
and several generations had been robbed of their freedom.

Religion is no exception. Its sanctity should never be used as a
shield against honest self-criticism. I want in this chapter to examine five of the hazards to which specifically the Judeo-Christian
tradition has been prone. They are: hard texts, dualism, messianic
politics, the pursuit of power and the inability to see that there
is more than one perspective on reality. Each, I believe, must be
guarded against.

Hard Texts

Every religion based on a body of holy writings, a sacred scripture,
contains *hard texts*: passages which, if taken literally and applied

directly, would lead to results at odds with that religion's deepest moral convictions. There are passages in the Hebrew Bible, the New Testament and the Koran that, taken in isolation, are radically inconsistent with the larger commitments of Judaism, Christianity and Islam to the sanctity of life and the dignity of all persons as bearers of God's image.

Such texts need interpretation. The classic form of fundamentalism is belief in the literal meaning of texts, specifically that we can move *from text to application without interpretation*. We cannot. Interpretation is as fundamental to any text-based religion as is the original act of revelation itself. No word, especially the word of God, is self-explanatory. Exegetes and commentators are to religion what judges are to law. They are essential to the system, and they can make all the difference between justice and injustice, right and wrong.

Every text-based religion has its own traditions of interpretation. That is why fundamentalism is so profoundly untraditional. Rabbinic Judaism regarded the Oral Law (tradition and interpretation) as equal in authority to the Written Law (revelation, specifically the books of Moses). The rabbis held that Biblicism – accepting the authority of the written word while rejecting oral tradition, as did the Sadducees and Karaites – was heresy. They said, 'One who translates a verse literally is a liar.'[9] The point is clear: no text without interpretation, and no interpretation without tradition. Christianity contains a similar principle: 'The letter kills, but the spirit gives life' (2 Corinthians 3:6).

Jews, Christians and Muslims have wrestled with the meanings of their scriptures, developing in the process elaborate hermeneutic and jurisprudential systems. Medieval Christianity had its four levels of interpretation – literal, allegorical, moral and eschatological – paralleling the Jewish division into *peshat*, *remez*, *drush* and *sod*.[10] Islam likewise has its *fiqh*; its four schools of Sunni jurisprudence and their Shia counterparts; its principles of *taqleed*, *itjihad* and *qiyas*. In all of these systems the task is to relate the infinite Word to a finite world, to spell out details unspecified in the text, and to resolve seeming inconsistencies between one passage and another.

Interpretation is the lifeblood of all systems, including secular ones, that rely on canonical texts. That is what happened to all the biblical texts standardly quoted by the new atheists in their critique of the Bible, especially the wars against the Midianites and Amalekites, with their mandate for total destruction of populations, and Joshua's wars of conquest. In fact it is just these texts that allow us to see most clearly the power of exegesis to interpret details in the light of the whole.

In general, the Hebrew Bible is hostile to war. The prophets of Israel were the first people in history to see peace as an ideal. Already in the eighth century BCE, Isaiah and Micah speak of a time when 'Nation will not take up sword against nation, nor will they train for war any more' (Isaiah 2:4; Micah 4:3), and, 'They will neither harm nor destroy on all my holy mountain, for the Earth will be full of the knowledge of the Lord as the waters cover the sea' (Isaiah 11:9). This is the world's first literature of peace.

In 1 Chronicles 22:8, David is told by God he was not permitted to build the Temple, because 'you have shed much blood and have fought many wars'. War may sometimes be necessary, but it has no place in the domain of the holy. One who has 'shed much blood' may not build a house of God.

The sages ruled, early in the second century, that the entire biblical legislation relating to Israel's neighbours and enemies was no longer operative, because after Sennacherib's conquests and population transfers (722–705 BCE), the 'nations' against which Israel was commanded to wage war could no longer be identified. As Maimonides writes, 'their memory has already perished'.[11] We no longer know who is who. That chapter in Jewish history is closed, not to be reopened. As for Joshua's conquest of the land, the Talmud offers a radical interpretation, insisting that they were all prefaced by an offer of peace.[12] War was deemed never to be mandated except when the effort to make peace has been tried and has failed.

As for the Amalekites, about whom the Bible commands the Israelites to 'blot out their memory from under heaven', they too can no longer be identified,[13] because the nations of today are not the nations of biblical times. 'Amalek' survives as a symbol of radical evil, a metaphor, not a people.[14] War, except in self-defence, no longer takes place on the battlefield; it becomes a struggle within the soul.[15] The biblical phrase 'the wars of the Lord' becomes in the Talmud a description of debate in the house of study.[16] The Talmud goes so far as to say, in connection with the drowning of the Egyptians at the Red Sea (Exodus 15), that the angels wished to sing a song of triumph but God silenced them with the words, 'My creatures are drowning – and you wish to sing a song?'[17] Israel's enemies have become 'my creatures'. In short, by a process of interpretation, itself confirmed by the course of history, all biblical texts relating to wars of conquest were rendered inoperative. If you seek to understand a religious ethic, never look at its written texts alone. Always seek to know how they were understood by the community of faith and how in practice they were applied. The difference is often great.

Living traditions constantly interpret their canonical texts. That is what makes fundamentalism – text *without* interpretation – an act of violence against tradition. In fact, fundamentalists and today's atheists share the same approach to texts. They read them directly and literally, ignoring the single most important fact about a sacred text, namely that its meaning is not self-evident. It has a history and an authority of its own. Every religion must guard against a literal reading of its hard texts if it is not to betray God's deeper purposes.

Dualism

The second danger within religion was vividly exemplified by two sensational discoveries of ancient manuscripts in the 1940s that revolutionised our understanding of sectarian Jewish and Christian groups in the era around the birth of Christianity. One was the library of a Jewish sect at Qumran, the Dead Sea Scrolls. The other was the find in the Upper Egyptian town of Nag Hammadi of a cache of early Christian codices. The Qumran sectarians may have been a branch of the movement known as the Essenes. Members of the group were disaffected by the official priesthood in Jerusalem and awaited a saviour known as the Teacher of Righteousness. The Nag Hammadi Christians were devotees of an esoteric doctrine known as Gnosticism. The find disclosed fifty-two texts from the first and second centuries including nine gospels, many of which had not been known before.

The two sects were significantly different, but they had one thing in common: they saw reality in starkly dualistic terms. There was a sharp separation between good and evil, light and dark, the saved and the damned, the children of light and the children of darkness, and little if any shading in between. The children of darkness, they believed, were currently in control. Humanity was in the grip of evil. The Qumran sectarians believed that this would be reversed after a massive convulsion in the affairs of humankind. The Gnostic Christians were more inclined to see evil as the natural condition of the world.

What both groups testify to is that the greatest danger to monotheism is not polytheism or atheism, but *dualism*. It arises out of a specific crisis of faith, namely the existence of evil. How can a just God allow unjust suffering to exist? There are many answers to this question, but there are times when the world seems too out of joint for the conventional answers to suffice. It is then that an unconventional answer appears: evil is an independent, active force, apart from and opposed to God. Dualism – which enters the West through Zoroastrianism, Manichaeism and Hellenistic Gnosticism – explains evil as the work of a mythic counterforce: the devil, the demiurge, Satan, the anti-Christ, the Prince of Darkness, and the many other names for the embodiment of evil.

Dualism is a faith of sharp distinctions: between body and soul, this world and the next, material and spiritual, substance and form. God is in heaven; on Earth, all too often, evil reigns.

Dualism is thus able to preserve the goodness of God while attributing the sufferings of the faithful to a malevolent force, protean in form and universal in reach.

As its name implies, dualism is not monotheism, despite the fact that it has appeared at times of crisis in all three Abrahamic faiths. It is a murderous creed. In medieval Christianity, for example, Jewry was seen as a demonic force responsible for the poisoning of wells, the spread of the plague, the death of children, the desecration of the host, and so on, and these accusations led to massacres and expulsions.[18] At the end of the nineteenth century, dualism reappeared in a secular form known as the Protocols of the Elders of Zion.[19] Though this myth originated in Tsarist Russia, it was used with devastating effect by Hitler, and continues to be popular today in many parts of the Middle East.

Dualism resolves cognitive dissonance by saying, in effect, 'It wasn't us, and it wasn't God, so it must be Them,' whoever the 'Them' happen to be. It turns penitential cultures into blame cultures, externalising evil and projecting it on a scapegoat, thereby redefining the faithful as victims. We, our nation or our people, are the victim of someone else's crime. Since there is little or no overt evidence of this, it follows that the children of Satan must be masters of disguise, practitioners of sorcery or more modern dark arts. From there it is a short step to seeing them as subhuman (for the Nazis, Jews were 'vermin, lice'; for the Hutus of Rwanda, the Tutsi were *inyenzi*, 'cockroaches'). They can then be killed without compunction. There is a straight line from dualism to demonisation to dehumanisation to genocide.

Dualism is the single most effective doctrine in persuading good people to do evil things. Those who have written most compellingly of hate, among them Aaron Beck, Frank Baumeister, Vamik Volkan and Mark Juergensmeyer, remind us that no one who does evil believes he or she is doing evil.[20] Those who commit mass murder see themselves as defending their people, avenging their humiliation, ridding the world of a pestilence and helping to establish the victory of truth, racial, political or religious. If attempted genocides did not have at least tacit popular support, they could not be committed. Dualism has the power to turn murder into a moral act. This is the logic of *altruistic evil*, and it is always potentially genocidal.

The most powerful antidote to dualism is monotheism, best defined in a verse in Isaiah (45:7): 'I form the light and create darkness, I bring prosperity and create disaster [*ra*, literally 'evil']; I, the Lord, do all these things.' By refusing to split light and dark, good and evil, into separate forces or entities, monotheism forces us to wrestle with the ambiguities of our own character, the necessity for moral choice and the inescapability of personal responsibility. Dualism relieves us of all these burdens. It is the supreme betrayal of monotheism.

Messianic Politics

The third danger is the politics of the end of days. Abrahamic monotheism, I have argued, lives in the cognitive dissonance between the world that is and the world that ought to be. Normally this gap is bridged by daily acts of altruism, the 'redemption of small steps'. This is *exodus politics*, the long, slow journey across the wilderness to redemption an act at a time, a day at a time. But sometimes the gap seems so large that it leads believers to hope for and expect a sudden denouement, a miraculous transformation of history, 'the world turned upside down'. This is the logic of the apocalypse, or *messianic politics*, that appears late in the Hebrew Bible in the book of Daniel, and in the New Testament in the book of Revelation.

One form of messianic politics took the form of the millenarian movements, people like the Ranters, the Hussites and the Levellers, studied by Norman Cohn in *The Pursuit of the Millennium*.[21] Cohn poses the question: Why did these movements arise, and to whom did they speak? Those particularly drawn to 'emotionally charged phantasies of a final, apocalyptic struggle' are, says Cohn, 'the populations of certain technologically backward societies which are not only overpopulated and desperately poor but also are involved in a problematic transition to the modern world, and are correspondingly dislocated and disoriented'.[22] The chief instigators are often 'certain politically marginal elements in technologically advanced societies – chiefly young or unemployed workers and a small minority of intellectuals and students'. The charismatic leaders who set such movements in motion offer their followers:

> Not simply a chance to improve their lot and escape from pressing anxieties – it was also, and above all, the prospect of carrying out a divinely ordained mission of stupendous, unique importance. This phantasy performed a real function for them, both as an escape from their isolated and atomized condition and as an emotional compensation for their abject status; so it quickly came to enthrall them in their turn. And what emerged then was a new group – a restlessly dynamic and utterly ruthless group which, obsessed by the apocalyptic phantasy and filled with the conviction of its own infallibility, set itself infinitely above the rest of humanity and recognized no claims save that of its supposed mission. And finally this group might – though it did not always – succeed in imposing its leadership on the great mass of the disoriented, the perplexed and the frightened.[23]

Ironically, given its religious origins, messianic politics has appeared in the modern world more often in secular guise, in the form of both the French and Russian revolutions. Both aimed at the complete reformation of society, both had moral or redemptive purposes, both were intended as a systematic overthrow of the previous order, and both were expected to initiate a lasting utopia. Both embraced terror. As Michael Walzer puts it, 'If messianism outlives religious faith, it still inhabits the apocalyptic framework that faith established. Hence the readiness of messianic militants to welcome, even to initiate, the terrors that precede the Last Days; and hence the strange politics of the worse, the better; and hence the will to sin, to risk any crime, for the sake of the End.'[24]

Messianic politics leads inevitably to disaster. It cannot do otherwise. For it is the attempt to bring the *end* of time *within* time, redemption to the as-yet-unredeemed human situation, to create utopia in real space and time.

Within Judaism it led to two disastrous rebellions against Rome, the Great Rebellion in 66 CE, and the Bar Kochba Rebellion sixty-six years later. The result of these two confrontations was the destruction of the Second Temple, the razing of Jerusalem and, according to the Roman historian Dio, 580,000 deaths. Prior to the Holocaust it was the greatest human catastrophe in Jewish history, and it led to an exile that lasted almost two thousand years. Thereafter, the efforts of the rabbis were directed to depoliticising Judaism and neutralising as far as possible the messianic idea.

The Lure of Power

The fourth danger is power. Politics and religion do not mix. They are inherently different activities. Religion seeks salvation, politics seeks power. Religion aims at unity, politics lives with diversity. Religion refuses to compromise, politics depends on compromise. Religion aspires to the ideal, politics lives in the real, the less-than-ideal. Religion is about the truths that do not change, politics is about the challenges that constantly change. Harold Wilson said, 'A week is a long time in politics.' The book of Psalms says, 'A thousand years are in your sight as yesterday when it is gone' (Psalm 90:4). When religion becomes political or politics becomes religious, the result is disastrous to religion and politics alike.

At the outset, as I have argued, Abrahamic monotheism involved the secularisation of power. In the pagan world the two were inevitably intertwined. The ruler was both head of state and head of the religion. He was either a demigod, or a child of the gods, or the chief intercessor with the gods. The Hebrew Bible secularised power, first by ascribing all ultimate authority to God. Human power was therefore delegated power, and it had moral limits. The people were entitled to rebel against tyrannical kings, a point that led eventually to both the English and American revolutions.

Second, power itself was divided by separating kingship from priesthood. Third, it was kept in check by the institution of the prophet who was mandated by God to criticise the corruption that power inevitably brings. The first Christians were non-political in a different way. They focused on the kingdom of heaven, not that of Earth. But there came a time when both Judaism and Christianity yielded to temptation. In Judaism the Hasmonean monarchs combined kingship with high priesthood. In Christianity the conversion of Constantine in the fourth century turned a religious sect into an imperial power.

In both religions it took historic calamity to restore the separation. In Judaism this came in the first century when internal factionalism fatally weakened the people in their struggle with Rome. Particularly chilling is the scene Josephus draws of Jerusalem under siege. The Jews were heavily outnumbered. There were 25,000 within the city, facing Titus' well-equipped and disciplined army of 60,000 soldiers. They might have held out, were it not that they too were split: the Zealots under Elazar ben Simon, an extremist faction led by Simon ben Giora, and a third force of Idumeans and others under John of Giscala. Josephus tells us that for much of the time these groups were more intent on attacking one another than the enemy outside the walls. They killed each other's men, destroyed one another's food supplies, and engaged in what Josephus calls 'incessant, suicidal strife'. At one point in his narrative he breaks off to lament, 'Unhappy city! What have you suffered from the Romans to compare with this?'[25]

As we noted above, the failed rebellion against Rome, together with its disastrous sequel, the Bar Kochba Rebellion (132–5 CE), left Jewish life in ruins. The institutions around which Israelite and Jewish life were organised in the days of the Bible had gone. There was now no compact nation, no sovereignty, no collective home. The age of priests, prophets and kings had gone. The Temple and its sacrifices were no more. In their place came a faith built around home, synagogue and school, that could be taken anywhere. Not until the rise of antisemitism throughout Europe towards the end of the nineteenth century were Jews to organise themselves politically again.[26] Yet, despite their dispersion, Jews and Judaism survived. They had made the fateful discovery that a religion can survive without power.

Sixteen centuries later, Christians made the same discovery. In 1517 the young priest Martin Luther nailed his 95 Theses to the door of All Saints Church in Wittenberg, setting in motion one of the great upheavals of European history. The Reformation created far-reaching changes in the political map of Europe, challenging the authority and power of Rome. For more than a century, Europe became a battleground, most savagely in the Thirty Years War, brought to an end by the Treaty of Westphalia in 1648. This was to have large consequences for Western culture.

The seventeenth century was, for Europe, the birth of the modern. It witnessed the rise of science (Bacon, Galileo, Newton), a new mode of philosophy (Descartes) and a new approach to politics (Hobbes, Locke). What they had in common was a search for basic principles that did not rest on religious foundations. Christianity, which had hitherto been spacious enough to encompass the Renaissance, could no longer be relied on, for how could it resolve disputes when it itself was the greatest single source of dispute? As Abraham Lincoln put it later, during the American Civil War, 'Both read the same Bible and pray to the same God, and each invokes His aid against the other.'[27] If two professing Christians, one Protestant, the other Catholic, could not resolve their disagreements without anathemas, excommunications and violence, then religion could not become the basis of a sustainable social order.

The secularisation of Europe happened *not* because people lost faith in God (not until Hegel and Nietzsche in the nineteenth century did anyone use the phrase 'the death of God'), but because people lost faith in the ability of religious believers to live peaceably together. More gradually, but also more extensively, Western Christianity had to learn what Jews had been forced to discover in the first century: how to survive without power.

The similarity of these two processes, so far apart in time, suggests the following hypotheses. First, *no religion relinquishes power voluntarily*. Second, *the combination of religion and power leads to internal factionalism, the splitting of the faith into multiple strands, movements, denominations and sects.* Third, *at some point the adherents of a faith find themselves murdering their own fellow believers*. Fourth, *it is only this that leads the wise to realise that this cannot be the will of God*. The Crusades – Christians against Muslims – did not provoke believers to abandon power, nor did the loss of the First Temple – Jews against Babylonians. It took the spectacle of Jew against Jew, Christian against Christian, to bring about the change. You do not learn to disbelieve in power when you are fighting an enemy, even when you lose. You do when you find yourself using it against the members of your own people, your own broadly defined creed.

Eventually people rediscover the founding insight of Abrahamic monotheism, that truth and power have nothing to do with one another. Truth cannot be proved by power. You cannot force people to be saved. Coerced agreement is not consent, said the rabbis.[28] Render to Caesar what is Caesar's, and to God what is God's, said Jesus (Matthew 22:21). There is no compulsion in religion, says the Koran (2:256).

Power is to be used not to impose truth, but to preserve peace. The religious significance of liberal democracy is precisely that it secularises power. It does not invite citizens to worship the state, nor does it see civic virtue as the only virtue. It recognises that politics is neither a religion nor a substitute for one. Liberal democratic politics *makes space for difference*. It recognises that within a complex society there are many divergent views, traditions and moral systems. It makes no claim to know which is true. All it seeks to do is ensure that those who have differing views are able to live peaceably and graciously together, recognising that none of us has the right to impose our views on others. Democratic politics has no higher aspiration than to allow individuals freedom to pursue the right as they see the right, with this proviso only, that they extend the same right to others, seeking the maximum possible liberty compatible with an equal liberty for all. Democratic politics is a religious achievement because it secularises power.

Single Vision

There is one last danger that applies to religious and secular alike. It was summed up by Isaiah Berlin:

> Few things have done more harm than the belief on the part of individuals or groups (or tribes or states or nations or churches) that he or she or they are in *sole* possession of the truth . . . and that those who differ from them are not merely mistaken, but wicked or mad: & need restraining or suppressing.[29]

The belief that 'there is one and only one true answer to the central questions which have agonised mankind' – which he attributes to Robespierre, Hitler and Stalin as well as the Crusaders – has been responsible for 'oceans of blood'. There is, says Berlin, only one antidote: 'Compromising with people with whom you don't sympathise or altogether understand is indispensable to any decent society.'[30]

Today, this fault is as likely to be found among the new atheists as among religious fundamentalists. They do indeed often take the view that those who differ from them are 'not merely mistaken, but wicked or mad, and need restraining or suppressing'.[31] Their inability to understand that, in Wallace Stevens's phrase, there are thirteen ways of looking at a blackbird, that there is more than one cognitive frame through which we understand and engage with reality, makes them not merely wrong but dangerously so.

The Hebrew Bible is constantly setting before us more than one perspective, never more pronouncedly so than the way it sets before us, at the very beginning, two completely different accounts of creation, one from a cosmological perspective, the other from a human one.

It is not incidental that Homo sapiens has been gifted with a bicameral brain that allows us to experience the world in two fundamentally different ways, as subject and object, 'I' and 'Me', capable of standing both within and outside our subjective experience. In that fact lies our moral and intellectual freedom, our ability to mix emotion and reflection, our capacity for both love and justice, attachment and detachment, in short, our humanity. It is this that the reductivist – the scientist who denies the integrity of spirituality, or the religious individual who denies the findings of science – fails to understand. This is what William Blake meant when he prayed, 'May God us keep, from single vision and Newton's sleep.'

The folly of the new atheists is typified by the remark of Sam Harris that the real danger lies in the religious moderates. They, he says, are the ones to give religion a good name; they are the people who lend credibility to the incredible. Religious moderation distracts us from the one truth of which he is unshakably convinced, namely that 'the very ideal of religious tolerance . . . is one of the principal forces driving us toward the abyss'.[32] The new atheism thus combines dualism (the scientific children of light versus the religious children of darkness), talk of apocalypse ('the abyss') and the belief that its adherents are 'in *sole* possession of the truth', Isaiah Berlin's definition of a fanatic.

The result of the banishment of religious moderates would be the squaring up of two sets of extremists, radical secularists on the one hand, religious radicals on the other, each convinced that their opponents are irredeemable, that there is only one perspective on reality and only one saving truth. The inevitable outcome is a *kulturkampf*, a war of cultures. You need to be completely ignorant of history to believe that any good can come of such a confrontation, when 'the best lack all conviction while the worst are full of passionate intensity'.

We need a strong, vigorous, challenging dialogue between religion and science on the massive problems confronting humanity in the unprecedentedly dangerous twenty-first century.[33] Each needs the other if it is to avoid hubris and intellectual imperialism. Bad things happen when religion ceases to hold itself answerable to empirical reality, when it creates devastation and cruelty on Earth for the sake of salvation in heaven. And bad things happen when science declares itself the last word on the human condition and engages in social or bio-engineering, treating humans as objects rather than as subjects, and substituting cause and effect for reflection, will and choice.

People learn. They realise that time and circumstance can lead them to drift from their founding principles and highest ideals, and they institute movements of *teshuvah*, *metanoia*, return. Jews learned from the bitter experience of factionalism that led to two defeats at the hands of Rome, and focused less on political power and military revolt than on the life of the spirit: on study, prayer and acts of kindness.

It was the Puritans, originally seen as religious zealots, who formulated the ideas and covenants that secured the most distinctively modern form of freedom: liberty of conscience. It was profoundly religious people who, as Alexis de Tocqueville discovered, took pride in the separation of church and state. Religious Christians like William Wilberforce led the fight against slavery. A religious Jew, Lewis Gompertz, created in 1824 the first animal welfare organisation, later known as the Royal Society for the Prevention of Cruelty to Animals. Islam, in Andalusia under the Umayyads, and in India under Akbar the Great, became a pioneer in religious tolerance.

Religions work best when they are open and accountable to the world. When they develop into closed, totalising systems and sectarian modes of community, when they place great weight on the afterlife or divine intervention into history, expecting the end of time in the midst of time, then they can become profoundly dangerous, for there is then nothing to check their descent into fantasy, paranoia and violence.

The answer is not no religion, which is impossible and undesirable since we are meaning-seeking animals, but the critical dialogue between religion and science, the necessary conversation between the twin hemispheres of our bicameral brain that alone can save us from danger and despair.

14

Why God?

Among all my patients in the second half of life . . . there has not been one whose problem in the last resort was not that of finding a religious outlook on life . . . and none of them had really been healed who did not regain his religious outlook.

Carl Jung[1]

If people lose their religion, nothing remains to keep them living in a society. They have no shield for their defence, no basis for their decisions, no foundation for their stability, and no form by which they exist in the world.

Giambattista Vico[2]

Moments of vital fusion between a living religion and a living culture are the creative events in history, in comparison with which all the external achievements in the political and economic orders are transitory and insignificant.

Christopher Dawson[3]

In January 2009 the British Humanist Association paid for an advertisement to be carried on the side of London buses. It read, 'There's probably no God.' It was that advertisement which finally persuaded me to write this book, because it raised the greatest of all existential choices: How shall we live our lives? By probability? Or by possibility? What has transformed humanity has been our capacity to remain open to the unlikely, the improbable. Never has this been more true than in the scientific discoveries of the past century.

Cosmology

Take creation. For more than two thousand years, religious thinkers had to face the challenge of the prevailing view, that of Aristotle, that there was no creation because the universe had no beginning in time. Matter was eternal. Moses Maimonides in the twelfth century says something interesting about this. His immediate response is that, if Aristotle were right, he would simply reinterpret Genesis 1. He has no difficulty in stating that religious faith is compatible with scientific truth, even when it seems to deny an item of faith as fundamental as creation.[4]

But he does not stop there. He says that in his view Aristotle has *not* proved the point. Maimonides was a huge admirer of Aristotle. He drew from his ideas in ethics, psychology and metaphysics. But he was critical enough to insist that just because a thinker is right about most things, he is not necessarily right about all. Maimonides remained unconvinced about the eternity of matter, and his scepticism was justified. In 1964, almost eight centuries after Maimonides wrote *The Guide for the Perplexed*, Arno Penzias and Robert Wilson identified the cosmic microwave background radiation of the universe, the remaining trace of the Big Bang 13.7 billion years ago, that finally proved that the universe did have an origin in time. Regardless of how it happened, there was an act of creation. Improbable but true.

Alongside this came the discovery that the entire physical universe, from the largest galaxies to the smallest particles, is governed by six mathematical constants: the ratio of electromagnetic force to the gravitational force between two electrons; the structural constant that determines how various atoms are formed from hydrogen; the cosmological constant; the cosmic antigravity force; the value that determines how tightly clusters of galaxies are bound together; and the number of spatial dimensions in the universe. Had the value of any of these constants been different by a small, almost infinitesimal degree, there would have been no universe capable of giving rise to life. Matter would have expanded too fast to coalesce into stars, or the universe would have imploded after the initial explosion, and so on. This fine-tuning of the universe for life became known as the 'anthropic principle'. It all seems too precise for it to have happened by mere chance.

This led several scientists, among them Lord Rees and Stephen Hawking, to resolve the problem by predicating an infinite number of parallel universes, each instantiating a different value for the various constants. Our universe is improbable only if it is the only one there is. If there were an infinity of them, at least one would fit the necessary parameters, and it happens to be ours.

This disposes of the improbability of the universe in which we live, but only by postulating another and higher improbability. For we have no reason to suppose that there are parallel universes, and we could never establish whether there were. If we could make contact with a parallel universe then, by definition, it would not be a parallel universe but part of our own, which simply turned out to be larger than we thought it was.

The improbability is multiplied by those scientists who argue that the universe was self-creating: it spun itself into being out of nothing. Again this is eminently possible. It is what the birth of the universe would look like according to the Bible if the words 'Let there be' were edited out – if, as it were, we were watching the event with vision but no sound. But it shows that to explain the existence of a universe that precisely fits the given mathematical parameters without acknowledging the existence of a creator, we are forced to hypothesise the existence of an infinity of self-creating universes for which we have no evidence whatsoever. The rule of logic known as Ockham's Razor – do not multiply unnecessary entities – would seem to favour a single unprovable God over an infinity of unprovable universes. Be that as it may, cosmology has become one of those areas in which the improbable has prevailed over previous conceptions of the probable.

The Argument from Life

So has biology. Among the more than a hundred billion galaxies, each with a hundred billion stars, only one planet thus far known to us, Earth, seems finely tuned for the emergence of life. And by what intermediate stages did non-life become life? There is a monumental gap between inanimate matter and the most primitive life form, bacteria, the simplest of which, mycoplasma, contains 470 genes. How did inert matter become living, self-reproducing life, and within a relatively short space of time? So puzzling was this that Francis Crick, co-discoverer of DNA and a convinced atheist, was forced to conclude that life did not originate on Earth at all. It came to Earth from Mars. Since no trace of life has yet been found on Mars, this too sounds like replacing one improbability with another.

How did life become sentient? And how did sentience grow to become self-consciousness, that strange gift, known only to Homo sapiens, that allows us to ask the question 'Why?' So many improbabilities had to happen that Stephen J. Gould was forced to the conclusion that if the process of evolution were run again from the beginning, it is doubtful whether Homo sapiens would ever have emerged.

You do not have to be religious to have a sense of awe at the sheer improbability of things. James Le Fanu, in *Why Us?*, argues that we are about to undergo a paradigm shift in scientific understanding. The complexities of the genome, the emergence of the first multicellular life forms, the origins of Homo sapiens and our prodigiously enlarged brain: all these and more are too subtle to be accounted for on reductive, materialist, Darwinian science.

Particularly unexpected was the result of the decoding of the human genome. It was anticipated that at least 100,000 genes would be found, allowing us to explain what made humans human, and establishing a one-to-one correlation between specific genes and physical attributes. Improbably, there turned out to be a mere 26,000 – not much more than the blind, millimetre-long roundworm *C. Elegans* that has 19,100.

Still more improbably, 'master' genes that orchestrate the building of complex life forms turn out to be the same across different species. The same genes that cause a fly to be a fly cause a mouse to be a mouse. A single gene, Pax 6, that in a mouse gives rise to a camera-type eye, when inserted into a fly embryo produces the compound eye characteristic of a fly. Far from being 'selfish', genes turn out to be ensemble players capable in mysterious ways of knowing contextually where they are and of what larger entity they are a part. Stephen J. Gould said that the significance of these results 'lies not in the discovery of something previously unknown – but in their explicitly unexpected character'.[5] Improbability again.

Nor are we any nearer an understanding of why the evolution of life as a biological phenomenon should give rise to an organism capable of self-consciousness, of thinking, reflecting, remembering, of asking the question 'Why?' This is perhaps the most improbable phenomenon of all, yet it is also the most consequential. Without that 'thinking and contemplating entity, man', wrote Diderot, the universe would be 'changed into a vast solitude, a phenomenon taking place obscurely, unobserved'.[6] In Homo sapiens, for the first time the universe became self-aware.

Stephen J. Gould and Richard Lewontin have argued that the higher states of consciousness are to human life what a spandrel is to a cathedral: an accidental by-product, a decorative motif. Can we prove otherwise? No. But we can say with some certainty that this is a very odd way of understanding the human condition. Human self-consciousness lies at the heart of all art, metaphysics, poetry; of all science, mathematics and cosmology; of everything that makes humanity different, distinct, unique. The least significant fact about Homo sapiens is that we have evolved to survive. So has everything else that lives. All that lives, said Spinoza, has a *conatus*, a will to live. What makes us different is that we are the meaning-seeking, culture-creating animal. That is constitutive of our humanity. To think of self-consciousness as a spandrel is as tone deaf as to think about a cathedral as a building to keep out the rain. A cathedral is a building constructed *ad majorem Dei gloriam*, 'for the greater glory of God'. Ignore that, and you will not understand what a cathedral is. Why should humanity be different?

Equally unexpected, and a direct consequence of the discovery of DNA, is the finding that virtually all life from the most primitive bacterium to us has a single source, DNA itself. Every living thing shares the same genetic script, what Francis Collins – head of the project to map the human genome – called 'the language of God'. Collins is just one of several distinguished scientists to have arrived at a religious conclusion, having embarked on a scientific journey. We now know the truth of a proposition that, though it proves no theological truth, nonetheless has deeply spiritual resonance, namely that unity begets diversity. The many derive from the One.

Nor does unity end there. Sustained reflection on the Earth's ecology has made us aware that life in all its almost unimaginable diversity is interlinked. Not only is all humanity part of a single fate – John Donne's 'any man's death diminishes me, because I am involved in Mankind'. So too is all of nature. Life is a series of interlinked systems in which each plays a part in the whole, and the loss of a single species may affect many others. Again, the many point to the One.

The sheer improbability of the scientific discoveries of the twentieth and twenty-first centuries is overwhelming. In 1894, Albert A. Michelson, the German-born American physicist, said, 'The more important fundamental laws and facts of physical science have all been discovered, and these are now so firmly established that the possibility of their ever being supplanted in consequence of new discoveries is exceedingly remote.' In 1900, speaking to the British Association for the Advancement of Science, Lord Kelvin said, 'There is nothing new to be discovered in physics now. All that remains is more and more precise measurement.' The long list of failed predictions should tell us to expect the unexpected. We are the unpredictable animal navigating our way through a universe that, from quantum physics to black holes to the Higgs boson, is stranger than any nineteenth-century scientist could have dreamed.

Everything interesting in life, the universe and the whole shebang is improbable, as Nassim Nicholas Taleb reminds us in *The Black Swan*, subtitled 'The Impact of the Highly Improbable'.[7] The book's title is drawn from the fact that people were convinced that, since no one had ever seen a black swan, they did not exist – until someone discovered Australia.

My favourite improbability is the fact that the man who *invented* probability theory, a brilliant young mathematician called Blaise Pascal, decided at the age of thirty to give up mathematics and science and devote the rest of his life to the exploration of religious faith.

None of this is intended as proof of the existence of God. The Bible itself satirises the Egyptian magicians who, unable to reproduce the plague of lice, declare, 'It is the finger of God' (Exodus 8:19). So much for the 'God of the gaps' – invoking God to explain the not-yet-scientifically-explicable. That is the way of the Egyptians, not the faith of Abraham. Science gives us a sense of wonder. It does not disclose the source and origin of that wonder. Maimonides said that science, by disclosing the vastness of the universe and the smallness of humankind, leads to the love and awe of God.[8] He did not say it leads to belief in God.

Contemplation of the natural universe is an intimation, no more and no less, of the presence of a vast intelligence at work in the universe, an intelligence capable of constantly surprising us, showing us that the more we know, the more we know we do not know, yet still beckoning us onwards to a point beyond the visible horizon.

The Argument from History

Thus science. What of history? How probable is it that one man who performed no miracles, uttered no prophecies, had no legion of disciples and wielded no power – Abraham – would become the most influential figure who ever lived, with more than half of the six billion people alive today tracing their spiritual descent from him? How probable is it that a tiny people, the children of Israel, known today as Jews, numbering less than a fifth of a per cent of the population of the world, would outlive every empire that sought its destruction? Or that a small, persecuted sect known as the Christians would one day become the largest movement of any kind in the world?

Nikolai Berdyaev (1874–1948) was a Russian Marxist who broke with the movement after the Russian Revolution and its aftermath. He became an unconventional Christian – he had been charged with blasphemy for criticising the Russian Orthodox Church in 1913 – and went into exile, eventually settling in Paris. In *The Meaning of History*, he tells us why he abandoned Marxism:

> I remember how the materialist interpretation of history, when I attempted in my youth to verify it by applying it to the destinies of peoples, broke down in the case of the Jews, where destiny seemed absolutely inexplicable from the materialistic standpoint ... Its survival is a mysterious and wonderful phenomenon demonstrating that the life of this people is governed by a special predetermination, transcending the processes of adaptation expounded by the materialistic interpretation of history. The survival of the Jews, their resistance to destruction, their endurance under absolutely peculiar conditions and the fateful role played by them in history: all these point to the particular and mysterious foundations of their destiny.[9]

Consider this one fact. The Bible records a series of promises by God to Abraham: that he would become a great nation, as many as the stars of the sky or the sand on the sea shore, culminating in the prophecy that he would become 'the father of many nations'. Yet in Deuteronomy 7:7, Moses makes a statement that seems flatly to contradict this: 'The Lord did not set his affection on you and choose you because you were more numerous than other peoples, for you are the fewest of all peoples.'

There seems no way of reconciling these two statements, none at any rate that could have been true at the time of the canonisation of the Mosaic books. Yet in the twenty-first century we can give precise meaning to these two prophecies. More than half of the six billion people alive today claim descent, literal or metaphorical, from Abraham, among them 2.2 billion Christians and 1.3 billion Muslims. Abraham did become 'the father of many nations'. Yet Jews – those whose faith is defined by the law of Moses – remain, at 13 million, 'the fewest of all peoples'. As the late Milton Himmelfarb once remarked, the total population of world Jewry is the size of the statistical error in the Chinese census.

Somehow the prophets of Israel, a small, vulnerable nation surrounded by large empires, were convinced that it would be eternal. 'This is what the Lord says, he who appoints the sun to shine by day, who decrees the moon and stars to shine by night . . . "Only if these decrees vanish from my sight," declares the Lord, "will Israel ever cease being a nation before me"' (Jeremiah 31:35–6). They were certain that their message of monotheism would eventually transform the imagination of humankind. There was nothing to justify that certainty then, still less after a thousand years of persecution, pogroms and the Final Solution. Yet improbably, Jews and Judaism survived.

King Frederick the Great once asked his physician, Zimmermann of Brugg-in-Aargau, 'Zimmermann, can you name me a single proof of the existence of God?'

The physician replied, 'Your majesty, the Jews.'

The Argument from Entropy

Consider the pattern of civilisation itself. One of the first historians to give a cyclical account of history, Giambattista Vico, argued that all civilisations were subject to a law of rise and decline. They are born in austerity. They rise to affluence and power. Then they become decadent and eventually decline. 'People first sense what is necessary, then consider what is useful, next attend to comfort, later delight in pleasures, soon grow dissolute in luxury, and finally go mad squandering their estates.' The only antidote to this, he argued, was religion, which motivates people to virtue and concern for the common good. Providence 'renews the piety, faith and truth which are both the natural foundations of justice, and the grace and beauty of God's eternal order'.[10]

It is an argument that has been repeated in our time by figures like Vaclav Havel and Jürgen Habermas. Havel, protesting the materialist conception of human life, argues that such a view leads inevitably to 'the gradual erosion of all moral standards, the breakdown of all criteria of decency, and the widespread destruction of confidence in the meaning of any such values as truth, adherence to principles, sincerity, altruism, dignity and honour'. He adds, 'If democracy is not only to survive but to expand successfully . . . it must rediscover and renew its own transcendental origins. It must renew its respect for the non-material order that is not only above us but also in us and among us.'[11]

Habermas, like Havel a secular intellectual, has nonetheless spoken of how 'enlightened reason' reaches a crisis when it discovers it no longer has sufficient strength 'to awaken, and to keep awake, in the minds of secular subjects, an awareness of the violations of solidarity throughout the world, an awareness of what is missing, of what cries out to heaven'. His conclusion is that 'Among modern societies, only those that are able to introduce into the secular domain the essential contents of their religious traditions which point beyond the merely human role will also be able to rescue the substance of the human.'[12]

There have been many superpowers: Spain in the fifteenth century, Venice in the sixteenth, Holland in the seventeenth, France in the eighteenth, Britain in the nineteenth, the United States in the twentieth. Yet Judaism has existed in some form for the better part of four thousand years, Christianity for two thousand, and Islam for fourteen centuries. Religions survive. Superpowers do not. Spiritual systems have the capacity to defeat the law of entropy that governs the life of nations.

We can trace this process in the present. Harvard sociologist Robert Putnam became famous in the late 1990s for a phrase he coined to describe the loss of social capital – networks of reciprocity and trust – in the liberal democracies of the West. He called it 'bowling alone'. More people were going ten-pin bowling, but fewer were joining teams and leagues. This was his symbol of the West's increasingly individualistic, atomistic, self-preoccupied culture. Things people once did together, we were now doing alone. Our bonds of belonging were growing thin.

In 2010, in his book *American Grace*, Putnam set out the good news that a powerful store of social capital still exists. It is called religion: the churches, synagogues and other places of worship that still bring people together in shared belonging and mutual responsibility.

An extensive survey carried out throughout the United States between 2004 and 2006 showed that frequent church- or synagogue-goers are more likely to give money to charity, regardless of whether the charity is religious or secular. They are also more likely to do voluntary work for a charity, give money to a homeless person, give excess change back to a shop assistant, donate blood, help a neighbour with housework, spend time with someone who is feeling depressed, allow another driver to cut in front of them, offer a seat to a stranger, or help someone find a job. Religious Americans are simply more likely than their secular counterparts to give of their time and money to others, not only within but also beyond their own communities.

Their altruism goes further. Frequent worshippers are also significantly more active citizens. They are more likely to belong to community organisations. Within these organisations they are more likely to be officers or committee members. They take a more active part in local civic and political life, from local elections to town meetings to demonstrations. They are disproportionately represented among local activists for social and political reform. They get involved, turn up and lead. The margin of difference between them and the more secular is large.

Tested on attitudes, religiosity as measured by church or synagogue attendance turns out to be the best predictor of altruism and empathy: better than education, age, income, gender or race. Religion creates community, community creates altruism, and altruism turns us away from self and towards the common good. Putnam goes so far as to speculate that an atheist who went regularly to church (perhaps because of a spouse) would be more likely to volunteer in a soup kitchen than a believer who prays alone. There is something about the tenor of relationships within a religious community that makes it an ongoing tutorial in citizenship and good neighbourliness.[13]

This is path-breaking research by one of the world's greatest sociologists, and it confirms what most members of religious congregations know, that they give rise to networks of support often breathtaking in their strength and moral beauty: visiting the sick, comforting the bereaved, helping individuals through personal crisis, supporting those in financial need, assisting people who have lost their jobs, caring for the elderly, and proving daily that troubles are halved and joys doubled when they are shared with others. Even today, religion still has the improbable power to renew the habits of the heart that drive civil society, defeating entropy and civilisational decline.

The Argument from Happiness

Thus far probability. But there was a second sentence adorning London buses courtesy of the British Humanist Association. In full the advertisement read, 'There's probably no God. Now stop worrying and enjoy your life.'

I am perplexed by this non sequitur. To me, faith is about, in the Bible's phrase, 'rejoicing in all the good the Lord your God has given you' (Deuteronomy 26:11). It is about celebration, gratitude, praise, thanksgiving and what Wordsworth and C. S. Lewis called being 'surprised by joy'. For many people, religion is an essential part of the pursuit of happiness. A host of surveys show that people who have religious faith and regularly attend religious services report higher life satisfaction and live longer than those who do not.[14]

For two generations, while Europe has secularised, it has witnessed the rise, especially among the young, of depressive illness, stress-related syndromes, drug and alcohol abuse, violent crime and attempted suicide. Stable families have been replaced by an almost open-ended range of variants, leaving in their wake troubled and disadvantaged children. Fewer people find themselves surrounded by the networks of support once provided by local communities. Robert Bellah and his co-authors, in *Habits of the Heart*, diagnosed the multiple ways in which our social ecology is being damaged 'by the destruction of the subtle ties that bind human beings to one another, leaving them frightened and alone'.[15]

The current preoccupation with happiness – a massive spate of books in recent years – testifies to a genuine questioning of whether we may not have taken a wrong turning in the unbridled pursuit of economic gain. The consumer society, directed at making us happy, achieves the opposite. It encourages us to spend money we do not have, to buy things we do not need, for the sake of a happiness that will not last. By constantly directing our attention to what we do *not* have, instead of making us thankful for what we do have, it becomes a highly efficient system for the production and distribution of unhappiness.

What do we know about happiness? There are basic preconditions: food, clothing, shelter, health, what Abraham Maslow called the physiological and safety needs.[16] Similarly, Moses Maimonides said that perfection of the body takes chronological precedence over perfection of the soul. It is impossible to focus on the higher reaches of spirituality if you are cold, hungry, homeless and sick. One of the things I respect about Judaism is its refusal to romanticise poverty.

But beyond a basic minimum, the relationship between income and happiness is slight. Research bears out Maslow's analysis that the higher needs are love and belonging, esteem and self-actualisation. The most significant determinants of happiness are strong and rewarding personal relationships, a sense of belonging to a community, being valued by others and living a meaningful life. These are precisely the things in which religion specialises: sanctifying marriage, etching family life with the charisma of holiness, creating and sustaining strong communities in which people are valued for what they are, not for what they earn or own, and providing a framework within which our lives take on meaning, purpose, even blessedness. Even Karl Marx admitted that religion was 'the heart of a heartless world, and the soul of soulless conditions'.

Two British authors, Richard Wilkinson and Kate Pickett, have argued recently that societies that are more equal tend to have higher reported life satisfaction.[17] Religious faith does not of itself create economic equality. But it does tell us that we are all equal in the sight of God. Each of us counts. A house of worship is one of the few places nowadays where rich and poor, young and old, meet on equal terms, where they are valued not for what they earn, but for what they are.

It makes a difference to happiness to know that we are at home in the universe, that we are here because someone wanted us to be, and that something of us will live on. The practices of religion – prayer as an expression of gratitude, ritual as enactment of meaning, sacred narrative as a way of understanding the world and our place within it, rites of passage that locate our journey as a shared experience connecting us to past and future generations, deeds of reciprocal kindness that bind us to a group in bonds of faith, loyalty and trust – create structures of meaning and relationship within which our individuality can flourish. This is where, for many of us, happiness is to be found.

'There's probably no God. Now stop worrying and enjoy your life' is one of the less profound propositions to have been produced by the collective intelligence of people who pride themselves on their intelligence. It is at least as true as saying, 'Exams don't matter, work is a waste of time, love does not last, commitment only leads to disappointment. Now stop worrying and enjoy your life.' Nothing worth striving for is easy, and nothing *not* worth striving for brings happiness. Pleasure, maybe; fun, perhaps; but happiness in any meaningful sense, no. If I wanted to stop worrying, I would not choose a world blind to my existence, indifferent to my fate, with no solace in this life or any other. Nor would I put my trust in those who ridiculed my deepest commitments.

The Greatest Improbability of All

Writing in 1832, the young Frenchman Alexis de Tocqueville made a mordant comment. 'Eighteenth century philosophers', he wrote, 'had a very simple explanation for the gradual weakening of beliefs. Religious zeal, they said, was bound to die down as enlightenment and freedom spread. It is tiresome that the facts do not fit this theory at all.'[18] Tocqueville was writing in the 1830s, in the full shock of his discovery that America – the very country that established the principle of separation of church and state – remained a deeply religious society. It still is. Today more Americans go weekly to a place of worship than do the people of Iran, a theocracy.[19]

The survival of religion is the greatest improbability of all. The world has changed beyond recognition since the Middle Ages. Religion has lost many of the functions it once had. To explain the world, we have science. To control it, we have technology. To negotiate power, we have democratic politics. To achieve prosperity, we have a market economy. If we are ill, we go to a doctor, not a priest. If we feel guilty, we can go to a psychotherapist; we have no need of a confessor. If we are depressed, we can take Prozac;

we do not need the book of Psalms. Schools and welfare services are provided by the state, not by the church. And if we seek salvation, we can visit the new cathedrals – the shopping malls – at which the consumer society pays homage to its gods.

Faith would seem to be redundant in the contemporary world. And yet far from disappearing, it is alive and well and flourishing, in every part of the world except Europe. In America there are mega-churches with congregations in the tens of thousands. In China today there are more practising Christians than members of the Communist Party and almost as many Muslims as there are in Saudi Arabia. In Russia, where religion was exiled for seventy years, a poll in 2006 showed that 84 per cent of the population believed in God.[20] And, as the editor of *The Economist* writes, whereas in the past religion was often associated with poverty, today 'the growth in faith has coincided with a growth in prosperity'.[21]

Why is this so? Because religion does what none of the great institutions of contemporary society does: not politics, not economics, not science and not technology. It answers the three great questions that any reflective human being will ask: Who am I? (the question of identity), Why am I here? (the question of purpose), and, How then shall I live? (the question of ethics and meaning).

Today's atheists – the neo-Darwinians, sociobiologists and evolutionary psychologists – all too often engage in a sustained act of self-contradiction. For them, what works is what survives: genes biologically, and 'memes' culturally. But manifestly, religion survives. Faith lives on. The religious in most countries have more children than the non-religious.[22] They are better at handing on their genes and memes to the next generation. Meanwhile, after three centuries of sometimes aggressive secularism, we have moved into what Jürgen Habermas calls a 'post-secular age'. Yet in defiance of all the evidence *on their own terms*, the new atheists argue that religion is an epiphenomenon, an accidental by-product of something else: once functional, now dysfunctional. If this were so, it would have disappeared long ago. Its survival is the supreme improbability.

The Defeat of Probability by the Power of Possibility

So if probability were the measure, there would be no universe, no life, no sentience, no self-consciousness, no humanity, no art, no questions, no poetry, no Rembrandt, no sense of humour, no sanctity of life, no love. How probable is it that the most primitive bacterium would one day evolve into a humanity capable of decoding the genome itself? Or that small religious groups would outlive great empires, that one day people would hold these truths self-evident that all men are created equal and are endowed by their Creator with certain unalienable rights, that slavery would be abolished, tyrannies would fall and apartheid would end?

Faith is the defeat of probability by the power of possibility. The prophets dreamed the improbable and by doing so helped bring it about. All the great human achievements, in art and science as well as the life of the spirit, came through people who ignored the probable and had faith in the possible.

How did this happen? It happened in the West because Abraham and his descendants believed in a God who stood outside the entire natural order, the domain of cause and effect and of probability itself. They believed in a God who defined himself in the phrase 'I will be what I will be', meaning, 'I will be what, where and how I choose' – hence, the God who defies predictability and probability. By setting his image on humanity, he gave us too the power to defy probability, to stand outside the taken-for-granted certainties of the age and live by another light. That belief gave the West its faith in the great duality charted by science and religion, the orderliness of the universe on the one hand, the freedom of humanity on the other.

'Once you eliminate the impossible,' said Sherlock Holmes, 'whatever remains, no matter how improbable, must be the truth.' That is the left-brain way of putting the argument. The sheer cumulative weight of the evidence from cosmology, biology, history, the decline and fall of civilisations, the failure of secular revolutions, the forces making for altruism in an age of individualism, even the pursuit of happiness itself – all these point towards the presence of a vast intelligence at work in the universe that has revealed itself directly or obliquely to our ancestors and through them to us. Despite E. O. Wilson's noble effort at 'consilience', a scientific theory-of-everything, there is no hypothesis remotely as simple, elegant and all-encompassing as the idea that an intelligent Creator endowed creation with creativity. For those who seek proof, this is as close as we can come, given our present state of knowledge of the universe and ourselves.

Speaking personally, however, as I have argued throughout, I believe that the demand for proof is misconceived. It came from the strange combination of events in the first century when two very different cultures, ancient Greece and ancient Israel, came together in the form of a synthesis that eventually encouraged people to believe that science and religion, explanation and interpretation, impersonal and personal knowledge, were the same sort of thing, part of the same world of thought. I have argued otherwise, that it is precisely because they are *not* the same sort of thing that the counterpoint between them gave and still gives human life its depth and pathos. We can no more dispense with either than we can with one of the two hemispheres of the brain.

If so, then the improbabilities that have accumulated are not proof of the existence of God but a series of intimations. Science does not lead to religious conclusions; religion does not lead to scientific conclusions. Science is about explanation. Religion is about interpretation. Science takes things apart to see how they work. Religion puts things together to see what they mean. They are different intellectual enterprises that engage different hemispheres of the brain. Science – linear, atomistic, analytical – is a typical left-brain activity. Religion – integrative, holistic, relational – is supremely a work of the right brain. This is meant only as a metaphor, but it is a powerful one.

The mutual hostility between religion and science is one of the curses of our age, and it is damaging to religion and science in equal measure. The Bible is not proto-science, pseudo-science or myth masquerading as science. It is interested in other questions entirely. Who are we? Why are we here? How then shall we live? It is to answer those questions, not scientific ones, that we seek to know the mind of God. But there is more to wisdom than science. It cannot tell us why we are here or how we should live. Science masquerading as religion is as unseemly as religion masquerading as science.

At their best, science and religion are both instances of the human passion to decode mysteries, constantly travelling in search of a destination that continues to elude us, that is always over the furthermost horizon. It is that willingness to search, ask, question, that makes us what we are. Wallace Stevens, in his poem *Thirteen Ways of Looking at a Blackbird*, wrote:

> I do not know which to prefer,
> The beauty of inflections
> Or the beauty of innuendoes,
> The blackbird whistling
> Or just after.

After the inflections, the innuendos remain, the hints, the intimations, Elijah's 'still small voice', Paul's 'through a glass darkly', Wordsworth's 'sense of something far more deeply interfused'. When all the scientific explanations are in, the great questions still remain.

Faith Is the Courage to Take a Risk

Somewhere just beyond the edge of the universe, at the far side of the knowable, there either is or is not the Presence who brought it, and life, and you, into being. You have to make a choice and it will affect the whole of your life.

You may say, I refuse to believe what I cannot test, what I cannot subject even in principle to some kind of proof. So be it. But the big decisions in life – as I learned from Bernard Williams and the Gauguin dilemma – are like that. You can never know in advance the facts that would make your decision the right one under the circumstances. That applies to the decision to marry, to have a child, to start a business, to undertake a research project, to write a symphony, to paint a picture. There is no creation without risk. What impresses me about the Bible is that it suggests that, *even for God*, creating humanity was a risk, and one that at least once he regretted having taken.

The same is true about the basic attitudes we take towards life. How can I know in advance, beyond doubt, whether it is right to trust people, to befriend them, to love, to forgive those who have harmed me, to grant those who have failed me a second chance, to act honourably, to resist temptation, to refrain from doing wrong even when I am sure I will not be found out, to make sacrifices for the sake of others, and to refuse to become cynical even when I know the worst about the world and the people in it? There is no 'rational choice', no decision procedure, to take the uncertainty out of such choices – not least because they affect not only what happens but also the kind of person I become.

To be human is to live in a world fraught with risk. We face a future that is unknowable, not just unknown. Faith is a risk and there is no way of minimising that risk, of playing it safe. Hamlet's soliloquy – 'For in that sleep of death what dreams may come?' – tells us that there is no death, let alone life, without risk. Those who are unprepared to take a risk are unprepared to live fully.

Faith is the courage to take a risk.

And what if I am wrong? I would rather have lived believing the best about humanity and the universe than believing the worst. It is perfectly possible and coherent to believe that there is no creative intelligence at work in the universe, or if there is, it is blind; that life is vicious, cruel and unjust; that *homo homini lupus est*,

'man is wolf to man'; that pessimism protects us from being disap-
pointed and cynicism is our best defence against being betrayed.

There is nothing irrational about believing that life has no
meaning, that we can make no significant difference to the world,
that life is short and death is long, so let us pursue what pleasures
we can while hardening ourselves against what malice and misfortune may bring; living, in short, as did the Hedonists, Epicureans
and Stoics of Greece of the third pre-Christian century. But these
are tired philosophies of life, to be found in civilisations nearing
their natural end.

There are, to be sure, secular humanists who live deeply altruistic lives, fighting injustice or poverty or disease, pursuing truth
or goodness or beauty for their own sake, without any super- or
infrastructure of belief about the larger metaphysics of existence. I – and I hope all religious believers – feel enlarged, indeed
blessed, by such people. To believe that religion holds a monopoly
of virtue is as narrow-minded as to believe that science holds a
monopoly of truth.

However, this does not mean that religious faith makes no
difference to the kind of people we become. Dozens of research
exercises have shown that students grow or shrink to fit the
expectations their parents and teachers have of them. When their
teacher believes they are capable of greatness and communicates
that in the classroom, students perform above the norm. When
they are written off as failures, they fail, or at least do worse than
they might have done otherwise.

Monotheism expects great things from us, and by doing so
makes us great. It calls us the image of God, the children of God,
God's covenantal partners. It challenges us to become co-builders
with God of a gracious society and a more just world. It tells us
that each of us is unique, irreplaceable, precious in God's sight.
We are not just the phenotype of a genotype, a member of a
species, to a biologist a specimen, to a government a source of
income, to an employer a cost, to an advertiser a consumer, and
to a politician a vote.

I see people transformed by this belief, spending their lives in gratitude to God for the gift of being alive and seeking to repay that debt by giving to others. I see them holding marriage sacred; I see them taking parenthood seriously as God told Abraham to take it seriously. I see them form communities on the basis of *chesed*, loving kindness. I see the power of faith to generate moral energies in a way nothing else does.

And when I see people grow taller under the sunlight of divine love than they might have done under a godless sky, then – like the searcher in Jorge Luis Borges' 'Approach to Al-Mutasim' – I find the traces that lead eventually to his presence: in people who do not act the way Marx, Darwin, Freud or their disciples taught us to expect. They are the flecks of gold amidst the dust. They are the signals of transcendence.

I cannot see that value attributed to the human person in any of the secular ideologies conjectured, let alone put into practice. How could there be? Biologically, as the neo-Darwinians remind us, we share 98 per cent of our genes with the primates and quite a lot of them with fruit flies. In any case, science deals with universal propositions, not with what James Joyce called epiphanies of the ordinary. The scientific method must screen out the uniqueness of the unique, the very thing poetry and art render radiant.

Homo sapiens, discovering God singular and alone, discovered the human being singular and alone. There is no greater dignity than that – we saw it in Pico Della Mirandola's *Oration*, the high point of the Renaissance view of man. Monotheism summons us, all of us, not an elite, to greatness.

I Believe

This, then, is my credo. I believe that the idea that the universe was created in love by the God of love who asks us to create in love is the noblest hypothesis ever to have lifted the human mind.

We are the meaning-seeking animal, the only known life form in the universe ever to have asked the question 'Why?' There is no single, demonstrable, irrefutable, self-evident, compelling and universal answer to this question. Yet the principled refusal to answer it, to insist that the universe simply happened and there is nothing more to say, is a failure of the very inquisitiveness, the restless search for that which lies beyond the visible horizon, that led to science in the first place.

The meaning of a system lies outside the system. Therefore the meaning of the universe lies outside the universe. That is why Abrahamic monotheism, belief in a God who transcends the physical universe and who brought it into being as an act of free creativity, was the first and remains the only hypothesis to endow life with meaning. Without that belief there is no meaning, there are merely individual choices, fictions embraced as fates. Without meaning there is no distinctively human life, there is merely the struggle to survive, together with the various contrivances human beings have invented to cover their boredom or their despair.

Without belief in a transcendent God – the God of freedom who acts because he chooses – it is ultimately impossible to sustain the idea that we are free, that we have choice, that we are made by our decisions, that we are morally responsible agents. Science leaves no space for human freedom, and when freedom ceases to exist as an idea, eventually it ceases to exist as a reality also. Those civilisations built on the abandonment of God and the worship of science – the French Revolution, the Soviet Union, the Third Reich and Chinese Communism – stand as eternal warnings of what happens when we turn a means into an end. Science as humility in search of truth is one thing. Science as sole reality is another. It can then become the most pitiless and ruthless of gods.

Without freedom, there is no human dignity: there is merely the person as thing, a biological organism continuous with all other organisms. The discovery of human dignity is perhaps the single most transformative idea given to the world by Abrahamic monotheism. That faith was the first to teach that every human being regardless of colour, culture or creed is in the image and likeness of God, the first to teach the sanctity of human life and the dignity of the human person, and to show how these ideals might be honoured and made real in the structures we build for our common life.

The God of Abraham is the God of surprises, the supreme power who intervened in history to liberate the powerless and set them on the long journey to freedom. He taught us the paradoxical truth that nations survive not by wealth but by the help they give to the poor, not by power but by the care they extend to the weak. Civilisations become invulnerable only when they care for the vulnerable.

Belief in God has historically been the only way to establish the moral limits of power. Belief in the sovereignty of God is infinitely preferable to belief in the sovereignty of humankind. Human beings worship. Sometimes they worship wealth, at other times power. Sometimes, as today, they worship the self. There are people who worship science itself. All these things are parts of life, not its totality, and any worship of the part rather than the whole has led in the past to disaster. Monotheism teaches us the single compelling truth that nothing is worthy of worship that is less than everything, the Author-of-all.

Abrahamic monotheism speaks on behalf of the poor, the weak, the enslaved. It tells a story about the power of human freedom, lifted by its encounter with the ultimate source of freedom, to create structures of human dignity. It bodies forth a vision of a more gracious world. It tells us that no one is written off, no one condemned to be a failure. It tells the rich and powerful that they have responsibilities to those who lack all that makes life bearable. It invites us to be part of a gentle revolution, telling us that influence is greater than power, that we must protect the most vulnerable in society, that we must be willing to make sacrifices to that end and, most daringly of all, that love is stronger than death. It sets love at the epicentre of the world: love of God, love of the neighbour, love of the stranger. If natural selection tells us anything, it is that this faith, having existed for longer than any other, creates in its followers an astonishing ability to survive.

Civilisations have come and gone: Mesopotamia, the Egypt of the pharaohs, Assyria, Babylon, Persia, the empire of Alexander the Great, and of the Caesars and Rome. In the modern world nation after nation rose to eminence: Venice, the Netherlands, France, Germany, Britain. They bestrode the narrow world like a colossus, then they faded, weary and spent. The faith of Abraham, some four thousand years old, continues to flourish, whether as Judaism, Christianity or Islam, looking as young as it ever did, having defied the predictions of centuries of intellectuals who pronounced its imminent demise.

Religion and science, the heritages respectively of Jerusalem and Athens, products of the twin hemispheres of the human brain, must now join together to protect the world that has been entrusted to our safekeeping, honouring our covenant with nature and nature's God – the God who is the music beneath the noise; the Being at the heart of being, whose still small voice we can still hear if we learn to create a silence in the soul; the God who, whether or not we have faith in him, never loses faith in us.

Epilogue: Letter to a Scientific Atheist

Dear Professor,

If you have followed me thus far, you will know I see science as one of the two greatest achievements of the human mind. Its achievements in the past century have been frankly astonishing, revealing a universe on the macro- and micro-scale almost beyond comprehension in its intricacy, detail, variety and complexity, from the universe of a hundred billion galaxies each with a hundred billion stars, to the human body, containing a hundred trillion cells, each with a double copy of the human genome with 3.1 billion letters, each enough, if transcribed, to fill a sizeable library of five thousand books.

How right Newton was when he said, 'I do not know what I may appear to the world, but to myself I seem to have been only like a boy playing on the sea-shore, and diverting myself in now and then finding a smoother pebble or a prettier shell than ordinary, whilst the great ocean of truth lay all undiscovered before me.'[1] We have seen a little more of the ocean since then, and we have only the dimmest intuition of what we might still discover as Newton's heirs voyage yet further across strange seas of thought.

Science fulfils three functions that I see as central to the Abrahamic faith. It diminishes human ignorance. It increases human power. And it exemplifies the fact that we are in God's image. God wants us to know and understand. He wants us to exercise responsible freedom. And he wants us to use the intellectual gifts he gave us. These are not reasons why scientists should become religious. They are reasons why religious people should respect scientists.

Yet with knowledge comes power, and with power, responsibility; and we know enough from history to be reasonably sure that responsibility is best exercised when diffused, when thoughtful minds from different disciplines and perspectives engage in respectful conversation as to how best to navigate our way as we travel to that one remaining undiscovered country called the future, unknown because unknowable, unknowable because we who make it are free.

My aim in writing this book has not been to convince you. As a Jew I do not believe we are called on to convert anyone. Besides which I come from a religious tradition whose canonical texts are all anthologies of arguments, and which coined the phrase 'arguments for the sake of heaven'. I recall the public conversation I had with the secular Israeli novelist Amos Oz, who began by saying, 'I'm not sure I'm going to agree with Rabbi Sacks about everything – but then, on most things I don't agree with myself.' (The other typically Jewish remark I cherish is Sidney Morganbesser's. In reply to the theological question, 'Why is there something rather than nothing?' he said, 'And if there were nothing, you'd also complain!')

I have tried simply to show you that religious faith is not absurd, that it does not involve suspension of our critical faculties, that it does not and should not seek to inhibit the free pursuit of science, that it does not rest on contradiction and paradox, that it does not force us to accept suffering as God's will for the world, and that it does not ask us to believe six impossible things before breakfast. It involves a mode of engagement with the world significantly different from that of science, but not incompatible with it. Least of all does it presume to tell scientists when they are right and when they are wrong. That is a scientific enterprise to be performed by scientific methodologies.

I do not regard atheism as an untenable stance towards the world. I have known some of the great atheists of our time, admired them deeply, and – as I hope I have shown in one or two places in this book – learned much from them, not least about religion itself. We disagreed, but I would not wish to live in a world in which people did not disagree. Disagreement is how knowledge grows. Living with disagreement is how we grow.

Yet I am troubled by the rancour that has entered the debate in recent years. We seem to have moved into an era of extreme and angry voices, of vituperative atheists and militant religious extremists, of people who deny the world of the spirit and those who challenge our very freedom, a clash of fundamentalisms that share a refusal to listen openly and intelligently to voices opposed to their own. If carried further, the result will be a world in which, to take Matthew Arnold's words from 'Dover Beach', there is

> neither joy, nor love, nor light,
> Nor certitude, nor peace, nor help for pain;
> And we are here as on a darkling plain
> Swept with confused alarms of struggle and flight,
> Where ignorant armies clash by night.

We can do better than that, even if there are fundamentals on which we disagree.

We are at the end of one chapter of history and are beginning to write the next with no idea of what kind of chapter it will be. We know this, that the end of the Cold War did not bring about the global spread of liberal democracy, the conquest of tyranny in the name of human rights, a greater equality within and between societies, or greater tolerance between conflicting views of the world.

The new communications technologies are changing almost everything we knew and not so long ago took for granted: the nation state, the idea of national cultures, the nature of politics and economics, the character of war and the fragility of peace, the structure of human groups, even, possibly, the architecture of the human brain. We suffer from information overload and attention deficit. The Internet makes it hard for us to distinguish between truth and rumour and is the most effective disseminator of paranoia and hatred yet invented.

The challenges humanity faces in the twenty-first century are legion: climate change, the destruction of biodiversity, the

responsible use of bio- and nano-technology, the extreme vulnerability of the international economy, and the power of spectacular acts of terror to achieve that most sought-after commodity
in an information-saturated age: the attention of the eyes of the
world. At almost every point, seemingly, we have moved from
stable equilibrium to those complex conditions charted by chaos
theory, where the beating of a butterfly's wing can set in motion
a tsunami.

We are in a desecularising and destabilising age. That brings
fear, and few things are worse than the politics of fear. It creates
a sense of victimhood and a willingness to demonise those with
and from whom we differ. One of its symptoms is the new secularism, so much angrier and intolerant than the old. Another is
the new religiosity that claims to be, but is not, a continuation of
the old. The best thing to do in such circumstances is for moderates of all sides to seek and find common ground.

In an age of fear, moderation is hard to find and harder to
sustain. Who wants to listen to a nuanced argument, when what
we want is someone to relieve us from the burden of thought
and convince us that we were right all along? So people mock.
They blame. They caricature. They demonise. In an age of anxiety, few can hear the still small voice that the Bible tells us is the
voice of God.

Hence Sam Harris's argument, mentioned in chapter 13,
that the real villains are the religious moderates. Get rid of the
moderates, the argument goes, and we can have a fair fight: scientific atheists versus religious Neanderthals. If Sam Harris knew
history, he would know the result of all such encounters. The
barbarians win. They always do.

You do not have to be an atheist to fear the new religiosity. I am
a believer, and I too fear it. I fear angry people who invoke God
and religion to justify their anger at a world that fails to meet
their expectations. I fear religion when it leads believers to brand
as heretics anyone whose understanding transcends theirs; when
it becomes adversarial, turning its followers against the world

instead of trying to mend the world; when it becomes involved
in partisan politics, dividing where it ought to unite; and when it
leads to tyrannical or totalitarian societies where barbaric punishments are exacted and human rights denied.

There is a difference between righteousness and self-righteous-
ness. The righteous are humble, the self-righteous are proud. The
righteous understand doubt, the self-righteous only certainty.
The righteous see the good in people, the self-righteous only the
bad. The righteous leave you feeling enlarged, the self-righteous
make you feel small. It is easy enough to befriend the former and
avoid the latter.

We need moderates, that is, people who understand that there
can be a clash of right and right, not just right and wrong. We
need people capable of understanding cognitive pluralism, that
is, that there is more than one way of looking at the world. We
need people who can listen to views not their own without feeling
threatened. We need people with humility.

That is why I ask for your understanding. E. O. Wilson wrote
his lovely little book about nature conservation, *The Creation*,
as a series of open letters to a Southern Baptist pastor. He
explains why:

> Because religion and science are the two most powerful forces in
> the world today, including especially the United States. If religion
> and science could be united on the common ground of biological
> conservation, the problem would soon be solved.[2]

Speaking personally, I do not think any real problems are soon
solved. The way is always long and hard. But the only way is together.
Religion and science, believer and sceptic, agnostic and atheist. For,
whatever our view of God, our humanity is at stake, and our future,
and how that will affect our grandchildren not yet born.

Religion and science share much, but in particular they share
faith. This sounds odd. After all, Richard Dawkins is on record
as saying:

I think a case can be made that faith, the principled vice of any religion, is one of the world's great evils, comparable to the smallpox virus but harder to eradicate. Faith is a great cop out.[3]

But that cannot be the full story. Listen to Max Planck, the Nobel Prize–winning physicist and founder of quantum theory:

Anybody who has been seriously engaged in scientific work of any kind realises that over the entrance to the gates of the Temple of science are written the words: *Ye must have faith*. It is a quality which the scientist cannot dispense with.[4]

Next, Einstein:

But science can only be created by those who are thoroughly imbued with the aspiration toward truth and understanding. This source of feeling, however, springs from the sphere of religion. To this there also belongs the faith in the possibility that the regulations valid for the world of existence are rational, that is, comprehensible to reason. I cannot conceive of a genuine scientist without that profound faith. The situation may be expressed by an image: science without religion is lame, religion without science is blind.[5]

Finally this by Friedrich Nietzsche:

It is still a metaphysical faith upon which our faith in science rests – that even we seekers after knowledge today, we godless anti-metaphysicians, still take our fire, too, from the flame lit by a faith that is thousands of years old, that Christian faith which was also the faith of Plato, that God is the truth, that truth is divine.[6]

Clearly Dawkins means something different by 'faith' than do the others. He thinks of faith as a refusal to ask questions. But faith as Planck, Einstein and Nietzsche understood it is the opposite: the courage and principled determination to go on asking questions despite the fact that there is no easy or immediate answer.

Faith has driven the scientific and religious imaginations along their different paths, but with the same basic refusal to rest content with what we know – with the same non-rational but not irrational willingness to travel to an unknown destination beyond the visible horizon, to attempt dimly to discern an order beneath the seeming chaos, to hear the music beneath the noise.

It is that courage to begin a journey not knowing where it will lead but confident that it will lead somewhere, that there really is a destination, an order, a faint but genuine melody, that is the faith not only of the scientist but of Abraham himself who heard a voice telling him to leave his land, his birthplace and his father's house, and did so, confident that the voice was not an illusion and the destination not a no-man's-land.

That restless faith, that sacred discontent, that principled iconoclasm, has driven the West to achieve what it has achieved. It is not a cultural universal. Many cultures, having achieved order, have not sought to move ever forwards. The truth is that most religious expressions in the history of humanity have been intensely conservative – here we stand and here we stay. God or the gods have been seen as endorsing the inevitability of the status quo.

The God of Abraham, the voice of the world-that-is-not-yet-but-ought-to-be, the God whose name ('I will be what I will be') *means* the unknowability of the future in a world constituted by freedom, is what scientists call a singularity, a one-off, a unique and world-changing event. And we, whether we are religious or not, are in some sense his heirs.

What might that mean, for us, here, now? Oddly enough, the Bible tells us very little about Abraham that might explain why he was chosen for the mission he undertook. It does not call him righteous, as it does in the case of Noah. It does not portray him as a miracle worker, as it does Moses. The only place in the Bible to explain why Abraham was chosen is this verse:

For I have chosen him, so that he will direct his children and his
household after him to keep the way of the Lord by doing what
is right and just.

This tells us three things about what it is to be an heir of Abraham.
First, it means that we are the guardians of our children's future.
We must ensure that they have a world to inherit. Today that
means political, economic and environmental sustainability.

Second, education – directing our children and our household
after us – is a sacred task. Teach children to love, and they will
have hope. Teach them to hate, and they will have only anger
and the desire for revenge. Thinking about the past leads to war.
Thinking about the future helps us to make peace.

Third, how do you keep the way of the Lord? By doing what is
right and just. That is the test. If religious people do what is right
and just, they are keeping the way. If they do not, then somehow
they have lost their way.

I think we can agree on those principles whether we believe in
the Lord or not.

In 1779 the German Enlightenment philosopher and art critic
Gotthold Lessing wrote a play, *Nathan the Wise*, that neatly encap-
sulates the problem of religious conflict and its solution in a way that
might be extended to the argument between believer and sceptic.

The play is set in the twelfth century in the Middle East. The
Muslim Sultan Saladin has won a victory against the Crusaders,
but it has cost him a great deal and there is an uneasy truce in
Jerusalem, with Muslims, Christians and Jews all eyeing one
another with suspicion.

He summons Nathan, a leading Jewish merchant, known
for his wisdom. 'Your reputation for wisdom is great,' says the
Sultan. 'The great religions, Judaism, Christianity and Islam, all
contradict one another. They cannot all be true. Tell me then,
which is best?'

Nathan recognises the trap immediately. If he says Judaism, he
insults the Sultan. If he says Islam, he denies his own faith. If

he says Christianity, he offends both. Nathan therefore does the Jewish thing. He tells a story.

There was once, he says, a man who possessed a priceless ring. Its stone was a lustrous opal that refracted light into a hundred colours. But it also had the mysterious power to make its wearer beloved of God and of man. The man passed the ring on to his most cherished son, and so it was handed down, generation after generation.

Finally it was inherited by a man who had three sons, each of whom he loved equally. Unable to choose between them, he secretly commissioned a jeweller to make two exact copies of the ring. On his deathbed, he blessed each son separately, and gave each a ring. Each son believed that he alone possessed the authentic ring.

The man died. After the funeral, one after the other of the sons claimed to be the one to whom their father had entrusted his most precious possession, the ring. There seemed no way of resolving the argument because no one could tell which was the original ring. All three were indistinguishable.

Eventually they brought the case before a judge, who heard the story and the history, and examined the rings. 'The authentic ring', said the judge in his verdict, 'had the power to make its wearer beloved of God and of man. There is therefore only one way each of you will know whether you have the genuine ring, and that is so to act as to become beloved of God and of man.'

'Bravo,' said the Sultan to Nathan, and let him go in peace.

Too simple, perhaps, too innocent an example of Enlightenment optimism. But it contains a truth. For if we believe in the God of Abraham, we know we cannot fully know God. We can merely see the effects of his acts. And that surely is true of the children of Abraham. We can see how, given their beliefs, people behave.

If they love and forgive, if they are open to others, if they respect their opponents as well as honouring their fellow believers, if they work for a better world by becoming guardians of the heritages of nature and culture, if they care about the future our grandchildren will inherit but we will not live to see, then they will be beloved of their fellow humans, and they will become true ambassadors of the God who loves those who perform acts of love.

That surely is an act of faith on which religion and science can agree. Let us join hands and build a more hopeful future.

Notes

Introduction

1. Albert Einstein, 'Science, philosophy and religion' (1940), in Albert Einstein and Alice Calaprice, *The Quotable Einstein*, Princeton, Princeton University Press, 1996.
2. See Jill Bolte Taylor, *My Stroke of Insight: A Brain Scientist's Personal Journey*, New York, Viking, 2008.
3. See, for example, Matt Ridley, *The Rational Optimist: How Prosperity Evolves*, New York, HarperCollins, 2010. On the difference, see Jonathan Sacks, *From Optimism to Hope: Thoughts for the Day*, London, Continuum, 2004.
4. Bernard Williams, *Shame and Necessity*, Berkeley, University of California, 1993, p. 166.
5. Ibid., p. 167. Pindar, *Pythian Odes*, IV: 263–9.
6. T. S. Eliot, 'What is a classic?' in Frank Kermode (ed.), *Selected Prose of T. S. Eliot*, New York, Harcourt Brace Jovanovich, 1975, p. 130.
7. Williams, *Shame and Necessity*, p. 167.
8. Ramin Jahanbegloo, *Conversations with Isaiah Berlin*, London, Halban Publishers, 2007, p. 110.

1. The Meaning-Seeking Animal

1. *Ideas and Opinions by Albert Einstein*, New York, Dell Publishers, 1954, p. 11.
2. Sigmund Freud and James Strachey, *Civilization and Its Discontents*, New York, W. W. Norton & Co., 2005, p. 76.
3. Ludwig Wittgenstein, *Notebooks, 1914–16*, 2nd ed., trans. G. E. M. Anscombe, Chicago, University of Chicago Press, 1979, p. 74e.
4. Tom Stoppard, *Arcadia*, London, Faber and Faber, 1993, Act 2, scene 7.
5. Thomas Nagel, a secular philosopher, puts it well. In response to those who say that the universe exists merely because it exists, he writes, 'To

me, it has always seemed an evasion. It requires that we leave the largest question unanswered – in fact, that we leave it unasked, because there is no such question. But there is: it is the question "What am I doing here?" and it doesn't go away when science replaces a religious worldview.' Thomas Nagel, *Secular Philosophy and the Religious Temperament: Essays 2002–2008*, Oxford, Oxford University Press, 2010, p. 8.

6. Jacques Monod, *Chance and Necessity: An Essay on the Natural Philosophy of Modern Biology*, New York, Vintage, 1972, p. 160.

7. Steven Weinberg, *The First Three Minutes: A Modern View of the Origin of the Universe*, New York, Basic, 1977, pp. 154–5.

8. Bertrand Russell, 'A Free Man's Worship', in *The Basic Writings of Bertrand Russell*, London, Routledge Classics, 2009, p. 39.

9. Ludwig Wittgenstein, *Tractatus logico-philosophicus*, London, 1922, 6.41.

10. Joseph Heller, *Good as Gold*, New York, Simon & Schuster, 1979, p. 74.

11. See Isaiah Berlin, *The Hedgehog and the Fox: An Essay on Tolstoy's View of History*, New York, Simon & Schuster, 1953.

12. See, for example, George Lakoff and Mark Johnson, *Metaphors We Live By*, Chicago, University of Chicago Press, 1980.

13. See Nassim Nicholas Taleb, *The Black Swan: The Impact of the Highly Improbable*, New York, Random House, 2007.

14. Viktor Frankl, *Man's Search for Meaning: An Introduction to Logotherapy*, New York, Simon & Schuster, 1984, p. 33.

15. Ibid., p. 86.

16. Viktor Frankl, *The Doctor and the Soul: From Psychotherapy to Logotherapy*, New York, Vintage, 1986, p. 104.

17. Ibid., p. 107.

18. Ibid., p. 13.

19. Babylonian Talmud, Berakhot 5b; Nedarim 7b; Sanhedrin 95a.

20. Jonathan Sacks, *To Heal a Fractured World: The Ethics of Responsibility*, New York, Schocken, 2005.

21. H. Richard Niebuhr, *The Responsible Self*, Louisville, KY, Westminster John Knox Press, 1999, p. 126.

22. Ibid., p. 94.

2. In Two Minds

1. Friedrich Nietzsche, *Human, All Too Human: A Book for Free Spirits*, trans. R. J. Hollingdale, Cambridge, Cambridge University Press, 1986, p. 251.
2. Martin Luther King and Susan Carson, *The Papers of Martin Luther King, Jr, Advocate of the Social Gospel: September 1948 – March 1963*, Berkeley, University of California Press, 2007, p. 108.
3. William Blake, letter to Thomas Butt, 22 November 1802, quoted in Geoffrey Keynes (ed.), *The Letters of William Blake*, London, Rupert Hart Davis, 1956, p. 79.
4. See Derrick De Kerckhove and Charles J. Lumsden, *The Alphabet and the Brain: The Lateralization of Writing*, Berlin, Springer-Verlag, 1988; Robert Ornstein, *The Right Mind: Making Sense of the Hemispheres*, New York, Harcourt Brace, 1997, pp. 26–42; Iain McGilchrist, *The Master and His Emissary: The Divided Brain and the Making of the Western World*, New Haven, CT, Yale University Press, 2009, pp. 276–9.
5. E. M. Forster, *Howards End*, New York, Signet Classics, 2007, ch. 33.
6. See David Diringer, *Writing*, London, Thames and Hudson, 1962; *The Alphabet: A Key to the History of Mankind*, London, Hutchinson, 1968; *The Story of the Aleph Beth*, New York, Yoseloff, 1958; Joseph Naveh, *Early History of the Alphabet: An Introduction to West Semitic Epigraphy and Palaeography*, Jerusalem, Magnes, Hebrew University, 1982; David Sacks, *The Alphabet: Unravelling the Mystery of the Alphabet from A to Z*, London, Hutchinson, 2003. See also David Shlain's fascinating *The Alphabet versus the Goddess: The Conflict between Word and Image*, New York, Viking, 1998.
7. Nicholas G. Carr, *The Shallows: How the Internet Is Changing the Way We Think, Read and Remember*, London, Atlantic, 2010; Richard Watson, *Future Minds: How the Digital Age Is Changing Our Minds, Why This Matters, and What We Can Do About It*, London, Nicholas Brealey Publishers, 2010; Clay Shirky, *Cognitive Surplus: Creativity and Generosity in a Connected Age*, New York, Penguin, 2010. Also see John G. Palfrey and Urs Gasser, *Born Digital: Understanding the First Generation of Digital Natives*, New York, Basic, 2008.
8. Walter J. Ong, *Orality and Literacy: The Technologizing of the Word*, London, Routledge, 2002.
9. Mishnah, Berakhot 1:1.
10. James Le Fanu, *Why Us?: How Science Rediscovered the Mystery of Ourselves*, London, HarperPress, 2009.

11. Norman Doidge, *The Brain That Changes Itself: Stories of Personal Triumph from the Frontiers of Brain Science*, New York, Viking, 2007. For a moving description of how one woman recovered full functions after a massive stroke that immobilised her entire left brain, see Jill Bolte Taylor, *My Stroke of Insight: A Brain Scientist's Personal Journey*, New York, Viking, 2008.

12. Joseph Needham, *Physics and Physical Technology*, Cambridge, Cambridge University Press, 1987, p. 14.

13. Richard E. Nisbett, *The Geography of Thought: How Asians and Westerners Think Differently – and Why*, New York, Free Press, 2003.

14. Carol Gilligan, *In a Different Voice: Psychological Theory and Women's Development*, Cambridge, MA, Harvard University Press, 1982.

15. Ibid., p. 173.

16. Lawrence J. Walker, 'Sex Differences in the Development of Moral Reasoning: A Critical Review', *Child Development*, 55.3, 1984, p. 677; Sara Jaffee and Janet Shibley Hyde, 'Gender Differences in Moral Orientation: A Meta-analysis', *Psychological Bulletin*, 126.5, 2000, pp. 703–26; Christina Hoff Sommers, *The War against Boys: How Misguided Feminism Is Harming Our Young Men*, New York, Simon & Schuster, 2000.

17. Steven Pinker, *The Blank Slate: The Modern Denial of Human Nature*, New York, Viking, 2002, pp. 337–71.

18. Simon Baron-Cohen, *The Essential Difference: The Truth about the Male and Female Brain*, New York, Basic Books, 2003.

19. Jerome Bruner, *Acts of Meaning*, Cambridge, MA, Harvard University Press, 1994.

20. Jerome Bruner, *Actual Minds, Possible Worlds*, Cambridge, MA, Harvard University Press, 1986.

21. Roy F. Baumeister, *The Cultural Animal: Human Nature, Meaning, and Social Life*, Oxford, Oxford University Press, 2005.

22. Martha Nussbaum, *Poetic Justice: The Literary Imagination and Public Life*, Boston, Beacon, 1995.

23. See Michael Polanyi, *Personal Knowledge: Towards a Post-critical Philosophy*, Chicago, University of Chicago Press, 1958; John Macmurray, *Persons in Relation*, Atlantic Highlands, NJ, Humanities International, 1991.

3. Diverging Paths

1. Cervantes, *Don Quixote*, 2, 62.
2. Harvey Cox, *The Future of Faith*, New York, HarperOne, 2009, p. 221.
3. Johann Gottfried Herder and Frank Edward Manuel, *Reflections on the Philosophy of the History of Mankind*, Chicago, University of Chicago Press, 1968; Heinrich Heine, *Sämtliche Werke*, Darmstadt, Wissenschaftliche Buchgesellschaft, 1992; Ernest Renan, *History of the People of Israel till the Time of King David*, Boston, Little, Brown, 1905; Matthew Arnold, *Culture and Anarchy*, Oxford, Oxford University Press, 2006; David J. Delaura, *Hebrew and Hellene in Victorian England: Newman, Arnold, and Pater*, Austin, University of Texas Press, 1969; Jacob Shavit, *Athens in Jerusalem: Classical Antiquity and Hellenism in the Making of the Modern Secular Jew*, London, Littman Library of Jewish Civilization, 1997. For a brief introduction, see Tessa Rajak, 'Jews and Greeks: the invention and exploitation of polarities in the 19th century', in her *The Jewish Dialogue with Greece and Rome: Studies in Cultural and Social Interaction*, Leiden, Brill, 2001, pp. 535–57.
4. There is a vast literature on the subject. See, for example, Martin Hengel, *The 'Hellenization' of Judaea in the First Century after Christ*, London, SCM Press, 1989; E. P. Sanders, *Judaism: Practice and Belief, 63 BCE – 66 CE*, London, SCM Press, 1992; Louis H. Feldman, *Jew and Gentile in the Ancient World: Attitudes and Interactions from Alexander to Justinian*, Princeton, NJ, Princeton University Press, 1993; Lee I. Levine, *Judaism and Hellenism in Antiquity: Conflict or Confluence*, Seattle, University of Washington Press, 1998; Martin Goodman, *Jews in a Graeco-Roman World*, Oxford, Clarendon, 1998; Tessa Rajak, *The Jewish Dialogue with Greece and Rome: Studies in Cultural and Social Interaction*, Leiden, Brill, 2001.
5. James Barr, *Biblical Faith and Natural Theology*, Oxford, Clarendon, 1994, p. 56.
6. I should say, by way of qualification, that a similar synthesis did take place within both Judaism and Islam between the eleventh and fourteenth centuries, in the wake of the rediscovery of key Greek philosophical texts, the emergence of medieval neo-Platonism and neo-Aristotelianism, and the unique period of religious tolerance, *convivencia*, in Al-Andalus, medieval Spain. Averroes in Islam, Maimonides in

Judaism – both born in Cordova – are the key figures. But the movement was shorter lived and more marginal in these two faiths than
in Christianity. In fact both Averroes and Maimonides were accused
of heresy in their lifetime, and their rationalism remained a minority
phenomenon in their respective faiths.

7. Jeremiah 31:29–30, 'In those days people will no longer say, "The
   parents have eaten sour grapes, and the children's teeth are set on edge."
   Instead, everyone will die for their own sin; whoever eats sour grapes –
   their own teeth will be set on edge.' Ezekiel 18:2–4, 'What do you people
   mean by quoting this proverb about the land of Israel: "The parents eat
   sour grapes, and the children's teeth are set on edge"? As surely as I live,
   declares the Sovereign Lord, you will no longer quote this proverb in
   Israel. For everyone belongs to me, the parent as well as the child – both
   alike belong to me. The one who sins is the one who will die.'

8. See the insightful study by Richard Kearney, *The God Who May Be:
   A Hermeneutics of Religion*, Bloomington, Indiana University Press,
   2001, pp. 20–38, from which these references are drawn.

9. Judah Halevi, *The Kuzari = Kitab Al Khazari: An Argument for the
   Faith of Israel*, New York, Schocken, 1964, Book I, p. 25.

10. Cicero, *De Natura Deorum*, ii. 34.

11. 'For the whole sensible world is like a kind of book written by the finger
    of God.' Hugh of St Victor, *De Tribus Diebus*. 'To conclude, therefore,
    let no man . . . think or maintain that a man can search too far or be
    too well studied in the book of God's word, or in the book of God's
    works; divinity or philosophy; but rather let men endeavour an endless
    progress or proficience in both.' Francis Bacon, *The Advancement of
    Learning* (1605). Charles Darwin quoted these words opposite the
    title page of *The Origin of Species*.

12. Babylonian Talmud, Berakhot 58a.

13. Maimonides, Introduction to *Eight Chapters*, the preface to his
    commentary to the Mishnah Tractate Avot.

14. Babylonian Talmud, Pesachim 94b.

15. The passage occurs in somewhat different forms in Babylonian Talmud,
    Sanhedrin 91b and Genesis Rabbah 34:10.

16. Max Weber, *Ancient Judaism*, New York, Free Press, 1967 (originally
    published 1952); Peter Berger, *The Sacred Canopy: Elements of a
    Sociological Theory of Religion*, New York, Anchor Books, 1990.

17. See, in greater detail, Jonathan Sacks, *Future Tense*, London, Hodder
    & Stoughton, 2009, pp. 207–30.

18. See John Rawls, 'Two Concepts of Rules', *The Philosophical Review*, vol. 64, 1955, pp. 3–13.

19. See Amos Funkenstein, *Theology and the Scientific Imagination: From the Middle Ages to the Seventeenth Century*, Princeton, Princeton University Press, 1986; Peter Harrison, *The Bible, Protestantism, and the Rise of Natural Science*, Cambridge, Cambridge University Press, 1998; Peter Harrison, *The Fall of Man and the Foundations of Science*, Cambridge, Cambridge University Press, 2007; R. Hooykaas, *Religion and the Rise of Modern Science*, Grand Rapids, MI, Eerdmans, 1972; Rodney Stark, *For the Glory of God: How Monotheism Led to Reformations, Science, Witch-hunts, and the End of Slavery*, Princeton, NJ, Princeton University Press, 2003.

20. Stephen Toulmin, *Cosmopolis: The Hidden Agenda of Modernity*, Chicago, University of Chicago Press, 1994.

21. On this see Sacks, *Future Tense*.

22. See my introduction in Jonathan Sacks, *The Authorised Daily Prayer Book of the United Hebrew Congregations of the Commonwealth: With a New Translation and Commentary*, London, Collins, 2007.

23. See Pamela Thurschwell, *Sigmund Freud*, London, Routledge, 2000, pp. 19–20; Greg Mogenson, *The Dove in the Consulting Room: Hysteria and the Anima in Bollas and Jung*, Hove, UK, Brunner-Routledge, 2003, pp. 71–82.

24. James Le Fanu, *Why Us?: How Science Rediscovered the Mystery of Ourselves*, London, HarperPress, 2009, p. 258.

4. Finding God

1. Ludwig Wittgenstein, *Philosophical Investigations*, New York, Macmillan, 1953, para. 109.

2. John Stuart Mill, *Nature*, London, Kessinger Publishing, 2010, pp. 28–30.

3. Genesis Rabbah 39:1. See Jonathan Sacks, *A Letter in the Scroll: Understanding Our Jewish Identity and Exploring the Legacy of the World's Oldest Religion*, New York, Free Press, 2000, pp. 51–60.

4. Maimonides, Mishneh Torah, Hilkhot Yesodei ha-Torah 8:1.

5. Babylonian Talmud, Shabbat 53b.

6. Bernard Williams, 'Tertullian's Paradox', in Anthony Flew and Alasdair MacIntyre (eds), *New Essays in Philosophical Theology*, London, SCM Press, 1955, pp. 187–211.

7. Maimonides, *Guide for the Perplexed*, Book III, 31.
8. George Steiner, *Language and Silence*, London, Faber & Faber, 1967.
9. Mark Roseman, *The Villa, the Lake, the Meeting: Wannsee and the Final Solution*, London, Allen Lane/Penguin, 2002.
10. See Léon Poliakov, *From Voltaire to Wagner*, London, Routledge and Kegan Paul, 1975; Nathan Rotenstreich, *Jews and German Philosophy: The Polemics of Emancipation*, New York, Schocken, 1984; Paul Lawrence Rose, *Revolutionary Antisemitism in Germany from Kant to Wagner*, Princeton, NJ, Princeton University Press, 1990.
11. Jonathan Glover, *Humanity: A Moral History of the Twentieth Century*, London, Jonathan Cape, 1999.
12. Jorge Luis Borges and Andrew Hurley, *Jorge Luis Borges: Collected Fictions*, New York, Viking, 1998, pp. 82–7.
13. Ludwig Wittgenstein, *Culture and Value*, Chicago, University of Chicago Press, 1980, p. 18e.
14. This was later published as a book: *The Condition of Jewish Belief: A Symposium*, Northvale, NJ, J. Aronson, 1989.
15. Stephen Jay Gould and Richard Lewontin, 'The Spandrels of San Marco and the Panglossian Paradigm: A Critique of the Adaptationist Programme', *Proceedings of the Royal Society of London, B*, 205, 1979.
16. Bernard Williams, *Moral Luck*, Cambridge, Cambridge University Press, 1981, pp. 20–39. Needless to say, this is a crude summary of an exquisitely subtle argument.
17. W. B. Yeats, 'The Choice', in *The Collected Poems of W. B. Yeats*, New York, Scribner, 1996, p. 209.
18. Viktor Frankl, *The Doctor and the Soul: From Psychotherapy to Logotherapy*, New York, Vintage, 1986, p. 13.

5. *What We Stand to Lose*

1. Leszek Kolakowski, *Religion*, London, Fontana, 1982, p. 215.
2. Most obviously Immanuel Kant in his principle that we treat rational beings as ends in themselves. See Immanuel Kant, *The Moral Law: Groundwork of the Metaphysic of Morals*, London, Routledge, 2007. But as I pointed out in the previous chapter, Kant expressed virulently antisemitic views. What is more, at his trial, Adolf Eichmann, often described as 'the architect of the Holocaust', showed himself to be a Kantian. As Emil Fackenheim puts it, he obeyed the two key Kantian principles: purity of motivation and universalisation. He was 'a

dutiful, idealistic mass-murderer, not merely a sadistic or opportunistic one'. And his 'maxim' of action was 'to make through his own will the Führer's will into universal law'. Emil Fackenheim, *To Mend the World: Foundations of Post-Holocaust Jewish Thought*, Bloomington, Indiana University Press, 1994, p. 270. When tested empirically under stress, the Kantian basis of respect for persons failed.

3. Friedrich Nietzsche, *The Gay Science: With a Prelude in Rhymes and an Appendix of Songs*, trans. Walter Kaufmann, New York, Vintage, 1974, Book III, para. 125, p. 181.

4. On Darwin's influence on Nietzsche, see John Richardson, *Nietzsche's New Darwinism*, Oxford, Oxford University Press, 2004. On the loss of faith of English intellectuals in the nineteenth century, see A. N. Wilson, *God's Funeral*, New York, W. W. Norton & Co., 1999.

5. Friedrich Nietzsche, et al., *Twilight of the Idols,* New York, Penguin Books, 1990, p. 81.

6. Friedrich Nietzsche, *The Will to Power*, trans. Walter Kaufmann, New York, Random House, 1967, para. 246, p. 142.

7. Ibid., para. 734, p. 389.

8. Friedrich Nietzsche, *Ecce Homo*, 'Why I Am a Destiny', p. 1.

9. Heinrich Heine, 'Zur Geschichte von Religion und Philosphie im Deutschland', *Sämtliche Schriften*, vol. 3, p. 505.

10. Will Durant, *The Story of Civilization V: The Renaissance*, New York, Simon & Schuster, 1954, 1.71 (italics added).

6. Human Dignity

1. Friedrich Nietzsche, *On the Genealogy of Morality*, ed. Keith Ansell-Pearson, trans. Carol Diethe, Cambridge, Cambridge University Press, 1994, Third Essay, 25:115.

2. Michel Foucault, *The Order of Things: An Archaeology of the Human Sciences*, New York, Vintage, 1973, p. 387.

3. *Oration on the Dignity of Man* (1486). The text is available at: http://www.wsu.edu:8080/~wldciv/world_civ_reader/world_civ_reader_1/pico.html. See Ernst Cassirer, Paul Oskar Kristeller and John Herman Randall, Jr, *The Renaissance Philosophy of Man*, Chicago, University of Chicago Press, 1948; M. V. Dougherty (ed.), *Pico della Mirandola: New Essays*, Cambridge, Cambridge University Press, 2008.

4. On del Medigo see Jacob J. Ross, *Sefer Behinat ha-dat*, Tel Aviv, Tel Aviv University Press, 1984; Harvey Hames, 'Elijah DelMedigo:

an archetype of the halakhic man?' in David Ruderman and Giuseppe Veltri, *Cultural Intermediaries: Jewish Intellectuals in Early Modern Italy*, Philadelphia, University of Pennsylvania Press, 2004, pp. 39–66.

5. *Free Inquiry Magazine*, vol. 17, no. 3, 1997; see Leon Kass, *Life, Liberty, and the Defense of Dignity: The Challenge for Bioethics*, San Francisco, Encounter Books, 2002.

6. Sigmund Freud, *Totem and Taboo*, London, Routledge, 2001.

7. Sigmund Freud, *The Future of an Illusion*, New York, W. W. Norton & Co., 1975.

8. Michael T. Ghiselin, *The Economy of Nature and the Evolution of Sex*, Berkeley, University of California Press, 1974, p. 247.

9. Stephen Jay Gould, *Wonderful Life*, New York, W. W. Norton & Co., 1989, p. 51.

10. Shakespeare, *Hamlet*, Act 2, scene 2, lines 303–12.

11. Nietzsche, *On the Genealogy of Morality*, Third Essay, 25:113.

12. The term derives from the work of Paul Ricoeur. See his *Freud and Philosophy: An Essay on Interpretation*, New Haven, CT, Yale University Press, 1970.

13. The most impressive treatment of the subject is Richard Weikart, *From Darwin to Hitler*, New York, Palgrave Macmillan, 2004. See also Dennis Sewell, *The Political Gene*, London, Picador, 2009.

14. Adolf Hitler, *Mein Kampf*, Munich, 1943, pp. 144–5, quoted in Weikart, *From Darwin to Hitler*, p. 211.

15. Quoted in ibid., p. 215.

16. The full story is told in Robert Jay Lifton, *The Nazi Doctors*, 2nd ed., New York, Basic Books, 2000, especially pp. 80–95.

17. Quoted in ibid., p. 134.

18. Primo Levi, *Survival in Auschwitz, The Nazi Assault on Humanity*, New York, Collier, 1961, p. 96.

19. Friedrich Nietzsche, *The Gay Science: With a Prelude in Rhymes and an Appendix of Songs*, trans. Walter Kaufmann, New York, Vintage, 1974, p. 344.

20. Babylonian Talmud, Eruvin 100b.

21. Friedrich A. Von Hayek and William Warren Bartley, *The Fatal Conceit: The Errors of Socialism*, Chicago, University of Chicago Press, 1989.

22. This is the point famously made by Robert Nozick in the passage about the 'experience machine' in *Anarchy, State, and Utopia*, New York, Basic Books, 1974, pp. 42–5. If we were offered the choice to

spend our life plugged into a machine that would simulate a stream of pleasurable experiences that we could not tell were not real, would we opt for this as against real life? Nozick assumes we would answer, 'No.'

23. See Nicholas Wolterstorff, *Justice: Rights and Wrongs*, Princeton, NJ, Princeton University Press, 2007.

7. The Politics of Freedom

1. John Plamenatz, *Man and Society*, London, Longman, 1963, pp. 45–88.
2. Christopher Hill, *The English Bible and the Seventeenth-Century Revolution*, London, Allen Lane, 1993.
3. See Dan Jacobson, *The Story of the Stories: The Chosen People and Its God*, New York, Harper & Row, 1982.
4. Eric Nelson, *The Hebrew Republic: Jewish Sources and the Transformation of European Political Thought*, Cambridge, MA, Harvard University Press, 2010.
5. Thomas Hobbes, *Leviathan*, Book 1, 11.
6. Lord Acton, 'The History of Freedom in Antiquity', *Essays in the History of Liberty: Selected Writings of Lord Acton*, ed. J. Rufus Fears, Indianapolis, Liberty Classics, 1985–8, pp. 5–28.
7. Hannah Arendt, *The Human Condition*, Chicago, University of Chicago Press, 1998, pp. 23–47.
8. Friedrich Nietzsche, *On the Genealogy of Morality*, ed. Keith Ansell-Pearson, trans. Carol Diethe, Cambridge, Cambridge University Press, 1994, Second Essay, pp. 35–6.
9. See Johannes Lindblom, *Prophecy in Ancient Israel*, Philadelphia, Muhlenberg, 1962; Michael Walzer, *Interpretation and Social Criticism*, Cambridge, MA, Harvard University Press, 1987.
10. See the works of Daniel Elazar in the section 'For Further Reading' on p. 336 of this book; also John Witte, Jr, *Religion and the American Constitutional Experiment: Essential Rights and Liberties*, Boulder, CO, Westview Press, 2000; Glenn A. Moots, *Politics Reformed: The Anglo-American Legacy of Covenant Theology*, Columbia, University of Missouri, 2010.
11. Inaugural address, 20 January 1961.
12. Inaugural address, 20 January 2009.
13. For classic covenant renewal thinking, see Reinhold Niebuhr, *The Irony*

of American History, New York, Scribner, 1952; and Robert Bellah, *The Broken Covenant: American Civil Religion in a Time of Trial*, New York, Seabury, 1975.

14. Joshua Berman, *Created Equal: How the Bible Broke with Ancient Political Thought*, Oxford, Oxford University Press, 2008.

15. Plato, *The Laws*, trans. Thomas Pangle, New York, Basic, 1980, p. 24.

16. Thomas Paine, *Political Writings*, ed. Bruce Kuklick, Cambridge, Cambridge University Press, 1997, p. 3.

17. Montesquieu, *The Spirit of the Laws*, vol. 1, book 20, sect. 7.

18. *Memoir, Letters, and Remains of Alexis de Tocqueville*, London, 1861, vol. 2, p. 397 (letter to M. De Corcelle, 2 July 1857). I owe this and the previous reference to Gertrude Himmelfarb, *The Roads to Modernity*, New York, Knopf, 2004, pp. 25–52.

19. Friedrich A. Von Hayek, *The Constitution of Liberty*, Chicago, University of Chicago Press, 1960; J. L. Talmon, *The Origins of Totalitarian Democracy*, New York, Praeger, 1960.

20. Oliver Goldsmith, 'The Traveller', in *The Poems and Plays of Oliver Goldsmith*, London, 1841, p. 4.

21. Talmon, *The Origins of Totalitarian Democracy*, p. 35.

8. Morality

1. Will and Ariel Durant, *The Lessons of History*, New York, Simon & Schuster, 1996, p. 51.

2. Martin Buber, *Good and Evil, Two Interpretations*, Gloucester, MA, Peter Smith, 1992, p. 142.

3. Adam Smith, *The Theory of Moral Sentiments*, Oxford, Clarendon, 1976, opening.

4. Frans de Waal, *The Age of Empathy: Nature's Lessons for a Kinder Society*, New York, Harmony, 2009, p. 79.

5. Dacher Keltner, *Born to Be Good: The Science of a Meaningful Life*, New York, W. W. Norton & Co., 2009, p. 232.

6. Robert Wright, *The Moral Animal: The New Science of Evolutionary Psychology*, New York, Pantheon, 1994.

7. Frans de Waal, *The Age of Empathy*, p. 91; Dacher Keltner, Jason Marsh and Jeremy Adam Smith, *The Compassionate Instinct: The Science of Human Goodness*, New York, W. W. Norton & Co., 2010, p. 19.

8. That animals are capable of compassion is taken for granted by Maimonides, *Guide for the Perplexed*, Book III, 48.

9. Voltaire, *Political Writings*, ed. David Williams, Cambridge, Cambridge University Press, 1994, p. 190.

10. Rousseau, *The Social Contract*, New York, Penguin, 2006.

11. Quoted in Robert Horwitz, *The Moral Foundations of the American Republic*, Charlottesville, University of Virginia Press, 1986, p. 213.

12. Leo Tolstoy and Jane Kentish, *A Confession and Other Religious Writings*, London, Penguin, 1987, p. 150.

13. A. N. Wilson, *God's Funeral*, New York, W. W. Norton & Co., 1999.

14. Elizabeth Anscombe, 'Modern moral philosophy', reprinted in G. E. M. Anscombe, Mary Geach and Luke Gormally, *Human Life, Action, and Ethics: Essays*, Exeter, UK, Imprint Academic, 2005, pp. 169–94.

15. Alasdair MacIntyre, *After Virtue*, London, Duckworth, 1981.

16. Allan Bloom, *The Closing of the American Mind: How Higher Education Has Failed Democracy and Impoverished the Souls of Today's Students*, New York, Simon & Schuster, 1987.

17. David Riesman, *The Lonely Crowd: A Study of the Changing American Character*, New Haven, CT, Yale University Press, 1961.

18. Plato, *The Republic*, Book 2, 2.359a–360d.

19. Edmund Burke, 'Letter to a member of the French assembly', *The Works and Correspondence of Edmund Burke*, London, F. & J. Rivington, 1852, vol. 4, p. 319.

20. Richard M. Weaver, *Ideas Have Consequences*, Chicago, University of Chicago Press, 1948.

21. Epicurus, *The Essential Epicurus: Letters, Principal Doctrines, Vatican Sayings, and Fragments*, ed. Eugene Michael O'Connor, Buffalo, NY, Prometheus, 1993; Carus Titus Lucretius and A. E. Stallings, *The Nature of Things*, London, Penguin, 2007.

22. Herschel Baker, *The Image of Man: A Study of the Idea of Human Dignity in Classical Antiquity, the Middle Ages, and the Renaissance*, New York, Harper & Row, 1961, pp. 84–8.

23. Bertrand Russell, *A History of Western Philosophy*, New York, Simon & Schuster, 1972, p. 258.

24. Michael Tooley, *Abortion and Infanticide*, Oxford, Clarendon, 1983.

25. Ian Dowbiggin, *A Concise History of Euthanasia: Life, Death, God, and Medicine*, Lanham, UK, Rowman & Littlefield, 2005; Anthony Gottlieb, *The Dream of Reason: A History of Western Philosophy from the Greeks to the Renaissance*, New York, W. W. Norton & Co., 2000.

26. Peter Singer, *Rethinking Life and Death: the Collapse of Our Traditional Ethics*, New York, St Martin's Griffin, 1996.

27. Charles Darwin, *The Descent of Man*, Princeton, NJ, Princeton University Press, 1981, pp. 158–84.
28. Ibid., p. 166.
29. David Sloan Wilson, *Darwin's Cathedral: Evolution, Religion, and the Nature of Society*, Chicago, University of Chicago Press, 2002.
30. Darwin, *The Descent of Man*, p. 162.
31. Michael Walzer, *Interpretation and Social Criticism*, Cambridge, MA, Harvard University Press, 1987, p. 6.
32. So, it should be said, did Darwin. See Adrian J. Desmond and James R. Moore, *Darwin's Sacred Cause: How a Hatred of Slavery Shaped Darwin's Views on Human Evolution*, Boston, Houghton Mifflin Harcourt, 2009.
33. John Stuart Mill, *On the Logic of the Moral Sciences*, Indianapolis, Bobbs-Merrill, 1965, p. 111.
34. Russell, *A History of Western Philosophy*, p. 19.
35. Plato, *The Republic*, 560–4.

9. Relationships

1. Genesis Rabbah 68:4.
2. Babylonian Talmud, Sotah 17a.
3. Quoted in Ferdinand Mount, *The Subversive Family: An Alternative History of Love and Marriage*, New York, Free Press, 1992, p. 2.
4. David Martin, *The Religious and the Secular: Studies in Secularization*, New York, Schocken, 1969; David Martin, *A General Theory of Secularization*, New York, Harper & Row, 1979; Charles Taylor, *A Secular Age*, Cambridge, MA, Harvard University Press, 2007.
5. Jill Kirby, *Broken Hearts: Family Decline and the Consequences for Society*, London, Centre for Policy Studies, 2002; David Popenoe, *War over the Family*, New Brunswick, NJ, Transaction, 2005.
6. Oliver James, *Britain on the Couch: Why We're Unhappier Compared with 1950 Despite Being Richer: A Treatment for the Low-Serotonin Society*, London, Arrow, 1998.
7. Babylonian Talmud, Berakhot 7a.
8. Hubert Dreyfus and Sean Dorrance Kelly, *All Things Shining*, New York, Free Press, 2011.
9. Buddhism values love, but in a somewhat different sense.
10. See James Barr, *Biblical Faith and Natural Theology: The Gifford Lectures for 1991, Delivered in the University of Edinburgh*, Oxford, Clarendon, 1993, p. 59.

11. Jeremiah 31:29–30; Ezekiel 18:2–4.
12. See Joshua Berman, *The Temple: Its Symbolism and Meaning Then and Now*, Northvale, NJ, Jason Aronson, 1995.
13. Abraham Joshua Heschel, *The Earth Is the Lord's, and the Sabbath*, New York, Harper Torch, 1966.
14. I have written more on this in Jonathan Sacks, *Covenant and Conversation, a Weekly Reading of the Jewish Bible: Genesis, the Book of Beginnings*, New Milford, NJ, Maggid & The Orthodox Union, 2009.
15. Midrash Tanhuma, Genesis 25.
16. Midrash Tehillim (Buber), to Psalm 92.
17. The roots *ch-v-h* and *ch-b-a* are semantically linked. The root *ch-b-a* is used earlier in the passage when the couple 'hide' from God (Genesis 3:8, 10).
18. Edmund Leach, *A Runaway World?* New York, Oxford University Press, 1968.
19. Robert Frost, 'Death of the Hired Man', in *Birches and Other Poems*, Mineola, NY, Dover Publications, 2001.

10. A Meaningful Life

1. Wallace Stevens, 'The Plain Sense of Things', in Wallace Stevens, *Collected Poetry and Prose*, New York, Literary Classics of the United States, 1997, p. 428.
2. Rebecca Goldstein, *36 Arguments for the Existence of God: A Work of Fiction*, New York, Pantheon, 2010, p. 308.
3. Leo Tolstoy, *A Confession*, trans. Jane Kentish, London, Penguin, 2008, p. 29.
4. Ibid., pp. 31–2.
5. Ibid., p. 54.
6. 'Religious faith and superstition are quite different. One of them results from *fear* and is a sort of false science. The other is a trusting.' Ludwig Wittgenstein, *Culture and Value*, trans. Peter Winch, Chicago, University of Chicago Press, 1980, p. 72e.
7. Shakespeare, *King Lear*, Act IV, scene 1.
8. Dylan Thomas, 'And Death Shall Have No Dominion', in Dylan Thomas, *Collected Poems 1934–1952*, London, Dent, 1952.
9. Albert Camus, *The Myth of Sisyphus*, London, Penguin Books, 2005, p. 1.

10. Ibid., p. 58.
11. Ibid., p. 119.
12. Ibid., p. 117.
13. Philip Rieff, *My Life among the Deathworks: Illustrations of the Aesthetics of Authority*, Charlottesville, University of Virginia Press, 2006.
14. This is the worldview associated with Richard Rorty and the post-modernists. See, for example, Richard Rorty, *Contingency, Irony, and Solidarity*, Cambridge, Cambridge University Press, 1991; Jean-François Lyotard, *The Postmodern Condition: A Report on Knowledge*, Minneapolis, University of Minnesota Press, 1984.
15. Roy A. Rappaport, *Ritual and Religion in the Making of Humanity*, Cambridge, Cambridge University Press, 1999, pp. 107–38.
16. Iris Murdoch, *The Sovereignty of Good*, London, Routledge and Kegan Paul, 1970, p. 84.
17. William Wordsworth, 'Lines Composed a Few Miles above Tintern Abbey', *The Poetical Works of William Wordsworth*, edited by Thomas Hutchinson, London, Henry Frowde, 1904, p. 206.
18. Vico's thesis is that we can only fully understand what we have made. Since we did not make nature, we can never achieve a full knowledge of it. We can, however, achieve a full knowledge of culture. Giambattista Vico, *New Science: Principles of the New Science Concerning the Common Nature of Nations*, trans. David Marsh, London, Penguin Classics, 1999. Maimonides articulated the same principle several centuries earlier, in *Guide for the Perplexed*, Book III, 21.
19. See the section 'For Further Reading', pp. 339–341 of this book, for the key books on happiness from which this section is drawn.
20. William Wordsworth, 'The World Is Too Much With Us', *The Poetical Works,* Hutchinson, ed, p. 259.
21. Tony Judt, *Ill Fares the Land*, London, Allen Lane, 2010, p. 1.
22. See http://www.civitas.org.uk/hwu/cohabitation.php.
23. Viktor Frankl, *The Doctor and the Soul*, New York, Vintage, 1986, p. 32.
24. Mishneh, Avot 1:14.
25. *Ideas and Opinions by Albert Einstein*, New York, Dell, 1954, p. 11.
26. Sigmund Freud, *Civilization and Its Discontents*, New York, W. W. Norton & Co., 2005, p. 76.
27. Ludwig Wittgenstein, *Notebooks 1914–1916*, 2nd ed., trans. G. E. M. Anscombe, Chicago, University of Chicago Press, 1979, 74e, 8.7.16.

28. Friedrich Nietzsche, *The Gay Science: With a Prelude in Rhymes and an Appendix of Songs*, trans. Walter Kaufmann, New York, Vintage, 1974, Book V, para. 373, p. 336.

11. Darwin

1. William P. Brown, *The Seven Pillars of Creation: The Bible, Science, and the Ecology of Wonder*, New York, Oxford University Press, 2010, p. 240.
2. Voltaire, *The Philosophical Dictionary*, selected and trans. H. I. Woolf, New York, Alfred A. Knopf, 1924.
3. Michael Polanyi, *Personal Knowledge*, Chicago, Chicago University Press, 1974, p. 405.
4. Max Planck, *Where Is Science Going?* trans. J. Murphy, London, Allen and Unwin, 1933.
5. Friedrich Nietzsche, *The Gay Science: With a Prelude in Rhymes and an Appendix of Songs*, trans. Walter Kaufmann, New York, Vintage, 1974, para. 125.
6. Sigmund Freud, *Totem and Taboo*, London, Routledge, 2001.
7. For a similar view about poetry, see Harold Bloom, *The Anxiety of Influence: A Theory of Poetry*, New York, Oxford Univeristy Press, 1973.
8. Maimonides, *Guide for the Perplexed*, Book I, 2.
9. Babylonian Talmud, Pesachim 54a; Genesis Rabbah 11:2.
10. George Gaylord Simpson, *The Meaning of Evolution, A Study of the History of Life and of Its Significance for Man*, New Haven, CT, Yale University Press, 1949.
11. Richard Dawkins, *The Blind Watchmaker*, London, Penguin, 1988, p. 6.
12. Steven J. Gould, 'Non-overlapping magisteria', *Natural History*, March 1997.
13. Babylonian Talmud, Shabbat 32a.
14. Albert Einstein, *Out of My Later Years (Essays)*, New York, Philosophical Library, 1950, p. 25.
15. Genesis Rabbah 10:8.
16. Timothy Ferris, *The Whole Shebang: A State-of-the-universe(s) Report*, New York, Simon & Schuster, 1997, p. 311.
17. Matt Ridley, *Genome: The Autobiography of a Species in 23 Chapters*, New York, HarperCollins, 1999, p. 21.

18. Francis Collins, *The Language of God: A Scientist Presents Evidence for Belief*, New York, Free Press, 2006.
19. Joseph Dov Soloveitchik and Michael S. Berger, *The Emergence of Ethical Man*, Hoboken, NJ, KTAV Publishing House, 2005.
20. Ecclesiastes Rabbah 7:13.
21. Genesis Rabbah 3:7; Rabbi Abraham Kook, Iggrot Re'iyah, vol. 1, 105–7.
22. Nahmanides, Commentary to Genesis 37:15, literally, 'an unwitting emissary of the Holy One'.
23. Charles Darwin, *Autobiographies*, London, Penguin, 2002, p. 50.
24. Adam Smith, *The Wealth of Nations*, Oxford, Oxford Paperbacks, 2008, Book I, II, 19.
25. Ibid., Book IV, II, 9.
26. Steven Johnson, *Emergence: The Connected Lives of Ants, Brains, Cities, and Software*, New York, Scribner, 2001.
27. Ibid., p. 59.
28. Simon Conway Morris, *Life's Solution: Inevitable Humans in a Lonely Universe*, Cambridge, Cambridge University Press, 2003, pp. 283–4.
29. This – the nature of divine foreknowledge and its compatibility or otherwise with human freedom – is a huge subject. See Maimonides, *Guide for the Perplexed*, Book III, 21, and the argument between Maimonides and Raavad, Mishneh Torah, Hilkhot Teshuvah 5:5.
30. Roy Baumeister, *The Cultural Animal: Human Nature, Meaning, and Social Life*, Oxford, Oxford University Press, 2005.
31. Bruno Snell, *The Discovery of the Mind*, Oxford, Blackwell, 1953.
32. Richard Dawkins, *The Selfish Gene*, Oxford, Oxford University Press, 1989, pp. 200–1.
33. Steven Pinker, *How the Mind Works*, London, Penguin, 1997, p. 52.

12. The Problem of Evil

1. Herbert N. Schneidau, *Sacred Discontent*, Berkeley, University of California Press, 1977, p. 2.
2. Reinhold Niebuhr, *The Irony of American History*, Chicago, University of Chicago Press, 2008, p. 138.
3. See John Bowker, *The Meanings of Death*, Cambridge, Cambridge University Press, 1991.
4. John Keats, letter to George and Georgiana Keats, Sunday 14 February

1819. 'Do you not see how necessary a World of Pains and troubles is to school an Intelligence and make it a Soul? A Place where the heart must feel and suffer in a thousand diverse ways!'

5. Mishneh Torah, Mattenot Ani'im 10:7.
6. Friedrich Nietzsche, *Twilight of the Idols and The Anti-Christ*, trans., with introduction and commentary, R. J. Hollingdale, London, Penguin, 1968, pp. 80–1.
7. Friedrich Nietzsche, *On the Genealogy of Morality*, ed. Keith Ansell-Pearson, trans. Carol Diethe, Cambridge, Cambridge University Press, 1994, Second Essay, p. 11.
8. Henry David Thoreau, *Walden*, Oxford, UK, Oxford World's Classics, 2008, ch. 1.
9. Genesis Rabbah 84:21.
10. Maimonides, *Guide for the Perplexed*, Book III, 12.
11. Nikolai Berdyaev, *The Meaning of History*, New Brunswick, NJ, Transaction, 2006, pp. 86–107.
12. John Cottingham, *The Spiritual Dimension*, Cambridge, Cambridge University Press, 2005, p. 23.
13. Christopher Dawson, *Religion and the Rise of Western Culture*, New York, Doubleday, 1991, p. 15.

13. When Religion Goes Wrong

1. Willam Blake, 'The Everlasting Gospel', c. 1818.
2. Blaise Pascal, *Pensées*, trans. A. J. Krailsheimer, London, Penguin, 1995, no. 813.
3. Quoted by Joseph Addison in *The Spectator*, vol. 6, p. 249.
4. C. S. Lewis, letter to Bede Griffiths, 20 December 1961.
5. Jonathan Glover, *Humanity: A Moral History of the Twentieth Century*, London, Jonathan Cape, 1999.
6. For a comprehensive statement of this argument, see David Berlinski, *The Devil's Delusion*, New York, Crown Forum, 2008.
7. Eric Hoffer, *The True Believer: Thoughts on the Nature of Mass Movements*, London, Secker and Warburg, 1951.
8. Scott Atran, *Talking to the Enemy*, London, Allen Lane, 2010.
9. Babylonian Talmud, Kiddushin 49a.
10. See Beryl Smalley, *The Study of the Bible in the Middle Ages*, Notre Dame, IN, Notre Dame University Press, 1964.
11. Maimonides, Mishneh Torah, Melakhim 5:4.

12. Ibid., 6:5.
13. See Avi Sagi, 'The punishment of Amalek in Jewish tradition: coping with the moral problem', *Harvard Theological Review* 87, pp. 323–46; Avi Sagi, *Yahadut: ben dat le-musar*, Israel, ha-Kibuts ha-me'uhad be-shituf Mekhon Shalom Hartman u-Merkaz Ya'akov Hertsog, 1998, pp. 199–219.
14. Levi Yitzhak of Berditchev, *Kedushat Levi*, Jerusalem, 2001, section on Purim; Gerald Cromer, 'Amalek as Other, Other as Amalek: Interpreting a Violent Narrative', *Qualitative Sociology*, 24:2, 2001, pp. 191–202.
15. Islam has a similar reinterpretation of the word *jihad*. See David Cook, *Understanding Jihad*, Berkeley, University of California Press, 2005.
16. Babylonian Talmud, Kiddushin 30b.
17. Babylonian Talmud, Megillah 10b.
18. The classic work is Joshua Trachtenberg, *The Devil and the Jews, the Medieval Conception of the Jew and Its Relation to Modern Antisemitism*, New Haven, CT, Yale University Press, 1943.
19. The best account is Norman Cohn, *Warrant for Genocide: The Myth of the Jewish World-Conspiracy and the Protocols of the Elders of Zion*, New York, Harper & Row, 1967.
20. Roy F. Baumeister, *Evil: Inside Human Cruelty and Violence*, New York, W. H. Freeman, 1997; Aaron T. Beck, *Prisoners of Hate: The Cognitive Basis of Anger, Hostility and Violence*, New York, HarperCollins, 1999; Vamik Volkan, *The Need to Have Enemies and Allies: From Clinical Practice to International Relationships*, Northvale, NJ, J. Aronson, 1988; Mark Juergensmeyer, *Terror in the Mind of God: The Global Rise of Religious Violence*, Berkeley: University of California Press, 2003.
21. Norman Cohn, *The Pursuit of the Millennium: Revolutionary Millenarians and Mystical Anarchists of the Middle Ages*, London, Paladin, 1970.
22. Ibid., pp. 285–6.
23. Ibid., p. 285.
24. Michael Walzer, *Exodus and Revolution*, New York, Basic, 1985, pp. 135, 145.
25. Flavius Josephus, G. A. Williamson and E. Mary Smallwood, *The Jewish War*, London, Penguin, 1981, p. 264.
26. For a balanced survey of the subject, see David Biale, *Power and Powerlessness in Jewish History*, New York, Schocken Books, 1986.

27. Abraham Lincoln, 'Second Inaugural Address', in Andrew Delbanco (ed.), *The Portable Abraham Lincoln*, New York, Viking, 1992, p. 321.
28. Babylonian Talmud, Shabbat 88a; Avodah Zarah 2b.
29. Isaiah Berlin, *Liberty*, ed. Henry Hardy, Oxford, Oxford University Press, 2002, p. 345.
30. Ibid., p. 346.
31. i.e. Richard Dawkins's famous remark, 'It is absolutely safe to say that if you meet somebody who claims not to believe in evolution, that person is ignorant, stupid or insane (or wicked, but I'd rather not consider that)', in a *New York Times* book review, 1989.
32. Sam Harris, *The End of Faith*, London, Free Press, 2006, p. 15.
33. See Fraser N. Watts and Kevin Dutton, *Why the Science and Religion Dialogue Matters: Voices from the International Society for Science and Religion*, Philadelphia, Templeton Foundation, 2006.

14. Why God?

1. Carl Jung, 'Psychotherapists or the clergy', *Collected Works*, vol. 11.
2. Giambattista Vico, *New Science: Principles of the New Science Concerning the Common Nature of Nations*, trans. David Marsh, London, Penguin Classics, 1999, p. 490.
3. Christopher Dawson, *Religion and the Rise of Western Culture*, New York, Doubleday, 1957, p. 224.
4. Maimonides, *Guide for the Perplexed*, Book II, 15.
5. James Le Fanu, *Why Us?: How Science Rediscovered the Mystery of Ourselves*, London: HarperPress, 2009, p. 141.
6. Dennis Diderot, *Rameau's Nephew and Other Works*, Indianapolis, Hackett Publishing, 2001, p. 292.
7. Nassim Nicholas Taleb, *The Black Swan: The Impact of the Highly Improbable*, New York, Random House, 2007.
8. Maimonides, Mishneh Torah, Hilkhot Yesodei ha-Torah 2:2.
9. Nikolai Berdyaev, *The Meaning of History*, New Brunswick, NJ, Transaction, 2006, p. 86.
10. Vico, *New Science,* p. 489
11. Vaclav Havel, *The Art of the Impossible*, trans. Paul Wilson, New York, Fromm International, 1998, p. 179.
12. Jürgen Habermas, *An Awareness of What Is Missing: Faith and Reason in the Post-Secular Age*, Cambridge, UK, Polity, 2010, p. 5.

13. Robert Putnam, *Bowling Alone: The Collapse and Revival of American Community*, New York, Simon & Schuster, 2000; Robert Putnam, David E. Campbell and Shaylyn Romney Garrett, *American Grace: How Religion Divides and Unites Us*, New York, Simon & Schuster, 2010.

14. Jonathan Haidt, *The Happiness Hypothesis: Finding Modern Truth in Ancient Wisdom*, New York, Basic, 2006, p. 88; E. Diener, et al., 'Subjective well-being: three decades of progress', *Psychological Bulletin*, 125, 1999, pp. 276–302; D. G. Myers, 'The funds, friends, and faith of happy people', *American Psychologist*, 55, 2000, pp. 56–67.

15. Robert Bellah, et al., *Habits of the Heart: Individualism and Commitment in American Life*, Berkeley, University of California Press, 1985, p. 284.

16. Abraham H. Maslow, 'A Theory of Human Motivation', *Psychological Review*, 50:4, 1943, pp. 370–96.

17. Richard Wilkinson and Kate Pickett, *The Spirit Level*, London, Penguin, 2010.

18. Alexis de Tocqueville, *Democracy in America*, New York, The Modern Library, 1981, vol. I, part II, ch. 9, p. 185.

19. Putnam, et al., *American Grace*, p. 9.

20. John Micklethwaite and Adrian Wooldridge, *God Is Back: How the Global Rise of Faith Is Changing the World*, London, Allen Lane, 2009, pp. 1–27.

21. Ibid., p. 16.

22. Eric Kaufmann, *Shall the Religious Inherit the Earth?: Demography and Politics in the Twenty-First Century*, London, Profile, 2010.

Epilogue

1. Sir David Brewster, *Memoirs of the Life, Writings, and Discoveries of Sir Isaac Newton*, Thomas Constable, Edinburgh, 1855, vol. II, ch. 27, p. 407.

2. Edward O. Wilson, *The Creation: An Appeal to Save Live on Earth*, New York, W. W. Norton & Co., 2006, p. 5.

3. Richard Dawkins, 'Is science a religion?' *The Humanist*, January/February 1997.

4. Max Planck, *Where Is Science Going? With a Preface by Albert Einstein*, trans. J. Murphy, London, Allen and Unwin, 1933, p. 217.

5. Albert Einstein, 'Science, Philosophy and Religion: A Symposium', Albert Einstein, *Ideas and Opinions*, New York, Bonanza Books, Crown Publishing Co., 1984, p. 46.
6. Friedrich Nietzsche, *The Gay Science: With a Prelude in Rhymes and an Appendix of Songs*, trans. Walter Kaufmann, New York, Vintage, 1974, Book V, 344, p. 283.

For Further Reading

It would be impossible to provide a full bibliography for the subjects covered in this book. They are vast, and each has generated a huge literature. The following are some of the, mainly contemporary, works I found helpful in reflecting on these issues. I have itemised them by chapter and topic.

Introduction

CRITICS OF RELIGION

Barker, Dan, *Godless: How an Evangelical Preacher Became One of America's Leading Atheists*, Berkeley, CA, Ulysses Press, 2008.

Dawkins, Richard, *The Blind Watchmaker*, London, Penguin, 1991.

Dawkins, Richard, *The God Delusion*, London, Bantam, 2006.

Dennett, Daniel, *Breaking the Spell: Religion as a Natural Phenomenon*, London, Penguin, 2006.

Dennett, Daniel, *Darwin's Dangerous Idea: Evolution and the Meanings of Life*, London, Penguin, 1996.

Grayling, A. C., *Against All Gods: Six Polemics on Religion and an Essay on Kindness*, London, Oberon, 2007.

Harris, Sam, *The End of Faith: Religion, Terror, and the Future of Reason*, London, Free Press, 2005.

Harris, Sam, *Letter to a Christian Nation*, London, Bantam, 2007.

Hitchens, Christopher, *God Is Not Great: The Case Against Religion*, London, Atlantic Books, 2007.

Hitchens, Christopher (ed.), *The Portable Atheist: Essential Readings for the Nonbeliever*, Cambridge, MA, Da Capo, 2007.

Humphrys, John, *In God We Doubt: Confessions of a Failed Atheist*, London, Hodder & Stoughton, 2008.

Mills, David, *Atheist Universe: The Thinking Person's Answer to Christian Fundamentalism*, Berkeley, CA, Ulysses Press, 2006.

Onfray, Michel, *In Defence of Atheism: The Case Against Christianity, Judaism and Islam*, New York, Arcade, 2007.

Russell, Bertrand, *Why I Am Not a Christian: And Other Essays on Religion and Related Subjects*, London: Routledge, 1979.

Smith, George H., *Atheism: The Case against God*, Buffalo, NY, Prometheus Books, 1989.

Stenger, Victor, *God: The Failed Hypothesis*, Amherst, MA, Prometheus Books, 2007.

Stenger, Victor, *The New Atheism: Taking a Stand for Science and Reason*, Amherst, MA, Prometheus Books, 2009.

DEFENDERS OF RELIGION

Andrews, Edgar, *Who Made God? Searching for a Theory of Everything*, Darlington, UK, EP Books, 2009.

Armstrong, Karen, *The Case for God*, London, Bodley Head, 2009.

Berlinski, David, *The Devil's Delusion: Atheism and Its Scientific Pretensions*, New York, Crown Forum, 2008.

Berry, R. J. (ed.), *Real Scientists, Real Faith: 17 Leading Scientists Reveal the Harmony between Their Science and Their Faith*, Oxford, Monarch Books, 2009.

Collins, Francis S., *Belief: Readings on the Reason for Faith*, New York, HarperOne, 2010.

Collins, Francis S., *The Language of God: A Scientist Presents Evidence for Belief*, New York, Free Press, 2006.

Copan, Paul and William Lane Craig, *Contending with Christianity's Critics: Answering New Atheists and Other Objectors*, Nashville, TN, B. & H. Academic, 2009.

Cornwell, John, *Darwin's Angel: A Seraphic Response to the God Delusion*, London, Profile, 2008.

Cottingham, John, *Why Believe?* London, Continuum, 2009.

Craig, William Lane, *Reasonable Faith*, Wheaton, IL, Crossway Books, 2008.

Crean, Thomas, *God Is No Delusion: A Refutation of Richard Dawkins*, San Francisco, Ignatius Press, 2007.

Eagleton, Terry, *Reason, Faith, and Revolution: Reflections on the God Debate*, New Haven, CT, Yale University Press, 2009.

Egan, Joe, *The Godless Delusion: Dawkins and the Limits of Human Sight*, Bern, Peter Lang, 2009.

Flew, Anthony, and Roy Varghese, *There Is a God: How the World's Most Notorious Atheist Changed His Mind*, New York, HarperOne, 2008.

Ganssle, Gregory, *A Reasonable God*, Waco, TX, Baylor University Press, 2009.

Gumbel, Nicky, *Is God a Delusion?: What Is the Evidence?* Oxford, UK, Alpha International, 2008.

Hahn, Scott, *Answering the New Atheism*, Steubenville, OH, Emmaus Road Publishers, 2008.

Hart, David Bentley, *Atheist Delusions: The Christian Revolution and its Fashionable Enemies*, New Haven, CT, Yale University Press, 2010.

Keller, Timothy, *The Reason for God: Belief in an Age of Scepticism*, New York, Dutton, 2008.

Leahy, Michael Patrick, *Letter to an Atheist*, Thompsons Station, TN, Harpeth River Press, 2007.

Markham, Ian S., *Against Atheism: Why Dawkins, Hitchens and Harris Are Fundamentally Wrong*, Hoboken, NJ, Wiley-Blackwell, 2010.

McGrath, Alister, *The Dawkins Delusion*, Downers Grove, IL, InterVarsity Press, 2007.

McGrath, Alister, *Dawkins' God: Genes, Memes, and the Meaning of Life*, Oxford, Blackwell, 2005.

Novak, Michael, *No One Sees God*, New York, Doubleday, 2008.

Polkinghorne, John, *Belief in God in an Age of Science*, New Haven, CT, Yale University Press, 2003.

Polkinghorne, John, *Questions of Truth: Fifty-One Responses to Questions About God, Science and Belief*, Louisville, KY, Westminster/John Knox Press, 2009.

Polkinghorne, John, and Thomas Oord, *The Polkinghorne Reader: Science, Faith and the Search for Meaning*, London, SPCK, 2010.

Poole, Michael, *The New Atheism: Ten Arguments That Don't Hold Water*, Oxford, UK, Lion Hudson, 2009.

Robertson, David, *The Dawkins Letters: Challenging Atheist Myths*, Christian Focus Publications, 2007.

Ward, Keith, *The Big Questions in Science and Religion*, West Conshohocken, PA, Templeton Press, 2008.

Ward, Keith, *God, Chance and Necessity*, Oxford, Oneworld, 1996.

Ward, Keith, *The God Conclusion: God and the Western Philosophical Tradition*, London, Darton, Longman & Todd, 2009.

Ward, Keith, *God: A Guide for the Perplexed*, Oxford, Oneworld, 2002.

Ward, Keith, *Pascal's Fire: Scientific Faith and Religious Understanding*, Oxford, Oneworld, 2006.

Ward, Keith, *Why There Is Almost Certainly a God: Doubting Dawkins*, Oxford, Lion, 2008.

OTHER

Cottingham, John, *The Spiritual Dimension*, Cambridge, Cambridge University Press, 2005.

Cox, Harvey Gallagher, *The Future of Faith*, New York, HarperOne, 2009.

Fergusson, David, *Faith and Its Critics*, Oxford, Oxford University Press, 2009.

Goldstein, Rebecca, *36 Arguments for the Existence of God: A Work of Fiction*, New York, Pantheon, 2010.

Hecht, Jennifer Michael, *Doubt: A History: The Great Doubters and Their Legacy of Innovation, from Socrates and Jesus* to *Thomas Jefferson and Emily Dickinson*, San Francisco, HarperSanFrancisco, 2003.

Hunter, James Davison, *To Change the World: The Irony, Tragedy, and Possibility of Christianity in the Late Modern World*, New York, Oxford University Press, 2010.

Kaufmann, Eric, *Shall the Religious Inherit the Earth?: Demography and Politics in the Twenty-First Century*, London, Profile, 2010.

Lennox, John C., *God's Undertaker: Has Science Buried God?*, Oxford, UK, Lion, 2007.

Micklethwait, John, and Adrian Wooldridge, *God Is Back: How the Global Revival of Faith Is Changing the World*, New York, Penguin, 2009.

Nagel, Thomas, *Secular Philosophy and the Religious Temperament: Essays 2002–2008*, Oxford, UK, Oxford University Press, 2010.

Robinson, Marilynne, *Absence of Mind*, New Haven, CT, Yale University Press, 2010.

Taylor, Charles, *A Secular Age*, Cambridge, MA, Belknap of Harvard University Press, 2007.

Tippett, Krista, *Einstein's God: Conversations about Science and the Human Spirit*, New York, Penguin, 2010.

Wilson, Edward O., *The Creation: An Appeal to Save Life on Earth*, New York, W. W. Norton & Co., 2006.

Wolpert, L., *Six Impossible Things before Breakfast: The Evolutionary Origins of Belief*, London, Faber & Faber, 2006.

Wright, Robert, *The Evolution of God*, London, Little, Brown, 2009.

1. The Meaning-Seeking Animal

Baumeister, Roy F., *The Cultural Animal: Human Nature, Meaning, and Social Life*, Oxford/New York, Oxford University Press, 2005.

Baumeister, Roy F., *Meanings of Life*, New York, Guilford Press, 1991.

Bell, Derrick A., *Ethical Ambition: Living a Life of Meaning and Worth*, London, Bloomsbury, 2002.

Bortolotti, Lisa, *Philosophy and Happiness*, New York, Palgrave MacMillan, 2009.

Britton, Karl, *Philosophy and the Meaning of Life*, Cambridge, Cambridge University Press, 1969.

Cottingham, John, *On the Meaning of Life*, London/New York, Routledge, 2003.

Durant, Will (ed.), *On the Meaning of Life*, London, Williams and Norgate, 1933.

Eagleton, Terry, *The Meaning of Life: A Very Short Introduction*, Oxford, Oxford University Press, 2008.

Ferry, Luc, *Man Made God: The Meaning of Life*, Chicago, University of Chicago Press, 2002.

Flanagan, Owen J., *Self Expressions: Mind, Morals, and the Meaning of Life*, New York, Oxford University Press, 1996.

Frankl, Viktor E., *The Doctor and the Soul: From Psychotherapy to Logotherapy*, trans. Richard and Clara Winston, New York, Vintage Books, 1986.

Frankl, Viktor E., *Man's Search for Meaning: An Introduction to Logotherapy*, trans. Ilse Lasch, Boston, Beacon Press, 1992.

Frankl, Viktor E., *The Unheard Cry for Meaning: Psychotherapy and Humanism*, New York, Simon & Schuster, 1978.

Greive, Bradley Trevor, *The Meaning of Life*, Kansas City, MO, Andrews McMeel Publishers, 2002.

Klemke, E. D. (ed.), *The Meaning of life*, New York, Oxford University Press, 1981.

Thagard, Paul, *The Brain and the Meaning of Life*, Princeton, NJ, Princeton University Press, 2010.

Young, Julian, *The Death of God and the Meaning of Life*, London, Routledge, 2003.

2. In Two Minds

RIGHT BRAIN, LEFT BRAIN

Damasio, Antonio R., *Descartes' Error: Emotion, Reason, and the Human Brain*, New York, Putnam, 1994.

Damasio, Antonio R., *Self Comes to Mind: Constructing the Conscious Brain*, New York, Pantheon, 2010.

Decety, Jean, and William John Ickes, *The Social Neuroscience of Empathy*, Cambridge, MA, MIT, 2009.

Doidge, Norman, *The Brain that Changes Itself: Stories of Personal Triumph from the Frontiers of Brain Science*, New York, Viking, 2007.

Jaynes, Julian, *The Origin of Consciousness in the Breakdown of the Bicameral Mind*, Boston, Houghton Mifflin, 1976.

McGilchrist, Iain, *The Master and His Emissary: The Divided Brain and the Making of the Western World*, New Haven, CT, Yale University Press, 2009.

Ornstein, Robert E., *The Right Mind: Making Sense of the Hemispheres*, New York, Harcourt Brace, 1997.

Pink, Daniel H., *A Whole New Mind: Why Right-Brainers Will Rule the Future*, New York, Riverhead, 2006.

Schiffer, Fredric, *Of Two Minds: The Revolutionary Science of Dual-Brain Psychology*, New York, Free Press, 1998.

Shlain, Leonard, *The Alphabet versus the Goddess: Male Words and Female Images*, London, Penguin, 2000.

Taylor, Jill Bolte, *My Stroke of Insight: A Brain Scientist's Personal Journey*, New York, Viking, 2008.

OTHER TEXTS REFERRED TO

Baron-Cohen, Simon, *The Essential Difference: The Truth about the Male and Female Brain*, New York, Basic, 2003.

Bruner, Jerome S., *Acts of Meaning*, Cambridge, MA, Harvard University Press, 1994.

Bruner, Jerome, *Actual Minds: Possible Worlds*, Cambridge, MA, Harvard University Press, 1986.

Bruner, Jerome S., *Making Stories: Law, Literature, Life*, New York, Farrar, Straus and Giroux, 2002.

Gilligan, Carol, *In a Different Voice: Psychological Theory and Women's Development*, Cambridge, MA, Harvard University Press, 1993.

Nisbett, Richard E., *The Geography of Thought: How Asians and Westerners Think Differently – and Why*, New York, Free Press, 2003.

Nussbaum, Martha Craven, *Poetic Justice: The Literary Imagination and Public Life*, Boston, Beacon, 1995.

Pinker, Steven, *The Blank Slate: The Modern Denial of Human Nature*, New York, Viking, 2002.

3. Diverging Paths

Barr, James, *Biblical Faith and Natural Theology: The Gifford Lectures for 1991*, Oxford, Clarendon, 1993.

Boman, Thorleif, *Hebrew Thought Compared with Greek*, Philadelphia, Westminster, 1960.

Funkenstein, Amos, *Theology and the Scientific Imagination: From the Middle Ages to the Seventeenth Century*, Princeton, NJ, Princeton University Press, 1986.

Harrison, Peter, *The Bible, Protestantism, and the Rise of Natural Science*, Cambridge, Cambridge University Press, 1998.

Harrison, Peter, *The Fall of Man and the Foundations of Science*, Cambridge, Cambridge University Press, 2007.

Hooykaas, R., *Religion and the Rise of Modern Science*, Grand Rapids, MI, Eerdmans, 1972.

Stark, Rodney, *For the Glory of God: How Monotheism Led to Reformations, Science, Witch-hunts, and the End of Slavery*, Princeton, NJ, Princeton University Press, 2003.

Stark, Rodney, *One True God: Historical Consequences of Monotheism*, Princeton, NJ, Princeton University Press, 2001.

Stark, Rodney, *The Victory of Reason: How Christianity Led to Freedom, Capitalism, and Western Success*, New York, Random House, 2005.

Toulmin, Stephen Edelston, *Cosmopolis: The Hidden Agenda of Modernity*, Chicago, University of Chicago Press, 1994.

6. *Human Dignity*

Fukuyama, Francis, *Our Posthuman Future: Consequences of the Biotechnology Revolution*, New York, Farrar, Straus and Giroux, 2002.

Habermas, Jürgen, *The Future of Human Nature*, Cambridge, Polity, 2006.

Human Cloning and Human Dignity: an Ethical Inquiry, Washington, DC, President's Council on Bioethics, 2002.

Kass, Leon (ed.), *Being Human: Core Readings in the Humanities*, New York, W. W. Norton & Co., 2004.

Kass, Leon, *Life, Liberty, and the Defense of Dignity: The Challenge for Bioethics*, San Francisco, Encounter, 2002.

Kass, Leon, *Toward a More Natural Science: Biology and Human Affairs*, New York, Free Press, 1985.

Kateb, George, *Human Dignity*, Cambridge, MA, Belknap of Harvard University Press, 2011.

Kraynak, Robert P., and Glenn E. Tinder, *In Defense of Human Dignity: Essays for Our Times*, Notre Dame, IN, University of Notre Dame Press, 2003.

Lewis, C. S., *The Abolition of Man*, New York, Macmillan, 1978.

Meilaender, Gilbert, *Neither Beast nor God: The Dignity of the Human Person*, New York, Encounter, 2009.

Pico della Mirandola, Giovanni, *Oration on the Dignity of Man*, Chicago, Gateway Editions, 1956.

Sandel, Michael J., *The Case against Perfection: Ethics in the Age of Genetic Engineering*, Cambridge, MA, Belknap of Harvard University Press, 2007.

Soulen, R. Kendall, and Linda Woodhead, *God and Human Dignity*, Grand Rapids, MI, Eerdmans, 2006.

Wolterstorff, Nicholas, *Justice: Rights and Wrongs*, Princeton, NJ, Princeton University Press, 2008.

7. *The Politics of Freedom*

Acton, Lord, *Selected Writings of Lord Acton*, ed. J. Rufus Fears, Indianapolis, Liberty Classics, 1985–8.

Berman, Joshua, *Created Equal: How the Bible Broke with Ancient Political Thought*, Oxford, Oxford University Press, 2008.

Cohen, Stuart, *The Three Crowns: Structures of Communal Politics in Early Rabbinic Jewry*, Cambridge, Cambridge University Press, 1990.

Elazar, Daniel Judah, *Covenant and Civil Society: The Constitutional Matrix of Modern Democracy*, New Brunswick, NJ, Transaction, 1998.

Elazar, Daniel Judah, *Covenant and Commonwealth*, New Brunswick, NJ, Transaction, 1996.

Elazar, Daniel Judah, *Covenant and Constitutionalism: The Great Frontier and the Matrix of Federal Democracy*, New Brunswick, NJ, Transaction, 1997.

Elazar, Daniel Judah, *Covenant and Polity in Biblical Israel: Biblical Foundations and Jewish Expressions*, New Brunswick, NJ, Transaction, 1995.

Elazar, Daniel Judah, *Covenant in the Nineteenth Century: The Decline of an American Political Tradition*, Lanham, MD, Rowman & Littlefield, 1994.

Elazar, Daniel Judah, *The Covenant Tradition in Politics*, New Brunswick, NJ, Transaction, 1995.

Elazar, Daniel Judah (ed.), *Kinship and Consent: The Jewish Political Tradition and its Contemporary Uses*, Washington, DC, University Press of America, 1983.

Elazar, Daniel Judah, and John Kincaid, *Covenant and Polity*, Philadelphia, Center for the Study of Federalism, Temple University, 1979.

Hayek, Friedrich A. Von, *The Constitution of Liberty*, Chicago, University of Chicago Press, 1960.

Hayek, Friedrich A. Von, and William Warren Bartley, *The Fatal*

Conceit: The Errors of Socialism, Chicago, University of Chicago Press, 1989.

Hill, Christopher, *The English Bible and the Seventeenth-Century Revolution*, London, Allen Lane, 1993.

Hill, Christopher, *Milton and the English Revolution*, New York, Viking Press, 1977.

Hill, Christopher, *The World Turned Upside Down: Radical Ideas during the English Revolution*, New York, Viking Press, 1972.

Miller, Perry, *The New England Mind: The Seventeenth Century*, Cambridge, MA, Harvard University Press, 1954.

Nelson, Eric, *The Hebrew Republic: Jewish Sources and the Transformation of European Political Thought*, Cambridge, MA, Harvard University Press, 2010.

Plamenatz, John Petrov, *Man and Society, Political and Social Theory*, New York, McGraw-Hill, 1963.

Rosenblatt, Jason P., *Renaissance England's Chief Rabbi: John Selden*, New York, Oxford University Press, 2006.

Sacks, Jonathan, *The Home We Build Together*, London, Continuum, 2009.

Sacks, Jonathan, *The Politics of Hope*, London, Jonathan Cape, 1997.

Talmon, J. L., *The Origins of Totalitarian Democracy*, New York, Praeger, 1960.

8. Morality

Axelrod, Robert, *The Evolution of Co-operation*, London, Penguin, 1990.

Baggett, David, and Jerry L. Walls, *Good God: The Theistic Foundations of Morality*, New York, Oxford University Press, 2011.

Garcia, Robert K., and Nathan L. King, *Is Goodness without God Good Enough?: A Debate on Faith, Secularism, and Ethics*, Lanham, MD, Rowman & Littlefield, 2009.

Harris, Sam, *The Moral Landscape: How Science Can Determine Human Values*, New York, Free Press, 2010.

Hauser, Marc D., *Moral Minds: How Nature Designed Our Universal Sense of Right and Wrong*, New York, Ecco, 2006.

MacIntyre, Alasdair C., *After Virtue: A Study in Moral Theory*, London, Duckworth, 1981.

Ridley, Matt, *The Origins of Virtue*, London, Viking, 1996.

Stout, Jeffrey, *The Flight from Authority: Religion, Morality, and the Quest for Autonomy*, Notre Dame, IN, University of Notre Dame Press, 1981.

Waal, Frans de, *The Age of Empathy: Nature's Lessons for a Kinder Society*, New York, Harmony, 2009.

Wade, Nicholas, *The Faith Instinct: How Religion Evolved and Why It Endures*, New York, Penguin, 2009.

Walzer, Michael, *Interpretation and Social Criticism*, Cambridge, MA, Harvard University Press, 1987.

Walzer, Michael, *Thick and Thin: Moral Argument at Home and Abroad*, Notre Dame, IN, University of Notre Dame Press, 1994.

Wright, Robert, *The Moral Animal: The New Science of Evolutionary Psychology*, New York, Pantheon, 1994.

9. Relationships

Barton, Stephen C., *The Family in Theological Perspective*, Edinburgh, T. & T. Clark, 1996.

Browning, Don S., M. Christian Green and John Witte, *Sex, Marriage, and Family in World Religions*, New York, Columbia Univeristy Press, 2006.

Broyde, Michael J., and Michael Ausubel, *Marriage, Sex, and Family in Judaism*, Lanham, MD, Rowman & Littlefield, 2005.

Buber, Martin, *I and Thou*, New York, Scribner, 1958.

Farley, Margaret A., *Just Love: A Framework for Christian Sexual Ethics*, New York, Continuum, 2006.

George, Robert P., and Jean Bethke Elshtain, *The Meaning of*

Marriage: Family, State, Market, and Morals, Dallas, Spence Publishers, 2006.

Macmurray, John, *The Form of the Personal*, London, Faber, 1961.

Macmurray, John, *Persons in Relation*, Atlantic Highlands, NJ, Humanities, 1979.

Mount, Ferdinand, *The Subversive Family: An Alternative History of Love and Marriage*, New York, Free Press, 1992.

Rogers, Carl R., *On Becoming a Person: A Therapist's View of Psychotherapy*, Boston, Houghton Mifflin, 1961.

Ross, Jacob Joshua, *The Virtues of the Family*, New York, Free Press, 1994.

Waal, Anastasia de, *Second Thoughts on the Family*, London, Civitas, Institute for the Study of Civil Society, 2008.

Wilson, James Q., *The Marriage Problem: How Our Culture Has Weakened Families*, New York, HarperCollins, 2002.

Witte, John, *From Sacrament to Contract: Marriage, Religion, and Law in the Western Tradition*, Louisville, KY, Westminster John Knox, 1997.

Witte, John, and Eliza Ellison, *Covenant Marriage in Comparative Perspective*, Grand Rapids, MI, Eerdmans, 2005.

10. A Meaningful Life

Ben-Shahar, Tal, *Happier: Learn the Secrets to Daily Joy and Lasting Fulfillment*, New York, McGraw-Hill, 2007.

Ben-Shahar, Tal, *The Pursuit of Perfect: How to Stop Chasing Perfection and Start Living a Richer, Happier Life*, New York, McGraw-Hill, 2009.

Bok, Derek Curtis, *The Politics of Happiness: What Government Can Learn from the New Research on Well-Being*, Princeton, NJ, Princeton University Press, 2010.

Bok, Sissela, *Exploring Happiness: From Aristotle to Brain Science*, New Haven, CT, Yale University Press, 2010.

Brümmer, Vincent, and Marcel Sarot, *Happiness, Well-Being*

and the Meaning of Life: A Dialogue of Social Science and Religion, Kampen, The Netherlands, Kok Pharos Publishing House, 1996.

Cahn, Steven M., and Christine Vitrano, *Happiness: Classic and Contemporary Readings in Philosophy*, Oxford, Oxford University Press, 2007.

Charry, Ellen T., *God and the Art of Happiness*, Grand Rapids, MI, Eerdmans, 2010.

Dalai Lama and Howard Cutler, *The Art of Happiness: A Handbook for Living*, London, Coronet, 1999.

Diener, Ed, and Robert Biswas-Diener, *Happiness: Unlocking the Mysteries of Psychological Wealth*, Malden, MA, Blackwell, 2008.

Emmons, Robert A., *Thanks!: How the New Science of Gratitude Can Make You Happier*, Boston, Houghton Mifflin, 2007.

Gilbert, Daniel Todd, *Stumbling on Happiness*, New York, Alfred A. Knopf, 2006.

Graham, Carol, *Happiness around the World: The Paradox of Happy Peasants and Miserable Millionaires*, Oxford, Oxford University Press, 2009.

Haidt, Jonathan, *The Happiness Hypothesis: Finding Modern Truth in Ancient Wisdom*, New York, Basic, 2006.

Hanson, Rick, and Richard Mendius, *Buddha's Brain: The Practical Neuroscience of Happiness, Love and Wisdom*, Oakland, CA, New Harbinger Publications, 2009.

Hecht, Jennifer Michael, *The Happiness Myth: The Historical Antidote to What Isn't Working Today*, New York, HarperOne, 2008.

Layard, P. Richard G., *Happiness: Lessons from a New Science*, London, Penguin, 2006.

Lyubomirsky, Sonja, *The How of Happiness: A Scientific Approach to Getting the Life You Want*, New York, Penguin, 2008.

McMahon, Darrin M., *Happiness: A History*, New York, Atlantic Monthly, 2006.

Minirth, Frank B., and Paul D. Meier, *Happiness Is a Choice: The*

Symptoms, Causes, and Cures of Depression, Grand Rapids, MI, Baker, 2007.

Nettle, Daniel, *Happiness: The Science behind Your Smile*, Oxford, Oxford University Press, 2005.

Ricard, Matthieu, *Happiness: A Guide to Developing Life's Most Important Skill*, New York, Little, Brown, 2006.

Rubin, Gretchen Craft, *The Happiness Project: Or Why I Spent a Year Trying to Sing in the Morning, Clean My Closets, Fight Right, Read Aristotle, and Generally Have More Fun*, New York, HarperCollins, 2009.

Russell, Bertrand, *The Conquest of Happiness*, London, George Allen & Unwin, 1948.

Seligman, Martin E. P., *Authentic Happiness: Using the New Positive Psychology to Realize Your Potential for Lasting Fulfillment*, New York, Free Press, 2002.

Seligman, Martin E. P., *Learned Optimism*, New York, Pocket, 1998.

Tirosh-Samuelson, Hava, *Happiness in Premodern Judaism: Virtue, Knowledge, and Well-being*, Cincinnati, Hebrew Union College, 2003.

Twerski, Abraham J., *Happiness and the Human Spirit: The Spirituality of Becoming the Best You Can Be*, Woodstock, NY, Jewish Lights Publishers, 2007.

11. Darwin

EVOLUTION AND CREATION

Alexander, Denis, *Creation or Evolution: Do We Have to Choose?*, Oxford, Monarch, 2008.

Alexander, Denis, *Rebuilding the Matrix: Science and Faith in the 21st Century*, Grand Rapids, MI, Zondervan, 2003.

Aviezer, Nathan, *Fossils and Faith: Understanding Torah and Science*, Hoboken, NJ, KTAV Publishing House, 2001.

Barbour, Ian G., *When Science Meets Religion: Enemies, Strangers, or Partners?* San Francisco, HarperSanFrancisco, 2000.

Brown, William P., *The Ethos of the Cosmos: The Genesis of Moral Imagination in the Bible*, Grand Rapids, MI, Eerdmans, 1999.

Brown, William P., *The Seven Pillars of Creation: The Bible, Science, and the Ecology of Wonder*, Oxford, Oxford University Press, 2010.

Cantor, G. N., and Marc Swetlitz, *Jewish Tradition and the Challenge of Darwinism*, Chicago, University of Chicago Press, 2006.

Collins, Francis S., *The Language of God: A Scientist Presents Evidence for Belief*, Detroit, Thomson/Gale, 2007.

Dowd, Michael, *Thank God for Evolution: How the Marriage of Science and Religion Will Transform Your Life and Our World*, New York, Viking, 2008.

Goodman, Lenn Evan, *Creation and Evolution*, London, Routledge, 2010.

Haught, John F., *God after Darwin: A Theology of Evolution*, Boulder, CO, Westview, 2008.

Haught, John F., *Making Sense of Evolution: Darwin, God, and the Drama of Life*, Louisville, KY, Westminster John Knox, 2010.

Haught, John F., *Science and Religion: From Conflict to Conversation*, New York, Paulist, 1995.

Hayward, Alan, *Creation and Evolution*, Minneapolis, MN, Bethany House, 1995.

Larson, Edward J., *The Creation-Evolution Debate: Historical Perspectives*, Athens, University of Georgia, 2007.

Larson, Edward J., *Trial and Error: The American Controversy over Creation and Evolution*, New York, Oxford University Press, 2003.

Miller, Kenneth R., *Finding Darwin's God: A Scientist's Search for Common Ground between God and Evolution*, New York, Cliff Street, 1999.

Miller, Kenneth R., *Only a Theory: Evolution and the Battle for America's Soul*, New York, Viking, 2008.

Newell, Norman Dennis, *Creation and Evolution: Myth or Reality?*, New York, Columbia University Press, 1982.

Polkinghorne, John, *An Evolving Creation*, Edinburgh, University of Edinburgh, Institute for Advanced Studies in the Humanities, 2009.

Ruse, Michael, *But Is It Science?: The Philosophical Question in the Creation/Evolution Controversy*, Buffalo, NY, Prometheus, 1988.

Ruse, Michael, *The Evolution-Creation Struggle*, Cambridge, MA, Harvard University Press, 2005.

Sarfati, Jonathan D., and Mike Matthews, *Refuting Evolution 2*, Niles, IL, Master, 2002.

Scott, Eugenie Carol, *Evolution vs. Creationism: An Introduction*, Westport, CT, Greenwood, 2004.

Slifkin, Nosson, *The Challenge of Creation: Judaism's Encounter with Science, Cosmology, and Evolution*, Ramat Bet Shemesh, Israel, Zoo Torah, 2006.

Slifkin, Nosson, *The Science of Torah: The Reflection of Torah in the Laws of Science, the Creation of the Universe and the Development of Life*, Brooklyn, NY, Targum, 2001.

Stove, D. C., *Darwinian Fairytales: Selfish Genes, Errors of Heredity, and Other Fables of Evolution*, New York, Encounter, 2007.

DARWINIAN AND NEUROSCIENTIFIC ACCOUNTS OF RELIGION

Atran, Scott, *In Gods We Trust: The Evolutionary Landscape of Religion*, Oxford, Oxford University Press, 2002.

Beauregard, Mario, and Denyse O'Leary, *The Spiritual Brain: A Neuroscientist's Case for the Existence of the Soul*, New York, HarperOne, 2007.

Boyer, Pascal, *Religion Explained: The Evolutionary Origins of Religious Thought*, New York, Basic, 2001.

Feierman, Jay R., *The Biology of Religious Behavior: The Evolutionary Origins of Faith and Religion*, Santa Barbara, CA, Praeger/ABC-CLIO, 2009.

Hamer, Dean H., *The God Gene: How Faith Is Hardwired into Our Genes*, New York, Doubleday, 2004.

McNamara, Patrick, *The Neuroscience of Religious Experience*, Cambridge, Cambridge University Press, 2009.

Newberg, Andrew B., and Mark Robert Waldman, *Born to Believe: God, Science, and the Origin of Ordinary and Extraordinary Beliefs*, New York, Free Press, 2007.

Newberg, Andrew B., and Mark Robert Waldman, *How God Changes Your Brain: Breakthrough Findings from a Leading Neuroscientist*, New York, Ballantine, 2009.

Newberg, Andrew B., Eugene G. D'Aquili, and Vince Rause, *Why God Won't Go Away: Brain Science and the Biology of Belief*, New York, Ballantine, 2001.

Tremlin, Todd, *Minds and Gods: The Cognitive Foundations of Religion*, New York, Oxford University Press, 2006.

Wade, Nicholas, *The Faith Instinct: How Religion Evolved and Why It Endures*, New York, Penguin, 2009.

Wilson, David Sloan, *Darwin's Cathedral: Evolution, Religion, and the Nature of Society*, Chicago, University of Chicago Press, 2007.

12. The Problem of Evil

Adams, Marilyn McCord, and Robert Merrihew Adams, *The Problem of Evil*, Oxford, Oxford University Press, 1990.

Bernstein, Richard J., *Radical Evil: A Philosophical Interrogation*, Cambridge, UK, Polity, 2002.

Feinberg, John S., *The Many Faces of Evil: Theological Systems and the Problems of Evil*, Wheaton, IL, Crossway, 2004.

Hick, John, *Evil and the God of Love*, New York, Harper & Row, 1978.

Inwagen, Peter van, *The Problem of Evil: The Gifford Lectures Delivered in the University of St Andrews in 2003*, Oxford, Clarendon, 2006.

Kelly, Joseph F., *The Problem of Evil in the Western Tradition: From the Book of Job to Modern Genetics*, Collegeville, MN, Liturgical, 2002.

Larrimore, Mark J., *The Problem of Evil: A Reader*, Oxford, Blackwell, 2001.

Matuštík, Martin Joseph, *Radical Evil and the Scarcity of Hope: Postsecular Meditations*, Bloomington, Indiana University Press, 2008.

Nadler, Steven M., *The Best of All Possible Worlds: A Story of Philosophers, God, and Evil*, New York, Farrar, Straus and Giroux, 2008.

Neiman, Susan, *Evil in Modern Thought: An Alternative History of Philosophy*, Princeton, NJ, Princeton University Press, 2002.

Patterson, David, and John K. Roth, *Fire in the Ashes: God, Evil, and the Holocaust*, Seattle, University of Washington, 2005.

Plantinga, Alvin, *God, Freedom, and Evil*, Grand Rapids, MI, Eerdmans, 1977.

Rorty, Amélie, *The Many Faces of Evil: Historical Perspectives*, London, Routledge, 2001.

Urban, Linwood, and Douglas N. Walton, *The Power of God: Readings on Omnipotence and Evil*, New York, Oxford University Press, 1978.

Wright, N. T., *Evil and the Justice of God*, Downers Grove, IL, InterVarsity Press, 2006.

13. When Religion Goes Wrong

Armstrong, Karen, *The Battle for God*, New York, Alfred A. Knopf, 2000.

Avalos, Hector, *Fighting Words: The Origins of Religious Violence*, Amherst, MA, Prometheus, 2005.

Baumeister, Roy F., *Evil: Inside Human Cruelty and Violence*, New York, W. H. Freeman, 1997.

Beck, Aaron T., *Prisoners of Hate: The Cognitive Basis of Anger, Hostility, and Violence*, New York, HarperCollins, 1999.

Cohn, Norman, *The Pursuit of the Millennium: Revolutionary*

Millenarians and Mystical Anarchists of the Middle Ages, New York, Oxford University Press, 1970.

Girard, René, *The Scapegoat*, Baltimore, Johns Hopkins University Press, 1986.

Girard, René, *Violence and the Sacred*, Baltimore, Johns Hopkins University Press, 1977.

Juergensmeyer, Mark, *Terror in the Mind of God: The Global Rise of Religious Violence*, Berkeley, University of California Press, 2000.

Kimball, Charles, *When Religion Becomes Evil*, San Francisco, HarperSanFrancisco, 2002.

Meyer, Marvin W., and Wolf-Peter Funk, *The Nag Hammadi Scriptures*, New York, HarperOne, 2007.

Nelson-Pallmeyer, Jack, *Is Religion Killing Us?: Violence in the Bible and the Quran*, London, Continuum, 2003.

Pagels, Elaine H., *The Gnostic Gospels*, New York, Random House, 1979.

Pagels, Elaine H., *The Origin of Satan*, New York, Random House, 1995.

Reich, Walter, *Origins of Terrorism: Psychologies, Ideologies, Theologies, States of Mind*, Washington, DC, Woodrow Wilson Center, 1998.

Schwartz, Regina M., *The Curse of Cain: The Violent Legacy of Monotheism*, Chicago, University of Chicago Press, 1997.

Stern, Jessica, *Terror in the Name of God: Why Religious Militants Kill*, New York, Ecco, 2003.

Talmon, J. L., *The Origins of Totalitarian Democracy*, New York, Praeger, 1960.

Volf, Miroslav, *Exclusion and Embrace: A Theological Exploration of Identity, Otherness, and Reconciliation*, Nashville, TN, Abingdon, 1996.

Volkan, Vamik D., *The Need to Have Enemies and Allies: From Clinical Practice to International Relationships*, Northvale, NJ, J. Aronson, 1988.

14. Why God?

COSMOLOGY

Barrow, John D., and Frank J. Tipler, *The Anthropic Cosmological Principle*, Oxford, Oxford University Press, 1986.

Davies, P. C. W., *The Cosmic Blueprint*, New York, Unwin Paperbacks, 1989.

Davies, P. C. W., *God and the New Physics*, New York, Simon & Schuster, 1983.

Davies, P. C. W., *The Goldilocks Enigma: Why Is the Universe Just Right for Life?*, Boston, Houghton Mifflin, 2008.

Davies, P. C. W., *The Mind of God: The Scientific Basis for a Rational World*, New York, Touchstone/Simon & Schuster, 1993.

Rees, Martin J., *Just Six Numbers: The Deep Forces that Shape the Universe*, New York, Basic, 2000.

Rees, Martin J., *Our Cosmic Habitat*, Princeton, NJ, Princeton University Press, 2003.

Schroeder, Gerald L., *Genesis and the Big Bang: The Discovery of Harmony between Modern Science and the Bible*, New York, Bantam, 1990.

Schroeder, Gerald L., *God According to God: A Physicist Proves We've Been Wrong about God All Along*, New York, HarperOne, 2009.

Schroeder, Gerald L., *The Hidden Face of God: How Science Reveals the Ultimate Truth*, New York, Free Press, 2001.

Schroeder, Gerald L., *The Science of God: The Convergence of Scientific and Biblical Wisdom*, New York, Free Press, 1997.

Spitzer, Robert J., *New Proofs for the Existence of God: Contributions of Contemporary Physics and Philosophy*, Grand Rapids, MI, Eerdmans, 2010.

SOCIOLOGY

Froese, Paul, and Christopher Bader, *America's Four Gods: What We Say about God – & What That Says about Us*, New York, Oxford University Press, 2010.

Putnam, Robert D., *Bowling Alone: The Collapse and Revival of American Community*, New York, Simon & Schuster, 2000.

Putnam, Robert D., David E. Campbell, and Shaylyn Romney Garrett, *American Grace: How Religion Divides and Unites Us*, New York, Simon & Schuster, 2010.

Roof, Wade Clark, *A Generation of Seekers: The Spiritual Journeys of the Baby Boom Generation*, San Francisco, HarperSanFrancisco, 1993.

Roof, Wade Clark, *Spiritual Marketplace: Baby Boomers and the Remaking of American Religion*, Princeton, NJ, Princeton University Press, 1999.

Stout, Jeffrey, *Blessed Are the Organized: Grassroots Democracy in America*, Princeton, NJ, Princeton University Press, 2010.

Wuthnow, Robert, *Acts of Compassion: Caring for Others and Helping Ourselves*, Princeton, NJ, Princeton University Press, 1991.

Wuthnow, Robert, *Boundless Faith: The Global Outreach of American Churches*, Berkeley, University of California Press, 2009.

Wuthnow, Robert, *Sharing the Journey: Support Groups and America's New Quest for Community*, New York, Free Press, 1994.

CONTEMPORARY REVIVAL OF RELIGION

Berger, Peter L., *The Desecularization of the World: Resurgent Religion and World Politics*, Washington, DC, Ethics and Public Policy Center, 1999.

Berger, Peter L., Grace Davie, and Effie Fokas, *Religious America, Secular Europe?: A Theme and Variations*, Surrey, UK, Ashgate, 2008.

Casanova, José, *Public Religions in the Modern World*, Chicago, University of Chicago Press, 1994.

Juergensmeyer, Mark, *Global Rebellion: Religious Challenges to the Secular State, from Christian Militias to Al Qaeda*, Berkeley, University of California Press, 2008.

Lilla, Mark, *The Stillborn God: Religion, Politics, and the Modern West*, New York, Alfred A. Knopf, 2007.

Micklethwait, John, and Adrian Wooldridge, *God Is Back: How the Global Revival of Faith Is Changing the World*, New York, Penguin, 2009.

Norris, Pippa, *Sacred and Secular: Religion and Politics Worldwide*, New York, Cambridge University Press, 2006.

Thomas, Scott, *The Global Resurgence of Religion and the Transformation of International Relations: The Struggle for the Soul of the Twenty-first Century*, New York, Palgrave Macmillan, 2005.

Appendix: Jewish Sources on Creation, the Age of the Universe and Evolution

This book is not specifically about Jewish faith, but for Jewish readers and others interested in how Judaism confronted some of the issues raised in the book, I include here some of the Jewish sources on science, creation and evolution that guided me in the presentation of the argument.

The Religious Importance of Studying Science

On seeing one of the sages of the nations of the world, one makes the following blessing: 'Blessed are you, Lord our God, King of the universe, who has given of his wisdom to mortal human beings.'

Babylonian Talmud, Berakhot 58a

If someone says to you, 'There is wisdom among the nations of the world,' believe it.

Midrash Eichah Rabbati 2:13

He who knows how to calculate the cycles and planetary courses, but does not, of him Scripture says, *but they regard not the work of the Lord, neither have they considered the operation of his hands* (Isaiah 5:12). How do we know that it is one's duty to calculate the cycles and planetary courses? Because it is written, *for this is your wisdom and understanding in the sight of the peoples* (Deuteronomy 4:6). What wisdom and understanding is in the sight of the peoples? Say, that is the science of cycles and planets.

Babylonian Talmud, Shabbat 75a

What is the way that leads to the love and awe of God? When someone contemplates His great and wondrous works and creatures, and from them obtains a glimpse of His wisdom which is incomparable and infinite, he will immediately love Him, praise Him, glorify Him, and long with an exceeding longing to know His great name, as David said *My soul thirsts for God, for the living God* (Psalm 42:3). And when he ponders these matters, he will recoil affrighted and realise that he is a small creature, lowly and obscure, endowed with slight and slender intelligence, standing in the presence of Him who is perfect in knowledge. And so David said, *When I consider your heavens the work of your fingers . . . what is man that you are mindful of him?* (Psalm 8:4–5).

> *Maimonides, Mishneh Torah, Hilkhot Yesodei ha-Torah 2:2*

Consequently, he who wishes to attain to human perfection must therefore first study logic, next the various branches of mathematics in their proper order, then physics, and lastly metaphysics.

> *Maimonides, The Guide for the Perplexed, Book I, 34*

Comment: The sages attached religious dignity and integrity to science, both as human wisdom and as an insight into the divine wisdom evident in the cosmos. The Babylonian Talmud sees the study of astronomy, for those who are capable of it, as a religious duty. Maimonides sees science as a way to the love and awe of God.

Literal and Non-Literal Readings of the Bible

The sages said, 'Whoever translates a verse literally is a liar' (Babylonian Talmud, Kiddushin 49a), expressing their dissent from those who disbelieved in the Oral Law and read the biblical text without reference to authoritative tradition. However, they also said (Shabbat 63a) that 'a text does not depart from its plain sense'. Beginning with Rav Saadia Gaon, medieval Jewish thinkers formulated general principles for when not to read a text literally.

> And so I declare, first of all, that it is a well-known fact that every statement in the Bible is to be understood in its literal sense except those that cannot be so construed for one of the following four reasons: it may, for example, either be rejected by the observation of the senses . . . or else the literal sense may be negated by reason.
>
> *Saadia Gaon, Sefer Emunot ve-Deot, Book VII*

Comment: The view of Saadia (882–942), shared by all the medieval philosophers, is that when a biblical text is incompatible with either reason or observation, that is sufficient evidence that it is to be read figuratively, allegorically, poetically or in some other way. Reason and observation, later to become the methodology of science, were regarded as reliable bases of knowledge, and it was taken as axiomatic that the Torah could not conflict with established truth.

Maimonides (1135–1204) repeatedly states that the creation narrative in Genesis 1 is not to be taken literally.

> Now, on the one hand, the subject of creation is very important, but on the other hand, our ability to understand these concepts is very limited. Therefore, God described these profound concepts, which His Divine wisdom found necessary to communicate to us, using allegories, metaphors, and imagery. The sages put it succinctly, 'It is impossible to communicate to man the stupendous immensity of the creation of the universe. Therefore, the Torah simply says, *In the beginning, God created the heavens and the Earth* (Genesis 1:1). But they pointed out that the subject is a deep mystery, as Solomon said, *It is elusive and exceedingly deep; who can discover it?* (Ecclesiastes 7:24). It has been outlined in metaphors so that the masses can understand it according to their mental capacity, while the educated take it in a different sense.
>
> *Maimonides, The Guide for the Perplexed, Introduction*

The account given in Scripture of the creation is not, as is generally believed, intended to be in all its parts literal . . . The literal meaning of the words might lead us to conceive corrupt ideas and to form false opinions about God, or even entirely to abandon and reject the principles of our faith. It is therefore right to abstain and refrain from examining this subject superficially and unscientifically . . . It is, however, right that we should examine the Scriptural texts by the intellect, after having acquired a knowledge of demonstrative science, and of the true hidden meaning of prophecies.

> *Maimonides, The Guide for the Perplexed, Book II, 29*

Comment: Maimonides holds that the entire creation narrative is an allegory not to be understood literally. Its true meaning is disclosed by the findings of natural science, though we will never be fully able to unravel its secrets. Maimonides elsewhere (*Guide*, Book III, 21) makes a distinction, very similar to that developed in the early eighteenth century by Giambattista Vico, that only the maker of a thing can fully understand it. To that extent, he would almost certainly have concurred that there will always be a margin of mystery when it comes to the understanding of the natural world and how it came into being.

These hesitations [in accepting an evolutionary view of the development of life] have nothing to do with any difficulty in reconciling the verses of Torah or other traditional texts with an evolutionary standpoint. Nothing is easier than this. Everyone knows that here, if anywhere, is the realm of parable, allegory and allusion. In these most profound matters people are willing to accept that the true meaning lies on the mystical plane, far above what is apparent to the superficial eye.

> *Rabbi Abraham Kook, Orot Ha-Kodesh, 559*

Comment: Rabbi Kook takes it as obvious that the creation account is not to be read literally. The resistances to contemporary science lie elsewhere.

The Age of the Universe

Heaven forbid that there should be anything in the Bible to contradict that which is manifest or proved . . . The question of eternity and creation is obscure, whilst the arguments are evenly balanced . . . If, after all, a believer in the Law finds himself compelled to admit an eternal matter and the existence of many worlds prior to this one, this would not impair his belief that this world was created at a certain epoch.

Judah Halevi, Kuzari, I:67

We do not reject the eternity of the universe because certain passages in Scripture confirm the creation, for such passages are not more numerous than those in which God is represented as a corporeal being, nor is it impossible or difficult to find for them a suitable interpretation. We might have explained them in the same manner as we did in respect to the incorporeality of God. We should perhaps have had an easier task in showing that the Scriptural passages referred to are in harmony with the theory of the eternity of the universe if we accepted this idea, than we had in explaining the anthropomorphisms in the Bible when we rejected the idea that God is corporeal.

Maimonides, The Guide for the Perplexed, Book II, 25

Comment: Both philosophers, Judah Halevi (1075–1141) and Maimonides, who on many other matters held diametrically opposite views, agreed that, were the eternity of the universe proved, it would not constitute an objection to their faith. Maimonides says that, had Aristotle succeeded in proving the eternity of the universe, he would have had no difficulty in reinterpreting Genesis 1. In fact, however, he maintained that Aristotle had not proved the point. He believed that the current state of science in his day, the twelfth century, was inconclusive on the matter, and therefore he saw no reason to modify his view that the universe had an origin in time. The correctness of this view was eventually established by Penzias and Wilson in 1964.

> Rabbi Judah bar Simon said: it does not say, 'It was evening,' but '*And* it was evening.' Hence we derive that there was a time-system prior to this.
>
> Rabbi Abbahu said: This teaches us that God created worlds and destroyed them, saying, 'This one pleases me; those did not please me.'
>
> Rabbi Pinhas said, Rabbi Abbahu derives this from the verse, 'And God saw all that He had made, and *behold* it was very good,' as if to say, 'This one pleases me, those others did not please me.'
>
> *Genesis Rabbah 3:7*

Comment: In this early rabbinic passage, Rabbi Judah infers from the word 'and', said of the first day of creation, that there must have been something prior to which it is added. Thus there were universes before this. Rabbi Abbahu, as understood by Rabbi Pinhas, derives the same principle from the Bible's use of the word 'behold', implying a sense of surprise. The implication is that God had previously created universes that were not 'very good'. This classic rabbinic exposition became an important source for Jewish thinkers in the Middle Ages faced with the challenge of Aristotle's belief in the eternity of matter, like Judah Halevi and Maimonides above.

> There were 974 generations before Adam.
>
> *Babylonian Talmud, Shabbat 88b*

Comment: On the basis of Proverbs 8, the rabbis said that the Torah preceded the creation of the world, and that God created the universe according to its blueprint. It existed for a thousand generations before it moved from heaven to Earth. Since there were twenty-six generations between Adam and Moses, it follows that there were 974 generations before Adam. This and the previous passage were invoked by Rabbi Israel Lipschitz (1782–1860) to show how new teachings about the age of the Earth, and the discovery of extinct species, vindicated ancient rabbinic teaching.

We are enabled to appreciate to the full the wonderful accuracy of our holy Torah when we see that this secret doctrine, handed down by word of mouth for so long, and revealed to us by the sages of the Kabbala many centuries ago, has been borne out in the clearest possible manner by the science of our generation.

The questing spirit of man, probing and delving into the recesses of the Earth, in the Pyrenees, the Carpathians, the Rocky Mountains in America and the Himalayas, has found them to be formed of mighty layers of rock lying upon one another in amazing and chaotic formations, explicable only in terms of revolutionary transformations of the Earth's surface.

Probing still further, deep below the Earth's surface, geologists have found four distinct layers of rock, and between the layers fossilised remains of creatures; those in the lower layers being of monstrous size and structure, while those in the higher and more recent layers being progressively smaller in size but incomparably more refined in structure and form.

Further, they found in Siberia in 1807, under the eternal ice of those regions, a monstrous species of elephant, some three or four times larger than those found at the present day; the skeleton may still be seen in the Zoological Museum at St Petersburg. Since that icy region is incapable of supporting any species of elephant, we must conclude either that the creature was swept there as a result of some cosmic upheaval, or that in some previous epoch the climate of Siberia had been warm enough to support elephants.

Similarly, fossilised remains of sea creatures have been found within the recesses of the highest mountains, and scientists have calculated that of every 78 species found in the Earth, 48 are species which are no longer found in our present epoch.

We know, too, of the remains of a giant creature discovered deep in the Earth near Baltimore, 17 ft long and 11 ft high, specimens of which have also been found in Europe, and which has been given the name 'mammoth'. Another giant creature whose fossilised remains have been found is the iguanodon, which stood 15 ft high and whose length extended to 90 ft. From its internal structure scientists have concluded that it was herbivorous. Another is the megalosaurus, which was slightly smaller than the iguanodon, but which was carnivorous.

From all this, we can see that all the Kabbalists have told us for so many centuries about the fourfold destruction and renewal of the Earth has found its clearest possible confirmation in our time.

And if we know how to look, we shall see that the holy Torah itself hints at these facts in its opening verses. The first verse refers to the original act of creation, while *the Earth was void and waste* refers to the epochs of upheaval and destruction which preceded our present age. The Torah passes over the intervening epochs in silence, because they have no immediate relevance to us; but *the spirit of God* which was *moving over the face of the waters* denotes the spirit of life which was, so to speak, waiting to re-enter the creation to be the vehicle of the glory of God. The ascending scale of being of the seven days of creation thus reflects the ascending scale of the great cosmic cycle . . .

In my opinion, the prehistoric men whose remains have been discovered in our time, and who lived long before Adam, are identical with those 974 pre-Adamite generations referred to in the Talmud (Shabbat 88 and Hagiga 14) and lived in the epoch immediately before our own.

This then is the meaning of the expression *from the eternity to eternity you are God* (Psalm 90), literally 'from world to world', for the divine spark enters into world after world, in ever-ascending order of perfection.

Rabbi Israel Lipschitz, Drush Or Ha-Chayim

Comment: A similar view, stated more briefly, is expressed by Rabbi Shalom Mordechai Schwadron (Techelet Mordechai to

Genesis 1:1). Rabbi Aryeh Kaplan takes up the idea that there were 974 generations before the creation of Adam.

> Adam was merely the first human being created in the latest cycle. According to these opinions, it would seem that man already had the physical and mental capacities that we possess as early as 974 generations before Adam, or some 25,000 years ago.
> *Aryeh Kaplan, Immortality, Resurrection, and the Age of the*
> *Universe, 21*

Evolution

Evolution did not figure in Jewish thought prior to Darwin, but in the twelfth century Maimonides noted the general evolutionary pattern evident both in natural and human history.

> When considering the divine acts, or the processes of nature, we get an insight into the prudence and wisdom of God as displayed in the creation of animals, with the gradual development of the movements of their limbs, and the relative positions of the latter, and we perceive also His wisdom and plan in the successive and gradual development of the whole condition of each individual ... Many precepts in our Law are the result of a similar course adopted by the same Supreme Being. It is, namely, impossible to go suddenly from one extreme to the other.
> *Maimonides, The Guide for the Perplexed, Book III, 32*

Rabbi Nissim ben Reuven (1320–80) argued that all creation evolved from a single substance, matter.

> At the beginning of creation, a unified substance was created for everything under the lunar sphere , ... this was because the will of God was to continue the nature of existence according to the possibilities, and not to create many things *ex nihilo*, since it is possible to make one substance that includes everything ... the

creation of two substances in the lower world *ex nihilo* would be without benefit; it suffices to have this wondrous and necessary origin.

Rabbi Nissim ben Reuven, Derashot Ha-Ran, 1

Rabbi Bachya ibn Pakuda (eleventh century, Spain) emphasises the structural unity of life, which testifies to its common origin.

> When we study the world, it shows us that it is entirely the plan of a Designer, the work of a single Creator. For we find that, with all the differences in its substances and elements, it shows uniformity in its effects and parts. The signs of the Creator's wisdom, manifest in the smallest as in the largest creatures, testify that they all have one wise Creator. If the world really had more than one Creator, diverse forms of wisdom would be manifest in its different parts and in its species and individuals.
>
>
>
> *Rabbi Bachya ibn Pakuda, Chovot Ha-Levavot, Shaar Ha-Yichud, 7*
>
>

Later commentators draw attention to the evolving nature of life as described in Genesis. Here, for example, is the comment of Rabbi Meïr Leibush ben Jehiel Michel Weiser (Malbim, 1809–79).

> Creation progressed from level to level: inanimate matter, plants, animals, and man. Everything that came earlier was a preparation for that which came later . . . It is known that also in rising up through the ladder of stages, creation did not proceed in discontinuous leaps, but rather through intermediate stages. Thus, coral is intermediate between inanimate matter and plants, polyps are intermediate between plants and animals, and monkeys are intermediate between animals and man.
>
>
>
> *Malbim to Genesis 1:20*
>
>

Similarly Rabbi Naftali Zvi Yehuda Berlin (Netziv, 1816–93) writes in terms that acknowledge micro-evolution and the nature

360

of life as an evolving phenomenon, foreseen and intended as such from the outset.

> *According to their kind* (Genesis 1:21). Scripture teaches that even though at the time of the Divine [creative] word, many kinds of sea creatures and birds emerged, none the less God continued to create other species from those that had already appeared, for example, the many varieties of chicken that eventually emerged from the first, all sharing the same essential constitution, and so with all other creatures.
>
> *Haamek Davar to Genesis 1:21*

> *That God created to do* (Genesis 2:3). According to the plain sense, not all things had reached their final end-point, since several things were subsequently changed in their nature. However, these changes were already contemplated then, so that God had already created them on that day [the seventh of creation] to do what they would later do.
>
> *Haamek Davar to Genesis 2:3*

Rabbi Arye Kaplan notes the unusual locution of the Torah when it describes the creation of fish and animals. The text does not say, *Let there be creatures* or *Let there be animals*, but *Let the water/ Earth bring forth* living creatures.

> This suggests that God did not actually create life at this time, but merely imparted to matter those unique properties that would make evolution take place, first to lower and then to higher forms of life, and eventually to man himself.
>
> *Aryeh Kaplan, 'Creative evolution', Faces and Facets, 83–4*

Rabbi Gedalia Nadel analyses the implications of a comment by Rabbi Ovadia Sforno (1470–1550), who argued that Genesis 2 implied that there was a two-stage creation of man.

And he blew into his nostrils the breath of life – a living soul, ready to accept the image of God . . . nevertheless, *and man was as a living being*, he was still only a living creature, unable to speak, until he was created in God's image and likeness.

Sforno, Commentary to Genesis 2:7

Regarding Sforno's basic point, that the creation of man in the image of God was the conclusion of a lengthy process, which began in a non-rational being under the category of animals, then proceeded to develop until it acquired human intellect, and also the physiological appearance of man with which we are familiar – it is reasonable that this is a correct description. The evidence of Darwin and of palaeontologists, regarding the existence of earlier stages, appears convincing . . .

As long as there is recognition of the Divine will that functions in nature via spiritual forces, there is no need whatsoever to negate the description of events that scientific investigation presents today. There are discoveries of skeletons of bipeds with a small skull, whose brain could not have been like the brain of the human being that we know. The man about which it is said, *Let us make man in our image*, was the final stage of a gradual process.

Rabbi Gedalia Nadel, Betorato shel Rav Gedalia, 100

Rabbi Abraham Kook sees the idea of evolution as essentially in harmony with the general Jewish view of the structure of time and history.

Evolution itself, moving upwards coordinately and undeviatingly from the lowest to the highest, demonstrates most clearly a prevision from afar – a preset purpose for all existence. Divine greatness is thereby enhanced and all the goals of faith confirmed, and trust in and service of the Divine is all the more justified – since all strives upwards and man has it in his power to improve and perfect himself and his world, he is manifestly thereby doing the will of his Creator. Spiritual perfection is thus seen to be in the centre of all existence.

Rabbi Abraham Kook, Orot Ha-Kodesh, 565

The idea that evolution shows that life emerged by chance does not impress the religious mind, which knows from many biblical examples that what appears to be random is in fact providential. The book of Esther, like the story of Joseph, is a providential narrative in which everything happens at the right time in the right way to bring about the fated end, yet the word 'God' does not appear in the book, and the festival to which it gave rise, Purim, means 'lotteries' or chance. In general, what appears to human eyes as chance is seen through the eyes of faith to be divinely intended. 'When the lot is cast in the lap, its entire verdict has been decided by God' (Proverbs 16:33). On this Malbim comments, 'There are things that appear given to chance but are actually providentially determined by God.'

Rabbi Eliyahu Dessler (1892–1953) takes this to be characteristic of appearance in general. We see the proximate causes of events, but the task of faith is to track them back to their source in the First Cause, God himself.

> Why was the world created in such a way that it appears as though it came about by way of evolution? However, this is the way of the revelation amidst the concealment. We see a long chain of cause and effect, which is the concealment. But it is up to us mentally to climb from the last to the first until we reach the First Cause, blessed be His name, and this is the revelation.
>
> *Rabbi Dessler, Michtav Me-Eliyahu, IV, 113*

The Views of Individual Thinkers

RABBI SAMSON RAPHAEL HIRSCH

Rabbi Samson Raphael Hirsch (1808–88), one of the leaders of nineteenth-century German Orthodoxy, wrote in the early days of the Darwin controversy, but saw immediately that, were Darwin's views to gain acceptance, they would in fact testify to increased wonder that God had created all life from a single source, using a mechanism both astonishingly simple yet capable of generating almost infinite diversity (the point I make in chapter 11).

> Even if this notion were ever to gain complete acceptance by the scientific world, Jewish thought ... would never summon us to revere a still extant representative of this primal form, as the supposed ancestor of us all. Rather, Judaism in that case would call upon its adherents to give even greater reverence than ever before to the one, sole God who, in His boundless creative wisdom and eternal omnipotence, needed to bring into existence no more than one single, amorphous nucleus, and one single law of adaptation and heredity in order to bring forth, from what seemed chaos but was in fact a very definite order, the infinite variety of species we know today, each with its unique character- istics that set it apart from all other creatures.
>
> Samson Raphael Hirsch, *The Educational Value of Judaism,*
> *Collected Writings, vol. 7, 264*

RABBI ABRAHAM ISAAC HACOHEN KOOK
Rabbi Abraham Kook (1865–1935) consistently took the view that evolution, though it seemed at first sight and to unsophis- ticated minds to be at odds with Jewish teaching, was in fact in accord with them, and people should be educated to see this. This is one of his many observations on the subject.

> My opinion on this is, that anyone with common sense should know that although there is no necessary truth in all of these new theories, at any rate we are not in the least bit obligated to deci- sively refute and oppose them, because the Torah's primary objec- tive is not to tell us simple facts and events of the past. What is most important is the Torah's interior – the inner meaning of the subjects – and this message will become greater still in places where

there is a counterforce, which motivates us to become strength-
ened by it. The gist of this has already been recorded in the words
of our earlier sages, headed by *The Guide for the Perplexed*, and
today we are ready to expand more on these matters.

It makes no difference for us if in truth there was in the world
an actual Garden of Eden, during which man delighted in an
abundance of physical and spiritual good, or if actual existence
began from the bottom upwards, from the lowest level of being
towards its highest, an upward movement . . .

And in general, this is an important rule in the struggle of ideas:
we should not immediately refute any idea which comes to contradict anything in the Torah, but rather we should build the palace of
Torah above it; in so doing we are exalted by the Torah, and through
this exaltation the ideas are revealed, and thereafter, when not pres-
sured by anything, we can confidently also struggle against it.

Rabbi Abraham Isaac Kook, Iggrot Ha-Re'iyah 134, 163–4

CHIEF RABBI DR J. H. HERTZ

In his *Commentary to the Pentateuch*, published in 1929, Rabbi
J. H. Hertz (1872–1946) gives a magisterial summary of Jewish
views on creation and evolution. He notes that 'while the *fact* of
creation has to this day remained the first of the articles of the
Jewish Creed, there is no uniform and binding belief as to the
manner of creation'. Citing Genesis 1, Psalm 104 and Proverbs
8:22–31, he shows how the Bible itself describes it differently
depending on perspective and context. That diversity continued
into the rabbinic period and beyond, now including midrashic,
philosophical and mystical approaches. *That* God created the
universe is central to Jewish faith. *How* he did so is not.

It follows that there is 'nothing inherently un-Jewish in the
evolutionary conception of the origin and growth of forms of
existence from the simple to the complex, and from the lowest
to the highest', provided we acknowledge that '*each stage is no
product of chance, but is an act of Divine will*, realising the divine
purpose, and receiving the seal of the divine approval'.

Hertz quotes Darwin's contemporary and co-discoverer of natural selection, Alfred Russel Wallace, whose approach was far more amenable to classic Jewish belief. Wallace argued that 'the unseen universe of Spirit' had intervened at least three times in the development of life: first in the creation of life from inorganic matter, second in the birth of consciousness, and third in the appearance of the higher mental faculties of humankind. Wallace believed that purpose was discernible in nature.

Hertz dismisses any inference from the prehuman origins of Homo sapiens. Man remains 'the goal and crown' of creation. 'Man, modern scientists declare, is cousin to the anthropoid ape. But it is not so much the descent, as the *ascent* of man, which is decisive. Furthermore it is not the resemblance, but the *differences* between man and the ape, that are of infinite importance.' The point of the biblical account 'is not to explain the biological origins of the human race, but *its spiritual kinship with God*'.

The aim of the Genesis creation account 'is not to teach scientific facts; but to proclaim highest religious truths respecting God, Man, and the Universe. The "conflict" between the fundamental realities of Religion and the established facts of Science is seen to be unreal as soon as Religion and Science each recognizes the true borders of its dominion.' He calls Genesis's declaration of man as the image of God 'the Magna Charta of humanity'.

RABBI JOSEPH SOLOVEITCHIK

The most profound exploration of the religious implications of evolution was undertaken by Rabbi Joseph Soloveitchik (1903–93) in his posthumously published *The Emergence of Ethical Man*. Far from seeing evolutionary biology as a threat to Judaism, he sees it as a vindication of Judaism as against the Greek tradition that influenced Christianity (and, he adds, the medieval Jewish philosophers). It was the Greeks who set man apart from nature in virtue of his powers of reason. Contemporary biology has restored man to nature where, according to the Hebrew Bible, he belongs.

According to the Torah, all life – plant, animal and human

– has a common origin, the Earth. 'The story of creation is a biography of nature' and we are part of nature. 'Man in the story of creation does not occupy a unique ontic position. He is, rather, a drop of the cosmos that fits into the schemata of naturalness and concreteness.' It is precisely the fact that we are part of nature that explains the Torah's emphasis on our 'biological integrity and welfare'. Death, in Judaism, is not the result of sin but of biology. It is because we are as much animal as divine that we need 'religious faith and commitment to a higher authority'.

As part of nature, we are commanded to 'serve and protect' nature, avoiding cruelty to animals, and acting as guardians of the integrity of the environment. 'As long as man lives within the bounds set by his Creator, which accentuate his naturalness, he remains *ben adam*, the son of Mother Earth, and may claim asylum in her lap.' It is the human encounter with the divine command that starts the dialogue out of which slowly emerges the ethical personality as we transcend our loneliness by recognising the integrity of the human other as a reflex of the divine Other.

It is impossible in brief summary to do justice to the subtlety and depth of Rabbi Soloveitchik's analysis. What is striking about it, as with all his work, is not only its scientific and philosophical sophistication and his taken-for-granted certainty that Judaism is compatible with modern science, but also his deep sense that modern science has liberated Judaism from certain Greek ideas that have long distorted its own self-understanding.

> I have always felt that due to some erroneous conception, we have actually misunderstood the Judaic anthropology and read into the Biblical text ideas which stem from an alien source . . . The sooner Biblical texts are placed in their proper setting – namely, the Oral Tradition with its almost endless religious awareness – the clearer and more certain I am that Judaism does not accent unreservedly the theory of man's isolationism and separatism within the natural order of things.
>
> *The Emergence of Ethical Man, 6*

Conclusion

The argument I have advanced in this book is within the spirit and substance of the Jewish philosophical mainstream as represented by Saadia, Judah Halevi and Maimonides in the Middle Ages, and Rabbis Hirsch, Kook, Hertz and Soloveitchik in the modern era. Needless to say, on this as on other fundamentals Judaism contains a range of views within the normative tradition, some more open to science than others. It is, though, striking how unthreatened these thinkers were by new developments in science, and that too has been part of my argument.

I end with a fascinating comment by the nineteenth-century Jewish mystic Rabbi Zadok haCohen of Lublin (1823–1900).

> Every day there are new interpretations of Torah, because every day, continually, God 'renews the work of creation'. Since the world was created according to the Torah ... presumably, the renewal of the world comes about through new aspects of Torah. That is why, after the blessing [in the morning prayers] 'creator of the heavenly lights' which speaks about the daily renewal of creation, the sages instituted a second blessing which is a form of blessing over the Torah ... in which we ask to know the new interpretations of Torah which come about through the new aspects of creation. (This is in accordance with an idea I heard, namely that [in the beginning] God wrote a book, the universe, and then wrote a commentary to the book, namely the Torah, because the Torah explains the possessions of God in creation.)
>
> *Rabbi Zadok haCohen, Tzidkat ha-Tzaddik, 92*

According to Rabbi Zadok, since the God of creation is the God of revelation, and since the Torah is itself a commentary on the natural world, every new scientific discovery generates new religious insight. By daily renewing creation, God is daily renewing revelation, our insight into his creative will.

For Further Reading

Aviezer, Nathan, *Fossils and Faith: Understanding Torah and Science*, Hoboken, NJ, KTAV Publishing House, 2001.

Aviezer, Nathan, *In the Beginning: Biblical Creation and Science*, Hoboken, NJ, KTAV Publishing House, 1990.

Blidstein, Gerald J., and Jacob J. Schacter, *Judaism's Encounter with Other Cultures: Rejection or Integration?*, Northvale, NJ, Jason Aronson, 1997.

Branover, Herman, and Ilana Coven Attia, *Science in the Light of Torah: A B'or Ha'Torah Reader*, Northvale, Jason Aronson, 1994.

Brill, Alan, *Thinking God: The Mysticism of Rabbi Zadok of Lublin*, New York, Michael Scharf Publication Trust of the Yeshiva University Press, 2002.

Cantor, G. N., and Marc Swetlitz, *Jewish Tradition and the Challenge of Darwinism*, Chicago, University of Chicago Press, 2006.

Carmell, Aryeh, and Cyril Domb, *Challenge: Torah Views on Science and Its Problems*, London, Association of Orthodox Jewish Scientists, 1976.

Funkenstein, Amos, *Theology and the Scientific Imagination: From the Middle Ages to the 17th Century*, Princeton, NJ, Princeton University Press, 1986.

Hertz, Joseph H., *The Pentateuch and Haftorahs: Hebrew Text, English Translation and Commentary*, London, Soncino, 1937.

Kaplan, Aryeh, and Y. Elkins, *Facets and Faces*, Jerusalem, Moznaim Publishers, 1993.

Kaplan, Aryeh, Yaakov Elman, and Israel Ben Gedaliah Lipschutz, *Immortality, Resurrection, and the Age of the Universe: A Kabbalistic View*, Hoboken, NJ, KTAV Publishing House in association with the Association of Orthodox Jewish Scientists, 1993.

Kelemen, Lawrence, *Permission to Believe*, Brooklyn, NY, Targum, 1991.

Kook, Abraham Isaac, and Ben Zion Bokser, *The Essential Writings of Abraham Isaac Kook*, Teanack, NJ, Ben Yehuda, 2006.

Landa, Judah, *Torah and Science*, Hoboken, NJ, KTAV Publishing House, 1991.

Levi, Yehudah Leo, *Torah and Science: Their Interplay in the World Scheme*, Nanuet, Jerusalem, Feldheim, 2006.

Schroeder, Gerald L., *Genesis and the Big Bang: The Discovery of Harmony between Modern Science and the Bible*, New York, Bantam, 1990.

Schroeder, Gerald L., *God According to God: A Physicist Proves We've Been Wrong about God All Along*, New York, HarperOne, 2009.

Schroeder, Gerald L., *The Hidden Face of God: How Science Reveals the Ultimate Truth*, New York, Free Press, 2001.

Schroeder, Gerald L., *The Science of God: The Convergence of Scientific and Biblical Wisdom*, New York, Free Press, 1997.

Shatz, David, and Joel B. Wolowelsky, *Mind, Body and Judaism: The Interaction of Jewish Law with Psychology and Biology*, New York, Michael Scharf Publication Trust of Yeshiva University Press, 2004.

Slifkin, Nosson, *The Challenge of Creation: Judaism's Encounter with Science, Cosmology, and Evolution*, Ramat Bet Shemesh, Israel, Zoo Torah, 2006.

Slifkin, Nosson, *Man and Beast: Our Relationships with Animals in Jewish Law and Thought*, Ramat Bet Shemesh, Israel, Zoo Torah, 2006.

Slifkin, Nosson, *Perek Shirah: Nature's Song*, Jerusalem, Urim, 2009.

Slifkin, Nosson, *Sacred Monsters: Mysterious and Mythical Creatures of Scripture, Talmud and Midrash*, Ramat Bet Shemesh, Israel, Zoo Torah, 2007.

Soloveitchik, Joseph Dov, *The Halakhic Mind: An Essay on Jewish Tradition and Modern Thought*, Ardmore, Seth, 1986.

Soloveitchik, Joseph Dov, and Michael S. Berger, *The Emergence of Ethical Man*, Jersey City, NJ, KTAV Publishing House, 2005.